LETTERS
FROM AN
AMERICAN
UTOPIA

LETTERS

FROM AN

AMERICAN

UTOPIA

*The Stetson Family and the
Northampton Association,
1843–1847*

EDITED BY

CHRISTOPHER CLARK

AND

KERRY W. BUCKLEY

University of Massachusetts Press
Amherst and Boston

2003016306
ISBN 1-55849-431-6

Designed by Dennis Anderson
Set in Janson Text
Printed and bound by The Maple-Vail Book Manufacturing Group

Library of Congress Cataloging-in-Publication Data

Letters from an American utopia : the Stetson family and the Northampton
Association, 1843–1847 / edited by Christopher Clark and Kerry W.
Buckley.
    p. cm.
Includes bibliographical references and index.
  ISBN 1-55849-431-6 (cloth : alk. paper)
    1. Northampton Association of Education and Industry—History. 2.
Northampton Association of Education and Industry—Biography. 3.
Stetson family—Correspondence. I. Clark, Christopher, 1953– II.
Buckley, Kerry W. (Kerry Wayne)

HX656.N75 L48 2004
974.4'23—dc22
                                                                2003016306

British Library Cataloguing in Publication data are available.

CONTENTS

PREFACE

ONE DAY IN April 1843 when the Connecticut River was swollen by flood-waters, a family reached the Hockanum ferry, near the foot of Mount Holyoke, riding on a lumber wagon. Having persuaded the ferrymen to take them across the fast-flowing river, the wagon's occupants set out across the flooded meadows, where poles marked the track toward the town of Northampton. On the wagon seat, with an infant girl in her arms, sat Dolly Witter Stetson, a woman in her mid-thirties. With her were her five other children and her husband James, a man of forty-two who had become used to uncomfortable journeys in poor weather. The Stetsons were removing to western Massachusetts from their home in Connecticut, but, more than simply moving house, they were embarking on a new way of life. Just a year earlier, a group of radical abolitionists and social reformers had started a utopian community at a place known as Broughton's Meadow, two and a half miles from the center of Northampton. The Stetson family was arriving to join this community, which was formally known as the Northampton Association of Education and Industry.

Utopian communities hold an unusual fascination for scholars, students, and general readers. The last decade or so has seen a significant flow of new books and articles about these movements, especially about the many communities that were founded in the United States during the nineteenth century. These studies draw on a wide array of source materials, from community records to promotional material and visitors' descriptions. Often, the letters and papers of community leaders are available, along with the letters or diaries of other figures who incidentally mentioned aspects of communal life. But direct, detailed evidence from regular community members is relatively hard to come by, and we know less than we would like to about the experiences of the men, women, and children who filled the ranks of communal groups. Now, thanks to the recent discovery of many of the Stetson family's letters, we have the opportunity to take a rare and valuable look into the lives of reformers and utopians, and to trace what happened to the riders in that wagon 170 years ago.

This volume gathers seventy-five letters, most of them written by Dolly

Stetson or her elder daughters to James A. Stetson while the family was living at the Northampton community between 1843 and 1846 and his work for the organization kept him in Boston or on the road. They were found in 1998 among family memorabilia in a house in the Stetsons' hometown of Brooklyn, Connecticut. With agreement from other family members, Mrs. Constance Beaman Renner arranged for them to be made available for scholarly use, and in 2000 the Stetson letters and some other artifacts were deposited in the collections of Historic Northampton Museum at Northampton, Massachusetts. Mrs. Renner's generosity has made this book possible, and we acknowledge it most warmly. Four further letters came to light in a private collection in September 2003, too late to be included here.

Historic Northampton has engaged in many programs to illustrate how local sources and perspectives can be used to illuminate broad historical issues. Its director, the historian Kerry Buckley, saw the Stetson letters, with their wide range of references and precise geographical and chronological focus, as serving this purpose very well. Christopher Clark had recently published *The Communitarian Moment: The Radical Challenge of the Northampton Association* (1995), a study of the Northampton community that had made extensive use of other recently discovered or little-known documentary sources, and so was well prepared to help bring the Stetson letters to a wider audience. Keen to exploit the evidence the letters provide about an array of issues of interest to historians and others, we invited two other scholars to contribute essays placing the letters in the context of their respective fields. Marjorie Senechal, director of the Northampton Silk Project, an interdisciplinary, academic, and community-based exploration of the history, art, science, and technology of silk and of its place in Northampton's own history, writes about the community's silk production. Paul Gaffney, an expert on race in nineteenth-century Massachusetts, shows how the Stetson letters shed light on race and race relations in the community and the locality. They demonstrate how the letters both add to our knowledge and need to be used along with other evidence if they are to be clearly interpreted.

With encouragement from Clark Dougan and Bruce Wilcox at the University of Massachusetts Press, we set about arranging for the letters' transcription and annotation. Kerry Buckley oversaw the transcription of the manuscript letters at Historic Northampton, which was commenced by Lydia Mitchell and then meticulously checked and completed by Marie Panik. Christopher Clark edited the resulting text and added the annotations that will help guide readers through the array of names and other references the letters contain. Clark also wrote an introduction and an interpretive essay of his own, drawing on the wider evidence that he had accumulated while writing *The Communitarian Moment*. As editors, we wish to acknowledge the contributions of all the individuals we have named to this book's preparation and production, together with Carl J. Guarneri, Carol A. Kolmerten, our copy editor Kay Scheuer, and managing editor Carol Betsch.

For the author of a historical work, the discovery of fresh documents relating to one's subject is both a constant hope and, for obvious reasons, a source of some apprehension. The finding of a substantial cache of letters actually written in the Northampton community was an exciting prospect, not just because such letters from utopian communities are generally so rare, but also because we already had some limited knowledge of the Stetsons from printed family memoirs and could now see what they had to say in their own words. The excitement was tempered, of course, by the prospect that the letters might undermine or contradict interpretations and conclusions that *The Communitarian Moment* had so recently reached.

On the whole, that did not happen. Rather, the Stetsons' letters tended to confirm patterns or explanations that the book had suggested. Still, there is no doubt that had they been available when it was being written, they would have considerably enriched *The Communitarian Moment*. They illuminate many details of life at the Northampton community also referred to in other sources, but in addition the Stetsons addressed three kinds of issues in particular that should shape our interpretation of the community and, by extension, of utopian communities more generally. They conducted a prolonged family negotiation over whether to stay at the community at all, providing invaluable evidence about family relationships and the terms on which men, women, and children conceived of their community participation. Second—and not simply because most of them were written by Dolly Stetson or her daughters—they offer some powerful insights into the status and aspirations of women in communal societies, insights that sharpen the more fragmentary conclusions on these themes that could be reached in *The Communitarian Moment*. Finally, the Stetson letters strongly confirm the book's tentative suggestion that disputes over "cultural" and behavioral issues, such as dancing, card-playing, courtship, and marriage, played a significant role in driving members away from the Northampton community and so, in the end, helping determine its fate.

But apart from their value as evidence, these letters deserve to be read in themselves. They constitute an extended conversation among family members in which news was shared, stories were told, hopes and fears expressed, and ideas discussed. If the spelling is erratic, the language has a richness and unaffected eloquence that nineteenth-century men and women prized and cultivated, perhaps especially among intimates. We meet James Stetson, an ambivalent family patriarch whose half-empty glass was sweetened by a wry sense of humor. There is Almira, the eldest of six children, who strove earnestly to work for her family and to acquire knowledge, and who wrote movingly of her dreams of a career in service to her ideals. Then there is Dolly Witter Stetson, the central figure in this collection, whom we first meet as she is about to embark on childbirth for the ninth time and whose relish for community life was shaped by a lively intelligence, a commitment to exploring reform ideals, and a down-to-earth view of family duties and household burdens. And appearing through the letters are other figures, among them the black abolitionists David Ruggles and Sojourner Truth, about whom we gain fresh insights, invaluable just because they are so unusual and tantalizing.

Of course we read these letters with hindsight informed by our knowledge of subsequent events that were unknowable to the writers. The Stetson correspondence captures a moment when ardent hopes and moral purpose joined to form a tangible community dedicated to social reform, and particularly the abolition of slavery. Like many of their fellow abolitionists, Dolly and James Stetson most likely hoped that their actions and example could achieve these objectives peacefully. Yet we know how fragile that moment was, and how innocent those hopes would prove to be of the massive bloodletting of the Civil War to come.

CHRISTOPHER CLARK
KERRY W. BUCKLEY

Letters
from an
American
Utopia

INTRODUCTION

"REAL COMMUNITY LETTERS"

A Family, Its Correspondence, and
a Utopian Community

CHRISTOPHER CLARK

MANY YEARS after their memorable journey to Northampton, the Stetsons' eldest child, Almira, who was fifteen in 1843, recalled her mother as she "hugged the baby and sat like a statue looking ahead" while the wagon braved the perils of river and flood. Casting her in a heroic role, firm against the elements, Almira drew attention to Dolly Stetson's determination to make a success of the family's new life, and signaled the central role of the Stetson family's women to its sense of identity and history.[1]

The image of the strong mother was commonplace enough in nineteenth-century autobiography and memorializing. Conventional social mores assigned the tasks of nurture, of moral and spiritual guidance, and of the foundations of character formation to women, particularly to mothers. Successful men often paid lavish tribute to their mothers' contributions to their achievements. Dolly's own son George R. Stetson, who was six years old when the family moved to Northampton, later wrote of his mother that "I feel my inadequacy to express in writing or speech my appreciation of her character and life."[2] It was appropriate that the strongest image Almira Stetson presented of her mother was at the moment of her steadfast advance—youngest daughter in her arms—toward a new way of life at the Northampton community. The family would later make their spell at Northampton a significant part of their collective memory, and the letters that they wrote while they were there—which they preserved, and which we can now read for ourselves—indicate Dolly Stetson's central role in taking them to the community and keeping them there in spite of various difficulties.[3]

To be sure, unlike some of the men, women, and children they joined at

I

Northampton, the Stetsons made a move that was not to prove permanent. Three years after arriving they left again, and a year after that, in 1847, most of them returned to their home at Brooklyn, in eastern Connecticut. Yet despite the temporary character of their stay at the community, it remained one of the central facets of the family's recollections. Privately printed memoirs that a son and granddaughter separately produced fifty, sixty, and seventy years after the Stetsons' journey to Northampton each emphasized its importance to them.[4] But their letters put us in a much better position to evaluate the family's sojourn at the Northampton community and, through that, add to our wider understanding of women and families in the reform movements of the mid-nineteenth century. The letters give an unusual and valuable insight into the lives of women living in a utopian community, and into their family relationships and hopes for the future. They also throw light on the circumstances and anxieties of women and men seeking to balance their own needs to earn a livelihood with the ideals of social reform that had motivated them to venture into a new way of life.

JAMES A. STETSON (1801–1893) and Dolly W. Stetson (1807–1899) had married in 1827 and set up home in the town of Brooklyn, Connecticut, where Dolly was born. James had moved there from Massachusetts in 1824 to establish himself as a chaise- and harness-maker. Their decision, after sixteen years of marriage, to cast their fortunes with the radical reformers at the Northampton community was rooted in an overlapping set of circumstances that shaped their lives during their years in Brooklyn. Three facets of their lives—their religion, their economic situation, and their family and kinship connections—shaped the move that they would make in 1843.

Dolly Stetson had grown up in a reasonably prosperous farm household. Her father, Ebenezer Witter, and her grandfather Nathan Witter before him, had owned a substantial farm of 350 or so acres on eastern Connecticut's pleasant, if not especially fertile, rolling uplands. Nathan Witter had been a deacon of Brooklyn's Congregational church. The family was quite well connected in the state and region. Ebenezer Witter had married Dolly Sharpe, whose brothers were successful farmers in the nearby settlements of Abington and Pomfret. Dolly Sharpe's sister, Dolly Stetson's aunt, was married to a prominent state official. Dolly Sharpe Witter apparently absorbed some consciousness of social distinction: she could write of one of her Brooklyn neighbors that she "possises a kind and generous spirit under an unpolished exterior."[5] Perhaps from principle, perhaps from the circumstances of her own marriage and life, Dolly Witter Stetson apparently inherited from her mother little of this sense of superiority. Her letters, at least, avoid such comments and convey, rather, a sense of equality.

One source for this egalitarianism was religion. Early nineteenth-century eastern New England was the seat of a growing Unitarian challenge to the Calvinist orthodoxy of the existing churches. Brooklyn was one of the first places in Connecticut to which the revolt spread, after a young pastor appointed in 1813 as colleague to the town's aged minister began to preach Unitarian views. Aided by the disestablishment of Connecticut's Congregational churches, by 1819 the Brooklyn parish had split apart. Although they were only a minority of church members, Unitarians had a majority in the society, the body that controlled church buildings and property, so the larger orthodox group were obliged to find a new place to worship. Among the early members of the new Unitarian congregation were Dolly Witter's parents, and the young girl followed them, drawing close to the church during her youth. In 1822 the church chose its new pastor, Rev. Samuel J. May, then the only Unitarian minister in the state. May's influence on the young Dolly Witter would be profound. Through him she would be drawn into a variety of educational and reform activities.

At church she also encountered the chaise-maker, James Stetson, who played bass viol for the choir. According to a family tradition, she fostered romantic hopes for a young lawyer she knew, but her parents guided her instead to this "honest mechanic." When Dolly and James married in 1827, Samuel May officiated. Among the wedding guests was Samuel's sister, Abby May, with whom Dolly would be friendly before May's own marriage to Bronson Alcott in 1830, and whose career as a mother and reformer would have some parallels to Dolly's. As Dolly went to housekeeping, the Mays and the Stetsons remained close; one year the minister's family boarded with the Stetsons. In a letter written seventeen years after her marriage, Dolly referred to her affection for the minister and his conduct of the wedding. But it was May's commitment and support for education, which reinforced the beliefs of Dolly's own family, together with his espousal of temperance, peace, and subsequently abolitionism, that would sweep the Stetsons during the early years of their marriage into a rapidly growing reform movement.[6]

Meanwhile, James Stetson's own fortunes, or misfortunes, largely determined his young family's ability to sustain itself and its standing. When he had arrived in Brooklyn in 1824 and set up a chaise-making shop with six journeymen or apprentices, he had been welcomed to a town that was seeking craftsmen to fulfill its needs for useful products and additional income. Brooklyn in the 1820s was, as it would remain, predominantly a town of farms and rural activities, but it had also been made the shire town of Windham County and had obtained some of the accoutrements of political and legal prominence: a courthouse and jail; a handful of lawyers and officials; and some of the businesses that a rural county seat could support. It also had a newspaper, which Samuel J. May would twice augment with short-lived but significant Unitarian periodicals under his editorship. James Stetson's chaise-making firm would help supply a small but steady local demand for two-wheeled carriages and wagons and for the leather harnesses and fittings that went with them.

Like some other local Unitarians, Stetson supported the minister's early efforts in the mid-1820s to promote temperance, and in 1825 he fired a wagon-painter who had been drinking on the job at his shop. Two months later the shop caught fire and burned, with the loss of several hundred dollars' worth of materials, and the disgruntled workman was suspected of arson. A Stetson family story related that the man was not caught, but nevertheless came to a sticky end. When an Englishman was later found drowned in the Connecticut River at Middletown, Brooklynites believed the body was that of the miscreant wagon-painter.

James Stetson's townsfolk came to his aid, helping in various practical and financial ways to resurrect his business. Legend had it that young Dolly Witter's contribution was a pound of linen thread, spun by her own hands; others donated or loaned materials and funds. By the time James and Dolly married, the chaise-making business was going again, but it is clear that it never ran without difficulty. James was now substantially in debt, and beholden to his creditors. After several years he made an assignment of his business to them, reorganizing his affairs, gaining time to pay what he owed, but also damaging his crumbling confidence in his own ability to maintain his trade and support a growing family. Dolly's father, Ebenezer Witter, was probably an important prop to his survival, if not necessarily to his self-esteem. Brooklyn's own fortunes faltered in the 1830s, and it would in due course lose its shire town status. James found himself competing in a tough regional and extra-regional market for wheeled vehicles, and needed to spend increasing amounts of time away from home to sell his products. The financial panic of 1837 and subsequent depression plunged many craftsmen and traders like him into chaos and bankruptcy. Stetson was forced to curtail his manufacturing activities and lost his workshop, valued at $200. Obliged to rely partially on family and neighborhood support, he had to look for new ways of making a living.[7]

Channels of local financial support and connections had been shaped in the 1830s by Brooklyn's rapid insertion into the campaign for the abolition of slavery. The campaign had been galvanized from Boston, by the publication in 1829 of David Walker's *Appeal to the Coloured Citizens of the World* and by the launch in 1831 of William Lloyd Garrison's paper, the *Liberator*, with its uncompromising condemnation of slavery as a sin. An abolitionist movement demanding the immediate, uncompensated emancipation of slaves spread quickly, and their location, principles, and family connections soon brought the Stetsons into it. In the adjoining town of Canterbury, Prudence Crandall had admitted a black child to her school for girls and, when the townspeople protested, had closed the school and reopened it again as a school for black children. Her stand against rising legal and violent persecution attracted the support of Samuel J. May, who offered assistance in conjunction with his Brooklyn neighbors, the brothers H. Egbert Benson and George W. Benson. May also alerted Garrison and other Boston abolitionists, and Crandall's case quickly became a cause célèbre of the abolition movement. Although she was eventually forced to abandon her school, Crandall's supporters ensured that she became a public martyr to bigotry and racial intolerance. The Crandall affair, its flurry of activity, and the nexus of connections it would help create helped put the Stetsons on the path that would, a decade later, take them to the Northampton community.[8]

George W. Benson was a Rhode Island merchant and manufacturer who had moved to Brooklyn to take up farming. Benson's father, George Benson, Sr., had long been prominent in the early antislavery movement and was one of the founders of the Windham Peace Society in 1826. As immediate-abolitionism gathered momentum in the early 1830s the Benson family became closely involved in it.[9] In 1833, while the Crandall affair was unfolding, George W. Benson married James Stetson's sister Catharine. The following year, after the *Liberator*'s editor had been drawn to Brooklyn several times by the campaign to support Crandall, William Lloyd Garrison married Benson's sister Helen. Through their minister and these marriages, James and Dolly Stetson now found themselves in a network of family and reform connections that drew them close to the growing radical abolitionist movement of the mid-1830s. In an 1837 letter to Benson, Garrison referred to "our esteemed friend [James] Stetson," and, as a family friend would later write, Dolly Stetson too was "a personal friend of S. J. May and other early anti-slavery leaders."[10]

But Dolly Stetson and the women around her could lay some claim to the status of "early anti-slavery leaders" themselves. When Prudence Crandall was jailed for a night at Brooklyn, one of the Benson sisters stayed with her and, according to George Stetson, Dolly and James spent the evening there in the cell with them. In 1834, in the aftermath of the Crandall affair, Dolly Stetson, the Benson sisters, and other local women founded the Brooklyn Female Anti-Slavery Society, of which Dolly would be president for five of its six years' existence.[11] The Bensons' household and those of other Brooklyn abolitionists, including Dolly and James Stetson's, became stopping-points for visiting lecturers and campaigners making their way through eastern Connecticut in the abolitionist cause. The Stetsons and their neighbors supported the establishment of the New England Anti-Slavery Society and its transmutation into the American Anti-Slavery Society, the founding of a Windham County society in 1836, and of the Connecticut Anti-Slavery Society in 1838. Like that of hundreds of others who raised funds, held fairs for the sale of goods, sold abolitionist papers, attended meetings, and drummed up signatures for petitions, their involvement helped the immediate-abolition movement gather momentum.

These activities provoked fierce opposition. Most northerners were indifferent or opposed to attempts to abolish slavery. Others argued variously that slavery would die out under competition from "superior . . . Yankee industry," that emancipation should be gradual and compensated, or that support should be directed to the American Colonization Society's efforts to have freed slaves resettled in Africa, their supposed homeland.[12] In Brooklyn, Samuel J. May's support for Prudence Crandall's right to teach black children, his advocacy of abolition, and his objection to racially segregated seating in church brought him into conflict with some of his parishioners. After spending a year as an antislavery lecturer, May departed in 1836 for a pastorate in Massachusetts. A split in the church also meant a split in the town, and the Brooklyn abolitionists were increasingly obliged to stand together for mutual support.[13] To make matters worse, the abolitionist movement itself was beginning to fracture in the late 1830s. Many evangelicals opposed the appearance of women as public speakers, while political abolitionists advocated the use of the electoral system and party politics to achieve emancipation measures. Their espousal of immediate abolition, and their close links with Garrison and his Boston-area supporters drew the Brooklynites toward abolitionism's radical wing, which advocated women's rights and rejected party politics, with its inevitable compromises, as an ineffective and morally corrupt means for obtaining reform. By the end of the decade these positions put them at odds with the majority of abolitionists in Connecticut. Radicals in Windham County and elsewhere found themselves exposed to community opposition. The Brooklyn Female Anti-Slavery Society ceased to function. Along with other considerations, this situation set the scene for the Stetsons' decision in 1843 to leave Brooklyn for Northampton.[14]

George W. Benson had moved his family to Northampton in 1841, and once there soon became engaged in a plan to start a community of like-minded reformers. The Northampton Association of Education and Industry, as it was formally called, commenced operations in April 1842, with Benson and other Connecticut abolitionists among its leading members. Neighbors from Brooklyn, including members of the Scarborough and Preston families, also joined the community. Indeed their removal from Brooklyn may have threatened James Stetson's local credit, which was already in a parlous state after his early disasters and the recent financial crisis. In 1841, too, Dolly Stetson's father died, further disturbing the family's patterns of local support and assistance. George W. Benson soon stepped in to help, proposing in the summer of 1842 that James Stetson should be appointed as the Northampton community's agent for selling the silk goods that it intended to manufacture. After some delay, Stetson accepted the position.

By that October, Stetson was on the road, peddling silk in various parts of New England and building his connections with the men, some of whom he already knew well, who were running the Northampton Association's business affairs. Early in 1843, as the community announced a revised constitution, including measures to provide support for all its members, James sought to persuade Dolly that he, she and their children should move together to live in the community. Writing to her on a printed copy of the Association's new constitution, James outlined his arguments for moving, specifying the advantages that he thought they would obtain, and also candidly identifying what he saw as drawbacks or reservations. After consideration, which James evidently left Dolly time for, she decided to accede to his suggestion. In

March 1843 the community voted to accept the Stetsons as members and, after a short wait for accommodation to be found for them, they set out on their April journey.[15]

The image of Dolly's upright deportment in the wagon crossing the river and meadows was apt. James had driven the move, but it was Dolly's decision to accept his proposal, and her determination that would make the family's transition to life in the Northampton community successful. In their own letters and in later family memoirs, husband and wife appear as strikingly different characters. James Stetson seems to have been an able man haunted almost to the point of timidity by the "Calamities" he had faced and the embarrassments they had brought him. "I never did a bad [i.e., unpleasant] job yet," he admitted, "but what I found it less terable in the Execution than I feared before I began." Dolly Stetson, on the other hand, was regarded as confident and energetic. "She moves like a power," commented Samuel J. May early in Dolly's married life. The impression was of an active, but anxious and perhaps vacillating husband whose best actions were determined and sustained by his wife's strength. So it was to prove at the Northampton community.[16]

TENS OF THOUSANDS of working men and women from the farms and towns of New England, the mid-Atlantic states, and the upper Midwest had joined antislavery societies in the 1830s or been touched by the impetus for social reform that the campaign to abolish slavery implied. Some thousands among them took steps in the early 1840s to explore the possibility that intentional communities could advance the cause of reform. During this decade (mostly in its first half) at least sixty such communities were founded across the northern United States, making it the most active period of the nineteenth century for attempts to create practical utopias.[17]

About half of these new communities were connected to a movement inspired by the French visionary Charles Fourier, and known in America as Fourierism or Associationism. Fourierists held that contemporary social ills derived from the burden of work that was unsuited to men and women's inherent inclinations, from the waste attributable to individual living arrangements, and from competitiveness. They advocated the creation of co-operative communities where competition could be eradicated and harmony established.[18] But even if they did not adopt Fourierism, other reformers, too, sought to change society by forming communities. A group led by the

Universalist minister Adin Ballou established the Hopedale Community at Milford, Massachusetts, in 1841 as a model of "practical Christianity" that could achieve social harmony and be replicated elsewhere (it was known formally as "Fraternal Community No. 1"). The same year some members of the Boston transcendentalist circle followed the former Unitarian minister George Ripley to create the Brook Farm community at West Roxbury, just outside the city.[19] The transcendentalist journal *The Dial*, and a host of reform newspapers from Garrison's *Liberator* to Horace Greeley's recently founded *New York Tribune*, carried articles about "community reform."

Abolitionist families and groups contemplated "community" principles as a way to change society, and some of them moved to Brook Farm, Hopedale, or the Fourierist communities in the faith that their efforts might speed up social change. The abolitionists who founded the Northampton community in the spring of 1842 were influenced by this ferment of ideas, and by the hope that cooperative action could achieve the ideals of harmony, equality, and justice that they had been pursuing in the antislavery movement. "The rights of all are equal," declared the Northampton Association's constitution, "without distinction of sex, color or condition, sect or religion." Early in 1843, as Dolly Stetson was considering James's proposal that they follow their Brooklyn associates to Northampton, her old acquaintance Abby May Alcott, sister of Samuel J. May, was moving with her small children to the short-lived Fruitlands community at Harvard, Massachusetts, conceived by her husband Bronson Alcott. The following spring Brook Farm adopted Fourier's principles and became one of the centers of the Associationist movement. During 1844 several joint conventions of the Massachusetts communities met to raise funds and garner support. For the first half of the 1840s community reformers could claim to be at the leading edge of a broader social change. "These attempts after a perfect society are plainly the most important things now doing," wrote Horace Greeley. "All other philanthropic effort is fragmentary and superficial."[20]

By the time the Stetsons joined it in April 1843, the Northampton Association had grown to about one hundred members and other residents, and was continuing to expand. It occupied a 470-acre site west of the center of Northampton that had previously belonged to the Northampton Silk Company, an ambitious but ill-fated effort to manufacture thread and other products from locally raised silk. The property included farm- and woodland, a four-story brick factory, a boarding house, various outbuildings, and several private houses that had either been purchased by the Association or were rented to provide living accommodation. A dam across the Mill River, the Connecticut River tributary that ran through the property, furnished water-power to the factory. Members worked at farming, lumbering, and various other trades, but the community's chief activity, which it hoped would be its main source of income, was the raising of raw silk and the manufacture of silk thread. Silk twisting and finishing took place in part of the factory, but the factory also contained living space for sixty or more people, a common kitchen and dining room, schoolrooms, and other spaces.[21]

In print, and sometimes even in private, the Northampton Association's friends and supporters could describe it in romantic tones as a sort of para-dise. Almira Stetson once referred to it as "Edendale," while an abolitionist visitor from eastern Massachusetts rhapsodized about "the paradisiacal na-ture of that lovely spot. It is Eden, Jr., to say the least." More prosaically, the singer Asa Hutchinson wrote of its "delightful situation . . . with water power and land sufficient to give employment to thousands. Everything in plain style, neat and good, excellent water and in great plenty." When the Stetsons eventually returned to Brooklyn in 1847, they consoled themselves that some of the town's scenery bore comparison with Northampton's. But the com-munity was evidently no place for the fainthearted. A Boston visitor wrote that "it does not strike a stranger agreeably. Everything seems huddled, un-comfortable and gloomy." As Dolly Stetson would reflect in 1844, when a new arrival compared the site with places he had seen in frontier Wisconsin, it could give a wild impression even in fair weather. Sojourner Truth thought it so forbidding when she arrived in November 1843 that she at first thought of leaving again as soon as she could. Frederick Douglass visited the com-munity on two occasions, and never forgot the "Spartan-like simplicity," its poor soil with "little or nothing upon it but stubby oaks and stunted pines," and "the rough and thorny ways" its members had chosen to tread.[22] The Association's rapid early growth and its survival against considerable finan-cial odds over nearly five years was a testament not to comfort or material prosperity, but to the determination and commitment of its members.

Their commitment is suggested by the fact that even some of the men and women who withdrew from the Northampton Association during the Stetsons' time there did so not to return to "individual" life, but in order to join other communities. James Stetson, however, turned out to be a hesitant, even reluctant communitarian. During the family's first year at Northampton, when they lived in a small house with one or two other families, James seems to have let the honest doubts he had expressed at the outset overcome any optimism he had felt about joining the community, and he became discouraged. He was skeptical of the Association's business arrangements, and may have quailed at the religious radicalism of some of his fellow members. His son George later claimed that "while he was in full sympathy with the reformatory measures of the community, and the men and women, yet for the first year or two, the conditions of his life and the character of his occupation were so different from his former customs that . . . he did not enjoy the change." Later on, though James by that time "appreciated the conditions of the community life more," the community's affairs were heavily hampered by debt and were being wound down.[23] In the meantime, it was the women in the family, Dolly Witter Stetson and their two eldest daughters, Almira and Mary, who sustained the enthusiasm for community life that kept the family at the Association and involved in its activities for almost three years.

To help market what was hoped would be an improved flow of silk products from the mill, the Association in the spring of 1844 asked James Stetson to set up a store in Boston, and to conduct his silk-selling activities there and in eastern New England. Somewhat to his relief, James took this opportunity to step out of the community life he found disagreeable, but the family's lack of means, and perhaps Dolly Stetson's insistence, meant that she and the children remained at Northampton. James's work had taken him away from home in the past, but now it would be for considerable lengths of time. It was to him during these absences that Dolly and the children wrote most of the letters that are collected here. Even when, after several months, it was determined that James should give up the Boston store and return to peddling silk on the road, he remained away from Northampton for significant periods, and the letters continued. Gaps in the correspondence, though, marked James's returns home, which became longer as the family's time in the community drew toward its close. Occasional hints in Dolly's letters suggest that personal friction may have grown up between James and one of the community's leaders, probably his brother-in-law George W. Benson; if so, it may be significant that James came back to spend more time at Northampton after Benson had formally left the Association in the summer of 1845.

The collection begins with a letter written in Brooklyn early in 1843, before Dolly Stetson and her children moved to Northampton. The bulk of the letters date from 1844 and 1845, when James Stetson was based in Boston and Dolly and the children were at the community. In the spring of 1846, the Stetsons withdrew from the community and Dolly moved with the children to rented rooms elsewhere in Northampton. Among the small number of letters from this period are some of the only examples that have come to light from the many that James wrote to his family while he was apart from them. By 1847, the Stetsons had returned to Brooklyn to take up farming. A final letter sent from Brooklyn that year marked the family's return to where it had begun.

The Stetsons mostly wrote their letters for one another, and so assumed knowledge and familiarity with people, attitudes, and concepts that might, in letters to strangers, have required more explicit elaboration. Their even, usually factual tone could mislead us into underestimating the striking commitment entailed in belonging to a community like that at Northampton in the 1840s. Part of that assumed knowledge and tacit understanding was the radicalism of the Stetsons' position and that of their fellow abolitionists. They had argued for the immediate, uncompensated abolition of slavery. They had criticized the politicians and clergy of the northern states who had refused to support those arguments, or who had acquiesced in policies and practices that accepted slavery or racial inequality. Some had withdrawn or "come-out" from churches with whose members or ministers they could not agree on the subject of slavery. Many radical abolitionists, including most of those at Northampton, had also since the late 1830s adopted nonresistance, the principle of disavowing any action or authority that was based directly or indirectly on the use of force. Garrison and his radical supporters attacked the United States Constitution as an implicit foundation for slavery that was, in Garrison's famous words, "a covenant with death and an agreement with hell." At the 1844 meetings of the American Anti-Slavery Society they would formally adopt a policy of disunion ("No Union with Slaveholders!") to extricate the northern states from complicity in southern sin. Before that, nonresistants and come-outers had attacked the orthodox churches and clergy as sectarian bigots more concerned with maintaining their congregations than with telling the unpopular truth about the crimes of slavery. As Garrison himself ironically expressed it after he and Association members were denied a meeting hall in Northampton for Fourth of July speeches in 1843, "We have committed crimes not easily to be forgiven, having opposed the sacred order of the clergy, and pleaded for good-for-nothing niggers!"[24]

The Northampton area was, indeed, no more friendly to radical abolitionists than Connecticut had been. A majority of the population opposed them. Democrats; people with connections to the South; Whigs, whose politics the radicals distrusted; the clergy of the orthodox churches, who regarded them as "infidels" and whom they attacked as covert supporters of slavery or upholders of "Jim Crow meetinghouses," with seating segregated by race; political abolitionists who condemned their rejection of politics; and evangelical abolitionists, who objected to their attacks on the clergy and their upholding of women's right to speak in public: all took issue with the Association's abolitionist, nonresistant reformers, whom they regarded as "fanatics." Erasmus D. Hudson, a Northampton community member and abolitionist lecturer, wrote of western Massachusetts as "this *priest ridden region*" where heaven and earth seem like "brass over our heads and iron under our feet." To many of the region's inhabitants, the antipathy was mutual. According to one local newspaper, the Association's "unhappy Garrisonians" and "disaffected community croakers" were alone in their discontent at the nation's fortunate condition and "withdrew to their unsocial home to . . . try to undermine the happy . . . institutions of our common country."[25]

Being in a community served several purposes for radical abolitionists. It was in some respects a retreat, a place where men and women hard-pressed in their own churches or localities could come among sympathetic friends. It was also a base for lecturing and campaigning in the area around, a center for activities that were intended to aggravate and annoy their wide array of opponents and ensure that the cause of abolition was not quietly forgotten. And in this sense as well as intrinsically, the very existence of a community of radical, nonsectarian exponents of human equality constituted a moral witness to the cause for which they were working.[26]

Although letters from utopian communities are rare, the Stetson collection is not unique. It takes its place alongside several similar collections, some of them long known about, but others only made available relatively recently. Marianne Dwight's letters from the Brook Farm community illustrated the life of a young elite single woman, while those of Mary Paul from the North American Phalanx were from a woman whose alternatives to community life would have been working in a mill or taking poorly paid household labor on a farm. Elizabeth Curson's unpublished letters from Brook Farm and the later Raritan Bay Union demonstrate one woman's different experiences in two communities, the first (like Dwight) as a single woman, the second (like

Dolly Stetson) as a married woman with a family. Though the Stetson letters are less revealing of sexual or emotional matters than the recently published diaries of Tirzah Miller of the Oneida Community, they still provide vivid evidence of the personal, family, and wider ties that shaped the lives of men and women who participated in communal ventures.[27]

In common with all these examples of surviving documents, the Stetsons' letters give us particularly rich evidence about the lives and attitudes of women in utopian communities. Indeed such materials have been critical to a reevaluation of women's community experience that has been under way in recent years. In an important study of women at New Harmony, Indiana, and other Owenite communities of the 1820s and 1840s, Carol A. Kolmerten stressed the negative aspects of communal life, especially for married women with families, who were often obliged to assume a double burden of work for the community and for their own households. The subsequent discovery of new documents written by Owenite women partly confirmed that interpretation, but also suggested that some women had different, more positive experiences. The Northampton letters of Dolly W. Stetson and her daughters likewise reflect the complexities of women's circumstances when they joined communities, but also clearly suggest that they could find benefits in the patterns of cooperative work and household arrangements that community life could offer.[28]

The Stetsons' letters lack some of the elements of direct reportage that can be found in accounts that were written for strangers or parents. At times, close reading and careful interpretation are required to tease out the subtler inflections of meaning in the family's exchanges. But there are compensations for this. Unlike some correspondents, the Stetsons were not simply painting rosy pictures of community life to convince or reassure skeptical relatives or friends of the validity of the choices they had made. Instead, their correspondence served as a vehicle for a richer, more complex set of dialogues within the family about the advantages and disadvantages of continuing to participate in "community reform."

FOLLOWING THE letters in this volume are three chapters in which historians analyze different facets of the evidence the Stetsons have provided us about the Northampton Association and the activities of its members, helping to place the community in the wider picture of social and political change in the 1840s. In my essay on marriage, education, and conduct at the community, I explore the interconnections between local and family circumstances, reform interests, and membership of the Northampton Association that drove the Stetsons to be participants there in the first place and shaped their experience of community life. The letters reflect a wider reality, similar to that facing many abolitionists and participants in utopian communities, in which reform ideals were intertwined with family and neighborhood conditions and with the struggle to make a livelihood. Indeed the Stetsons' first year at Northampton was marked by tragedy. Barely six months after they arrived, their son Ebenezer died of illness, a week or so after his tenth birthday. It was the third time the family had to face the death of a child.[29] Their letters hint that life in a community, rather than in their own individual household, may have enabled them to hitch this burden and their other daily and personal concerns to the purpose of reform. Community, they hoped, might help reconcile the tensions and conflicts within personal lives that made society unequal or obstructed the realization of a more just, humane world. That, at least, had been one of the objects behind forming intentional communities in the first place, and the Stetsons tried to make this vision work in their own lives as well as in that of the society around them.

At the heart of the Northampton Association's practical activities and plans were its efforts at silk production. Up to a point, this was merely fortuitous. The community had purchased the property, mill, and some of the equipment of the bankrupt Northampton Silk Company at a time when the 1830s bubble in silk manufacture and cultivation had recently burst. Silk cultivation and manufacture were in effect going concerns when the community commenced, and it seemed to make sense to continue with them as the source of much-needed revenue. Moreover, some of the community's members, including the Stetsons and their eastern Connecticut neighbors, came from a region of New England where silk raising and processing had been well-established parts of the rural economy in the decades before 1840. To abolitionists and nonresistants, silk production could also have a felicitous, deeper significance. Silk was a "free" product, untainted by the evils of slavery. The Northampton community sought to combine education and work for its members, particularly its children. The processes of raising silkworms, creating raw silk, and manufacturing silk products could offer object lessons in the creation of a harmonious and equal human society.[30]

Members hoped that the silk goods they made would become the community's largest source of income. In her essay on silk production at

Northampton, Marjorie Senechal uses the Stetson letters as a prism through which to examine the opportunities and difficulties it posed for the community. While James Stetson was engaged in selling silk thread from the store in Boston or from his peddler's cart, his children, particularly Almira, were involved in various aspects of producing it. Senechal reconstructs for us the processes of silk production and some of the techniques and equipment the Stetson children and their community colleagues would have used. To do so, she draws on nineteenth-century evidence, on her expertise gained from observing rural silk production in present-day Albania and other parts of the world, and on the experience of having her students recreate some of the devices that nineteenth-century silk producers would have employed. Her findings offer fresh insights into silk raising and manufacture in the 1840s, when an important transformation was about to overtake the American silk industry. They also provide some striking evidence about the problems that dogged the Northampton community's silk-making efforts and, consequently, its finances and ultimate viability.

The Northampton community was also a place where abolitionist ideas about a future American society freed from slavery could be worked out and put to a test. It provided a kind of laboratory for realizing the oft-proclaimed abolitionist ideal of upholding human equality. As a member wrote in 1844, "We are here endeavoring to apply to actual life the great Christian principle of the *Brotherhood of the Race*." Just as its constitution, in proclaiming human equality, implicitly promised to rectify gender imbalances and inequities, so the belief in the indivisibility of the human race suggested a commitment to racial equality. Opponents often seized on this aspect of the Association's character. A writer in the *Massachusetts Spy* in 1843 had described it as "an uncouth assemblage . . . , [where] representatives of the various nations of the earth, congregated beneath a wide-spreading pine tree to worship the God of their spiritual conceptions," while other critics were less subtle still in their condemnation of the community's interracial character.[31] In his essay in this volume, Paul Gaffney explores the dimensions of race at the community.

The Northampton Association was one of the very few places anywhere in the United States in the 1840s where men and women of European and African descent could live together on terms of equality, rather than of hierarchy, exploitation, or dependence. Among the Stetsons' close neighbors and associates at Northampton were the community's principal African American members, the abolitionist campaigner David Ruggles, the evangelist Sojourner Truth, and the fugitive slave Stephen C. Rush. Gaffney brings the new evidence revealed in the family's letters together with his detailed knowledge of African Americans in nineteenth-century western Massachusetts, to provide a carefully crafted analysis of the character and limits of racial interaction and equality in this community dedicated to freedom.

As they turn to the letters, readers will find for themselves that, not surprisingly, all these themes were intermixed throughout this substantial three-year correspondence. They will encounter familiar topics: men's and women's anxieties about their children and their aging parents; problems with rotten teeth and shortages of cash; the joys and loneliness of childbirth and baby-minding; the pressures of work, school, and family illness. They will encounter less familiar issues: the debates and anxieties of communal living, and even (toward the end) the attempted murder of a boarder in one of the community's houses. They will be able to listen to the voices of children as well as of adults, and to their sometimes scornful amusement at adult foibles. They will read of a nineteenth-century family's experiences of child death, the comings-and-goings of friends and neighbors, and efforts to shape and plan their own future. Yet in the Stetsons' case these mostly commonplace concerns were inflected by their adherence to a reform campaign, and by their membership in a close community of fellow campaigners whose character and exigencies added an extra dimension to their lives—a dimension that they chose to preserve and memorialize even after they had turned to other things.

Notes

I should like to thank all the individuals who contributed to the aspects of this book for which I was responsible: Marie Panik, Kerry Buckley, Paul Gaffney, Marjorie Senechal, Carl J. Guarneri, Carol A. Kolmerten, and—for their hospitality—Carol MacColl and Don Michak. Work to complete the book was facilitated by a Residential Fellowship at the University of Connecticut Humanities Institute and research leave from the University of Warwick, which I gratefully acknowledge.

1. Kate deNormandie Wilson, *Dolly Witter Stetson* (Brooklyn, Conn., 1907), 31.

2. George Ripley Stetson, *The Story of My Life, and Incidents Connected Therewith* (n.p., n.d.), 17. (It might be mentioned in passing that in this memoir Stetson notes that his middle name is from a family connection; he was not, apparently, named for the Unitarian minister George Ripley, who would found the Brook Farm community in 1841).

3. Stetson Family Correspondence, Manuscript Collection, Historic Northampton, Northampton, Mass. References are to letters in this collection unless otherwise indicated, and include the letter number assigned in this volume.

4. The three memoirs were George R. Stetson, "When I Was a Boy," in Charles A. Sheffeld, ed., *The History of Florence, Massachusetts, Including a Complete Account of the Northampton Association of Education and Industry* (Florence, Mass., 1895), 118–123; Wilson, *Dolly Witter Stetson*; and George Ripley Stetson, *The Story of My Life*.

5. Dolly Sharpe Witter to James A. Stetson and Dolly W. Stetson [hereafter JAS and DWS], August 28, 1845 (letter no. 65).

6. On Brooklyn's Unitarian controversy and Samuel J. May's reform activities, see Ellen D. Larned, *History of Windham County*, 2 vols. (1880; rpt. ed., Chester, Conn., 1976): 2: 461–465, 475–478. Dolly Stetson's regard for Samuel J. May apparently never dimmed. The Stetson collection at Historic Northampton includes two newspaper obituaries found among the materials accompanying the letters. One is of Dolly Stetson herself, published in 1899, but the other, which must have been kept deliberately after its publication in 1871, is of Samuel J. May.

7. On James Stetson's financial difficulties, see Wilson, *Dolly Witter Stetson*, 77–79. For the loss of his workshop, compare "Abstract of the Assessment Lists of the Town of Brooklyn," Town Clerk's Office, Brooklyn, Conn., for 1838, with that for 1837.

8. See Peter P. Hinks, ed., *David Walker's Appeal to the Coloured Citizens of the World* (University Park, Pa., 2000). On the Crandall affair, see "A Canterbury Tale," *The Abolitionist* [New-England Anti-Slavery Society] 1, no. 4 (April 1833); "The Black Law of Connecticut," ibid. 1, no. 9 (September 1833); "Miss Crandall's Second Trial," ibid. 1, no. 11 (November 1833): 161–170; and Samuel J. May, *Some Recollections of our Antislavery Conflict* (Boston, 1869), 42–56.

9. On the Benson family, see [Wendell Phillips Garrison] *The Benson Family of Newport, Rhode Island, together with an Appendix concerning the Benson Families in America of English Descent* (New York, 1872), 38–44, 51–54. George W. Benson's brother Henry Egbert Benson, who had been active in the Crandall campaign, died in 1837.

10. William Lloyd Garrison to George W. Benson, February 17, 1837, in *The Letters of William Lloyd Garrison*, ed. Walter M. Merrill and Louis Ruchames, 6 vols. (Cambridge, Mass., 1971–1981): 2:210. Giles B. Stebbins, "A Young Man in the Community," in Sheffeld, ed., *The History of Florence*, 128.

11. Brooklyn Female Anti-Slavery Society, Records, 1834–1840, Connecticut State Library, Hartford.

12. The quotation is from an article in the *Northampton Democrat* (Northampton, Mass.), reprinted in the *Liberator* (Boston), July 28, 1843.

13. On Samuel J. May, see *Memoir of Samuel Joseph May* (Boston, 1873); Douglas C. Stange, *Patterns of Antislavery among American Unitarians, 1831–1860* (Rutherford, N.J., 1977), 48; Donald Yacovone, *Samuel Joseph May and the Dilemmas of the Liberal Persuasion* (Philadelphia, 1991).

14. In a letter to George W. Benson on March 19, 1839, William Lloyd Garrison sent greetings to the Benson family and to other named individuals in Brooklyn: *The*

Letters of William Lloyd Garrison, ed. Merrill and Ruchames, 2:444. The fact that all the people Garrison named subsequently became connected with the Northampton Association is evidence of the close-knit character of this radical abolitionist group. Of eight Brooklyn individuals who subscribed in 1841 to the American Anti-Slavery Society's "one dollar pledge" fundraising campaign, four—including Dolly W. Stetson—joined the Northampton Association within the next two years; subscription lists were published in *National Anti-Slavery Standard* (New York), July 1, July 29, and September 9, 1841.

15. JAS to DWS, [February 20, 1843] (letter no. 2); William Adam to JAS, April 2, 1843, Northampton Association of Education and Industry, Records, 1836–1853, vol. 4, 21, American Antiquarian Society, Worcester, Mass.; as secretary of the association Adam wrote in connection with the Stetsons' impending arrival, but asked them to wait in Brooklyn until they heard from him again, evidently to permit accommodation to be found for them.

16. JAS to DWS, [February 20, 1843] (letter no. 2).

17. General works on utopian communities that discuss this period include Brian J. L. Berry, *America's Utopian Experiments: Communal Havens from Long-Wave Crises* (Berkeley, Calif., 1992); Yaacov Oved, *Two Hundred Years of American Communes* (New Brunswick, N.J., 1988); Donald E. Pitzer, ed., *America's Communal Utopias* (Chapel Hill, N.C., 1997); and Edward K. Spann, *Brotherly Tomorrows: Movements for a Cooperative Society in America, 1820–1920* (New York, 1988).

18. The standard work on American Fourierism is Carl J. Guarneri, *The Utopian Alternative: Fourierism in Nineteenth-Century America* (Ithaca, N.Y., 1991).

19. Edward K. Spann, *Hopedale: From Commune to Company Town, 1840–1920* (Columbus, Ohio, 1992); Anne C. Rose, *Transcendentalism as a Social Movement, 1830–1850* (New Haven, Conn., 1981); Richard Francis, *Transcendentalist Utopias: Individual and Community at Brook Farm, Fruitlands, and Walden* (Cambridge, Mass., 1997).

20. *New York Daily Tribune*, August 13, 1842.

21. Christopher Clark, *The Communitarian Moment: The Radical Challenge of the Northampton Association* (Ithaca, N.Y., 1995; Amherst, Mass., 2003), 2–3.

22. Almira Stetson to James A. Stetson, August 25, [1844] (letter no. 20); "Noggs," in *Essex County Washingtonian*, August 29, 1844; Dale Cockrell, *Excelsior: Journals of the Hutchinson Family Singers, 1842–46* (Stuyvesant, N.Y., 1989), 267; Henrietta Sargent to George Dixwell, March 1, 1843, Wigglesworth Family Papers, Box 3, Massachusetts Historical Society, Boston; *Narrative of Sojourner Truth; A Bondswoman of Olden Time* (Battle Creek, Mich., 1878), 120; Frederick Douglass, "What I Found at the Northampton Association," in Sheffeld, ed., *History of Florence*, 130.

23. George R. Stetson, *The Story of My Life*, 16.

24. William Lloyd Garrison to Edmund Quincy, July 6, 1843, in *The Letters of William Lloyd Garrison*, ed. Merrill and Ruchames, 3:170. "Come-outer" came from Revelation 18:4 (referring to Babylon): "And I heard another voice from heaven, saying, Come out of her, my people, that ye be not partakers of her sins, and that ye receive not of her plagues." "Nonresistant" derived from Christ's teaching in the

Sermon on the Mount, recorded in Matthew 5:39: "But I say unto you, That ye resist not evil: but whosoever shall smite thee on thy right cheek, turn to him the other also."

25. Erasmus D. Hudson to editor, in *National Anti-Slavery Standard*, January 19, 1843; Hudson to Abby Kelley, March 2, 1843, in Abby Kelley Foster Papers, Box 1, folder 6, American Antiquarian Society; *Northampton Democrat*, reprinted in *Liberator*, July 28, 1843.

26. I have discussed the functions of the community and the reform activities of its members in more detail in Clark, *The Communitarian Moment*, 86–95.

27. [Marianne Dwight Orvis] *Letters from Brook Farm, 1844–1847* (Poughkeepsie, N.Y., 1928); a new edition is currently in preparation by Joel Myerson. Mary Paul's letters are published in Thomas Dublin, *Farm to Factory: Women's Letters, 1830–1860* (New York, 1981); the Elizabeth Curson (Hoxie) letters are in Houghton Library, Harvard University, bMS Am 1175 (356–445); Robert S. Fogarty, ed., *Desire and Duty at Oneida: Tirzah Miller's Intimate Memoir* (Bloomington, Ind., 2000).

28. Carol A. Kolmerten, *Women in Utopia: The Ideology of Gender in the American Owenite Communities* (Bloomington, Ind., 1990); and idem, "Women's Experiences in the American Owenite Communities," in Wendy E. Chmielewski et al., eds., *Women in Spiritual and Communitarian Societies in the United States* (Syracuse, N.Y., 1993), 38–51; but see also Carol A. Kolmerten, "Voices from New Harmony: The Letters of Hannah Fisher Price and Helen Gregoroffsky Fisher," *Communal Societies* 12 (1992): 113–128. I have developed this theme in Christopher Clark, "A Mother and Her Daughters at the Northampton Community: New Evidence on Women in Utopia," *New England Quarterly* 75, no. 4 (December 2002): 592–621.

29. Ebenezer Witter Stetson (b. 1833) died at the Northampton Association on November 1, 1843. A daughter, Mercy Turner Stetson, had died of scarlet fever in 1834 at the age of three, and a son, James A. Stetson, Jr., died in January 1842, probably aged about two, also of scarlet fever.

30. Clark, *The Communitarian Moment*, 140–143.

31. William Bassett to Elizabeth Pease, July 22, 1844, Boston Public Library MS. A. 1.2.14.44 (emphasis in original); *Massachusetts Spy*, quoted in *Liberator*, November 24, 1843.

Stetson Family Correspondence, 1843–1847

Editorial Note

THE LETTERS reproduced here have been transcribed from originals discovered in a house in Brooklyn, Connecticut, in 1998 and deposited by Mrs. Constance Beaman Renner in the manuscript collections of Historic Northampton in 2000.

Original spellings have been retained throughout, except where the handwriting was unclear, in which cases modern spelling has been used. Like many of their contemporaries, the Stetsons employed dashes of various lengths as well as conventional marks to punctuate their writing, and simplified versions of these have been retained in the transcription. Crossings-out in the original are indicated in ~~strikethrough text~~; trivial mistakes and corrections have been omitted. Writers' insertions in the original have been silently placed in the text. Editorial insertions are placed in square brackets [ ]. A small number of letters have been torn or have parts missing; places where the original text has disappeared are indicated thus: /// .

The principal figures in this correspondence were:

James A. Stetson (1801–1893);

Dolly Witter Stetson (1807–1899);

and their children (all born in Brooklyn, Conn., except where stated):

Almira Benson Stetson, born May 22, 1828;

Mary S. Stetson, born December 8, 1831;

Ebenezer Witter Stetson, born October 22, 1833, died Northampton, Mass., November 1, 1843;

Sarah Frances Stetson, born August 16, 1835;

George Ripley Stetson, born May 11, 1837;

Lucy D. Stetson, born December 20, 1841;

James E. Stetson, born Northampton, Mass., April 24, 1844.

1. Mary, Sarah, Ebenezer, and Almira Stetson to James A. Stetson

Brooklyn Jan 13th 1843[1]

Dear Father

As the other children are going to write a few lines to you I thought that I would write and tell you How I have got along in my studies at school. I have got to Interrest In Arithmetic. we have got ~~to~~ through the bounderies in Geography we have been studying them for a great while and we have got all the bounderis in the world. I want to study the History of the United States very much and if you think it is best I will, for I could get the lessons at home some times you know. Our singing schools are united and Mr Bard is going to have us review all our ~~sums~~ Rules this Evening we got your letter last evening and were very much pleased at the story you told about your going to the meshine shop I can not think of any more to write now only that I am very well except a cold from your affectionate Daughter M. S. Stetson.

Sarah says that she can not write so she has composed this and I will write it for her she says

Dear father

I send my love to you and I wish that you would come home Dear father I wish that you would buy me a doll you know that [you] promised that if ~~I you~~ I would stay in the house one day you would get me one and I did not go out once that day.

Some poetry of Sarah's selecting

> Poor Lucy was so ill one day—
> That she could ne[i]ther walk nor play.
> And felt so heavy in her heart—
> She had to keep her cradle,

from your daughter
Sarah Stetson

My dear father,

I now have A few moments to spare as the rest of the chrildren are a going to write I will tell you about my studies. I have got to Practice and have got in Geography as far as Mary has and have been through the gramma[r] once and have got most through again I have got so I can skate pretty well but a thaw has been here and has swept away all the ice so we cannot skate

your affectionate son

Ebenezer W Stetson

Brooklyn Jan 13ᵗʰ 1843

My Dearly beloved Father,

Mother says that as all your letter's are ~~directed~~ addressed to "Wife and children" she does not think that she ought to answer them all and she thinks that you would be pleased to have a letter from all of us. so we thought that we would write and answer to your kind letter of the 9th which we received last night. We are pretty well except Lucy she had just got over a sick turn which we think was occasioned by her teeth when she seemed to have a dreadful cold but Mother has doctered her pretty smartly and she seems a great deal better today and I guess that she will get along nicely. We have had colds but have not been sick with them. Mother gave Ebenezer a sweat Saturday and that cured his cold. Grandmother is pretty well except a lame back she fell down three or four stairs the other day and hurt her back some, but not dangerously. Your eldest daughters Elizabeth and Sarepta are very well.[2] I think that you are well paid for the trouble of ~~writing~~ writeing if laughing would pay you we had quite a laugh over your epistle I rather think that I should be a good hand to go to Northhampton if there are so many fishes there for I can catch two to time though I might not be so good at fording the water as your Miss Ford is.[3] I should think that she was a wonder in a strange land. I do not like the idea very well of sleeping in the winter with the thermomerter 12 degrees below Zero with a window open, but so it is and who can help it. I am afraid if I should pursue the course of ~~your ——y~~ Mr Ruggles up there that I should be so smart that I should jump over the meeting house by spring and do not know but that I could lift it too.[4] I rather thought that the association people would either turn to fishes or salamanders or some other creatures—but I supposed that they are trying to see how far they can jump and not kill themselves. Mother says that she thinks that I had better lay my plans before you and I feel that if I can do any thing to help ~~allong~~ along that it is time that I should know what I am a going to do And first, If you do not conclude to ~~to~~ go to Northhampton in the spring, I do not see what I shall do unless I live out and that I do not want to do. unless you see ~~aut~~ aunt Sarah and see if she will fulfill her engagment to take me as an apprentice I think if I learn that trade that after I get learned I shall find employment any where where we should happen to pitch our tents. Mr Coe[5] says if we want to live all in a heap as we always have that I must go and learn the trade of the Misses Tracy over in Killingly but I think that I should learn it more ~~thougally~~ thougherly of Aunt Sarah but you must do with me whatever seemeth the good

But I have writen my part so good bye.

from your affectionate daughter. Almira Stetson

Addressed: James A Stetson / Boston / Mass

2. James A. Stetson to Dolly W. Stetson

[Feb 20, 1843]

My Dear Wife You see I am again detained here an other week this time to accomodate Doc[t] Hudson & Mr Adam to attend the convention at Manchister[6] with the horse they disign for me to take which horse by the way I am told is a very Lazy one so I must drag snail like for 5 or 600 miles through snow banks & I know not what Else through the coldest state in the union O! Dear it almost friezes me to think of it, but never mind I never ~~dreaded to do~~ did a bad job yet but what I found it less terable in the Execution than I feared before I began and a man who has lived through the terrour of asking his <u>wife of her parents</u>, and <u>a man to indorse for him at the Bank</u> and having the pay day come around with <u>nothing in his pocket to pay it with</u>, can live through any thing Else under the Canopy so I hope (as I have gone through all the above Calamities and more, too,) that I shall start next Monday morning with good spiritts and relying on the protection of him who has thus far protected me reach my jurneys End in saifty & find you all well but I must here from you before I Shall return so you must write as soon as you receive this and direct to Burlington Vt. where I hope to be the latter part of next week—You see by the first page of this sheet[7] that new Laws have been enacted for the regulation of the community for the year now entered upon which I hope you will consider upon and as I am about determind to remove unless you see some great objection to our doing so ~~to~~ as Early in the spring as possable, but I promise you to begin with that I will not Come here unless you think Best so you must make up your mind pro. or Con. for by it I shall

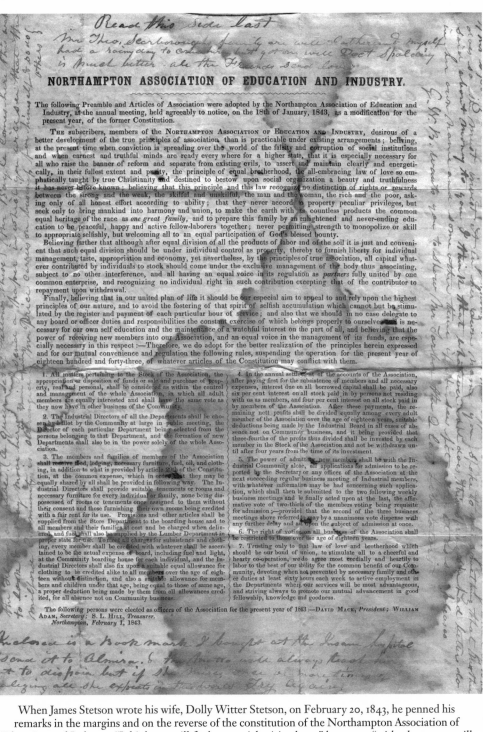

When James Stetson wrote his wife, Dolly Witter Stetson, on February 20, 1843, he penned his remarks in the margins and on the reverse of the constitution of the Northampton Association of Education and Industry. "I think you will find congenial spiritts here," he wrote, "with whome you will be happy and in whose projects you can hartily unite." (Courtesy, Historic Northampton)

be guided in order that you might be better able to do so I will give you my reasons for thinking it best to come. & first for yourself I think you will find congenial spiritts here with whome you will be happy and in whose projects you can hartily unite not in all perhaps but mainly & for myself if I could but see you happily situated (after the trials and crosses you have born since my reverses came upon us,) where you could injoy more rest more advantajes for mental & moral improvement which I Know you so much long for I should ~~I shoul~~ then be a happy man ~~always putting~~ the welfare of our children will always be uppermost in our minds & I am greatly mistaken if here is not the best place for them that we can possably expect to get, if they can but carry out the plan they propose in their different Schools I see not why our children may not be highly Educated in Body & Mind and when I say that I think these people deeply imbued with Religious principal I must say that I have my doubts wither the system they propose to persue will prove the best that might be adopted. to this our special care must turn & if we like not thair plan we need not adopt it but can pursue any other we choose. I must further say that it requires considerable faith to believe that thair business system will sucseed, as at presant arranged I do not think it can be very proffittable but I am fully persuaded that they intend to do the best they know, and not being bound to System they are free to amend when ever they shall see the need of amendment. I wish you would ask Mr Tarbox to show you Georges[8] last letter again and see if it is there stated that the Earnings of the community for the 8 months mentioned was 2900 Dollars over and above the pay of wages if it was the statement will be like the one made by the man that Saw 100 Bears and when his statement was doubted he put it at fifty and again at 25 & finally at one and when his friend said he now doubted his having seen any well said he I did see—<u>where one Set</u>—we either got a wrong impression or mistook or George made a mistatement I told him what [he?] wrote he said he was in a great hurry and might have writen a blind letter.—in the first part of the 4th provision of the printed Laws it is stated that after paying for the subsistance of members, &c—the subsistance therein mentioned is regulated by a Committee and is the Law for the presant year and provides first that all persons over the ages of 10 years shall be allowed ,,80 cents per week for board which in our family amounts to $166,,40—all under 10 years ,,40 for them $83..20—in all for Board $249,,60 all over 18 are to receive 20 Dollars from 14 to 18 = $14,, from 10 to 14 = $10,,00 from 6 to 10—$8,,00 under 6 $5,,00 which in all makes 90 Dollars for clothing for Board and clothing $338,,60 for our family if the community dont Earn Enough I cannot tell you where or who makes up the deficency if they Earn more the printed Laws show how it is to be disposed of thise are some of the facts in the case the people here seem sanguine of sucksess Mr Hayward is coming from Salem in the Spring & brings 1200 Dollars others are applying but without Capital.[9]—& now for the other side of the picture (if I may call this imperfect scrol a picture) & the First is our Beloved Mother. what is her wish concerning us? & how can we act so as best to discharge our duty to her you are her only Child & her happiness must be consulted by you can you lieve her in her old age to the mercy & Care of strangers that has taken care of you in your infancy I know you Cannot, nither Can I. what is to be done then will she Come with us or shall we stay with her? you & she must answer these questions and in doing it you must yeald yours to her wishes & happiness—again will the advantages for Intelectual & Physical Education of our children and ourselves recompense for the giving up of <u>some at least</u> of per<u>sonal freedom</u> and the possability of wrong or rather of scarc any Religious instruction I mean in preaching unless we go into town, which will undoubtedly create unplesant feelings in the minds of some here, & (another qustion is the opposition to the Clergy well founded <u>I am in doubt</u>) I mean the Extrem opposition but on the other hand how lame weak deficient ~~is the~~ and corrupt is the influence of the Orthodox preaching in Brooklyn & Every where and among allmost all sects must our Children be cramped by it,—Again if we have more light & think we have any influance in Extending that light ought we to come away from B.[10] & Extinguish that light by mingling it with the Meators that may Blaze up here for a while & then go out for Ever I am confounded myself & it will take your own Clear mind to lead me out of the Laberyanth I am almost ready to give up my manhood & say wherever you direct but keep me with you and I will submit.—I will only add that if we come here we can have a comfortabl tenement alone or go into Community house in the factory to the last I at presant am intierly apposed—I will state one thing more they propose to take schollars from abroad at $100,, per year that all under 18 are in the Educational department & receive no pay other than as above & thair Education—one thing more it snowed most all last week & is snowing niow (sunday) & has been very cold—tomorrow I hope to start Kiss Lucy for me give my love to all the Children & mother and believe me when I say that I Love you best of all yours J A. Stetson

Read this Side last

Mr Theo. Scarboroughs[11] family are well Catherine & myself had a rainy day to come here but got on well Doct Spalding is much better—all the Friends send love

G. W. Benson Sais that mother partly agrees to let him have some money this spring I do not know any thing about the affair & I will only say that if she does so she must invest it in her own name you spoke to me something that Mother said about money to you I think that whatever she does this spring she had better do in her own name and some other time if she sees fit alter it as she pleases

G.W.B. wants you to show Mr Tarbox the 2 last Liberators

I have attended meeting this afternoon Mr H Scarborough led in reading 5th 6th & 7th chapters of Geneses. I find quite a number of Transindental-ists. & they think the account of the Flood a fable (a queer set of Fellows these) Mr Boyle comes here this week to look & he may move here[12] I send a paper in which you will see that the Milford Community is all arranged in thair affairs Mr Price carries on business for himself & so do others[13]

Inclosed is a Book mark I bought at the Insane hospital I send it to Almira. & the motto will always teach her not to dispair but if she mises once or more times of realizing all she expects in this world Try Again.

Addressed: Mrs. Dolly A. Stetson / Brooklyn / Connecticut
Postmark: Northampton Ms. Feb 20

3. Dolly W. Stetson and Almira Stetson to James A. Stetson

Northampton April 21st [1844]
Sunday Morning

My Dear Husband

thinking you may be in Boston the first of the week[14] I seat myself to give you some account of matters that have occured here since you left—and first of all I am waiting with all the patiance I can for you to return to help me thro with my confinement or I know not why else it is that I am so long in this state of anxiety and waiting. I hope threfore that your business will admit of your returning by the last of this week—Aunt Mary has been quite tired out with the care of Aunt Ruth[15] she has been more unwell the week past and I do not know but her sands have allmost run out—Almira has been very sick all the fore past of last week—but is now nearly well— her sickness was something like the scarlet fever she had a very bad canker throat and a very high fever. I was quite alarmed about her for several days. I gave her a sweat which reduced the fever and George gave her some medicine that killed the canker very soon—the rest of the family have been pretty well—

The next day after you left Mr Mack came to me and wished to know if I was willing to exchange tenements with him.[16] I told him that he knew that I had always been willing to live in the factory but that you had objections to living there, and I should not decide any thing about it but that they must write to you. Mr Mack said that he felt himself pledged to raise 1000$ in the educational department that he had been promised a suitab[l]e place for the school and that he had advertised that they would be ready to receive shollars the first of May

After receiving your letter I read what you wrote about moveing both to George and Mr Mack—George was disposed not to do any thing about it untill you returned but Mr Mack was very anxious to move and he though[t] George did wrong not to write you more particularly about it the reasons why it was nessesary that we should move—Mr Mack suggested that we might move up to Samuel Hills house if I thought you would prefer it[17]—I told Mr Mack at last if he concientiously thought that the good of the Association required that we should move we would do it—As far as I was concerned I thought we had better move for I had Aunt Ruth and her nurse to board and she was liable to die and make much more work and Mary almost sick and Almira quite and I could not see how the family or myself were to be taken care of so I told Mr Mack if we were to be moved before the first of May the sooner we moved the better, accordingly at eleven o,clock yesterday word came that we would exchange tenements yesterday afternoon and so after picking up our clothes and getting things in a shape to be moved I went down to Catharines[18] and spent the afternoon leaving all for others to do— about sundown I came down to the upper story in the south east corner of the factory where I found my family and goods I think you will like the change very much it seems plesant to me to get up and have time to see to the washing and dressing the children before breakfast and have them look decent by breakfast time, and the noise I think is no more anoying than the whining and grunting of neighbours children

Monday Evening

I have now tried another day in my new home and am sure that for the present I am sure I shall like very much—after allmost seventeen years of more or less care of housekeeping concerns it is a great change to have no responsibility about what we shall eat and what we shall drink—It seems as if I was visiting only that I cannot make out whose guest I am—Almira is nearly well to day—Aunt Mary has got quite rested and has gone to stay to day with Aunt Ruth—the rest of us are as well as usual. All desire very much to have you get home and see how you will like it I am very much disappointed about the noise here I think I can truly say I have not spent so quiet a sunday since I have been in the Association a[s] I did yesterday—I hope you will be able to eff[ect] some arangement by which you can stay at home and that by our past experiances disappointments and trials we may grow to be a better and a happier family here and be prepared for a reunion with those of us who have gone in their innocence and purity to the world "where there shall be no more sorrow or crying and where all tears shall be wiped from every eye."

I have been very busy to day in fixing clothes for Thomas to go to Boston on Wednsday[19] I will leave the rest of the sheet to be filled tomorrow evening—

Tuesday Morning

The report is going the rounds this morning that the Hutchinsons are to be here on sunday likewise Gay and Remond[20]—I hope you will be at home—Mr Payne wishes me to request you to purchase a thermometer worth a dollar—[21] I should like to have you call upon Ann Mann and get Mary and Sarah some cheap and pretty Summer bonnets and pay for them out of the money due to me from the silk department—I am sensibly admonished that my time has fully come—Oh! that you were here

Wednesday Morn

Dear Father

I welcome you not only of by the name of <u>my</u> Father but as the Father of <u>six</u> happy and I trust good children The last to make up the six came into your charge last night quarter before twelve, it is a son and brother Aunt Nancy and Mary say that it is the exact picture of Ebenezer dark hair and all[22] Mother is very comfortable indeed <u>never</u> got along more comfortable. Aunt Nancy was the <u>sole</u> attendant The children know nothing about it yet. Lucy heard it cry and said there is the <u>baby</u> but nobody noticed it You <u>dont</u> know how relieved I feel not to have the housework to take charge of and every thing seems so much more as it ought to be and I think it is about as still here as it was at our old <u>home</u> Come back as soon as possible Saturday at the fartherest because it would be quite an erroneous idea for the <u>babe</u> to get <u>that</u> it had got no <u>Father</u> when it has It is so very <u>knowing</u> that I do not know but the says <u>Parder</u> an <u>Mother</u> (I should'nt wonder) from loving Almira

Addressed: Mr James. Stetson / Boston / Mass // Care Thomas.

4. Dolly W. Stetson to Anna Jackson

Northampton May 23[d] 1844

My Dear Anna[23]

haveing an opportunity to send a letter by Catharine I thought I would just tell you that we had not forggotten you but remembered you with the same love that we felt for you the times that are past. I have another son— he was born the twenty fourth of April. he is a fine growing child, but it does not seem to me that he can ever fill the place of Ebenezer that dear child whose birth gave such joy to us all, and who so seldom in his life did any thing to cause us sorrow. but why grieve for him his amiable disposition and good principles were such as I belive insured him a welcome to his Fathers house where "there are many mansions" adapted I believe to the condition and wants of all who are worthy to receive the joyous summons to "enter into the joy of their Lord[24]—We are all well and all the children send love to you—Mary has worked a book mark and sends it—as you use the Bible more than any other book I think a cross will be an appropriate mark for you— Sarah has made a chain for you and hopes you will like—George wanted to send you something but says he cant send any thing but love—and wishes you would come up here—Almira is so much engaged with work that she has not time to make any thing to send—but she wants to see you very much

I wish you would write or get some one to write me a long letter and tell me all about yourself how you are in "mind body and estate" or else come up here and tell me face to face which would be better—I expect Mother to spend the summer here with us—I hope you will see Catharine she can tell you much more than I have time to write

Husband is in Boston and will be seldom at home thro the summer—

My baby will not let me write any more so I must close wishing you every good gift both in this world and that which is to come

truly your friend

DW Stetson

Addressed: Anna Jackson / Providence // by Mrs Benson

5. Dolly W. Stetson to James A. Stetson

Sunday Afternoon

Dear Husband.

I believe that I must begin by saying that were are all well and hope these few lines will find you enjoying the same blessing.

the fact is you have acquired some how or another the art of writing so interesting letters that I feel some what embarrassed to know what to write. my imajineation (if I ever had any) has so long lain dorment that I find it impossible to arouse it into action, and my opportunities for observing the works of nature and art, are limited to the brick walls of my room or at most the prospect from my windows. The singing of the birds is drowned in— a,wah! a,wah! of the baby who fulfills the promise he gave when you were at home of being a very crying child. I know not why he should cry so much for he is a fine growing child and begins to look quite like a baby—the day that he was a month old he weighed eleven pounds. Lucy has cryed several times for Father to come home and George has been very indignant to say the least that you are not to come home soon—you have now been gone about as long as you have been usually on your peddleing expeditions and it seems to us all that you aught to return I had that thought Association was to keep families together instead of seperating them—

Mother does not come yet but I shall expect her every day this week—I am very impatient to have her come—for I do long to have liberty to do something where I see so much to be done as there is here—

I have not even been able to make you any shirts or collars but if you need them very much I will make them my first business—but I have constant applications to make this blouse and mend that and cut this dress and sew on this button so that unless you need them I shall be likely to neglect them for the wants that are constantly pressing me—I am glad that I am in the family here for I do not see how I could ever get along with my own family if I was expected to keep boarders and take care of my baby too—I want you to write where you board—how you succeed in business how your business agrees with your health and every thing that you think will interest me—the letters that you send to George or Mr Bassett[25] I never see—they are too much engaged in their own business to think that a woman can ever want to hear from her husband

Mary was rather disappointed that you did not mention the boquet of flowers that she sent to Nancy Atkins whether or not she was pleased with them—I suppose that you will see Lucy & [the Co?] and perhaps Doct Whitcomb and wife cannot you get the Doct to get a certificate from the select men of Brooklyn for the storage of the cannon and pay it over to the trustees of the fund—

Tomorrow completes seventeen years since we were married that is since our union was sanciond "according to law" in looking back on the past I find much to regreat and much to enjoy. many seasons of joy and many of sorrow. many omissions of duty if not commssions of crime on my part, "many things done that I ought not to have done and many things left undone that it was my duty to do" but there is one point where my conscience does not accuse me of neglect of duty and that is in "multiplying and replenishing [rest of letter torn off][26]

Addressed: pr Giles S[tebbins]

6. Almira B. Stetson to James A. Stetson

Northampton May 26th 1844.

My Dear Father,

We received your last letter by Mr Fuller.[27] He seems to be a very pretty young man His trade is the tailors but he only cuts, does not sew at all. Now I am going to write you a real community letter, and tell you all about every

Northampton May 26th 1844.

My Dear Father.

We received your last letter by Mr Buller. He seems to be a very pretty young man. His trade is the tailors but he only cuts, does not sew at all. Now I am going to write you a real community letter, and tell you all about every thing. Last Monday night Aunt Ruth died. The thursday before she was moved to the Factory and Mrs Bradbury took care of her. Mr Bradbury took the room that Oliver Paine used to have and Aunt Ruth had Mr Brigham's bedroom. Sunday she seemed more feeble, and Monday she complained of being very cold in the afternoon. Both her legs that had been swelled so burst open, and about seven quarts of water run from them and she died at seven that evening. Her friends had her carried to Westfield, and had the funeral there. We had about a fortnight ago there were two people come here from Western New York. gentleman and lady. They were married the week that they started. Mr Loomis is his name he is a great farmer and has come very highly recommended by Dr Joslyn who writes that "if he were there he should rather have him the half a dozen young men with $5000". They are real go ahead people and take hold of work as if they had some interest. They were very much disappointed in the looks of the place. Mrs Loomis says that she had no idea that there was a place in old Massachusetts that look so wild — and that her husband

In this letter dated May 26, 1844, Almira B. Stetson, the oldest of the Stetson children, writes to her father: "Now I am going to write you a real community letter, and tell you all about every thing." (Courtesy, Historic Northampton)

thing. Last Monday night Aunt Ruth died The thursday before she was moved to the Factory and Mrs Bradbury took care of her Mr Bradbury took the room that Oliver Paine used to have and Aunt Ruth had Mr Brighams bedroom.[28] Sunday she seemed more feeble and Monday she complained of being very cold in the afternoon both her legs that had been swelled so burst open, and about six or seven quarts of water run from them and she died at seven that evening.

Her friends had her carried to Westfield, and had the funeral there. We had about a fortnight ago there were two people came here, from Western New York, gentleman and lady They were married the week that they started Mr Loomis is his name he is a great [farmer?] and has come very highly recomended by Dr Joslyn who writes that "If he were here he should rather have him the half a dozen young men with $5000." They are real go ahead people and take hold of work as if they had some interest. They were very much dissapointed in the looks of the place Mrs Loomis says that she had no idea that there was a place in old Massachusetts that looks so wild—and that her husband who has been to Wisconsin feels transported back there it looks so uncivilised here. They appear to be very intelligent pleasant people. Theodore wishing to have his advice and so forth has taken them into his family.[29] Mr Hammonds family has come and got settled in Mr Adam's house they expect Mr Whipple in about a week I like them very much. I went over and help them some and have got quite well acquainted with them. He is by profession a portrait painter but he does almost any thing He has been white washing the rooms at the Factory, and the next job is the old Boarding house which is to be whashed on the outside. Mrs Hammond has a piano and is quite a singer.[30] I spent the evening there Friday and we had "dreams of future bliss" Mr Hammond wants to have the swamps in front of the factory and by his house drained and all the trees and brush in the swamp dug out with the stumps and a handsome fence round it and plant fruit trees in clusters and have a gravel ride round it and then have a flight of steps go from the foot of the hill through the woods up to the new community house, and have that beautiful spring in the woods brought to the middle of the garden and there have a fountain. Oh——when shall we see all this. But I feel assured that we shall see it some time. I mean to bring all my energies together to accomplish it. Mr [Kerr?] has come and has settled down with Uncle George.[31]

Doctor Hudson has left with his family, and Hiram Wells is to live there.[32]

George Ashley went down the other day to be married and found that he was obliged to be published in his own town and brought his intended home with him and the talk is that he will be married when Roxy is. Roxy is expecting Nickinson every day—she improves every day on the strength of his arrival.[33] Mr Wilson is here came last night, he says this place seems like his home.[34] James [Ryle?] has been here staid several days.[35]

I believe this is all the Community news I have to write, and Mother is going to write, so there is no domestic that I know of. The Miss Hayden's were admited for a year last night.[36] But I must tell you of my birth day present (as I call it.) Mr Charles May had a letter from his brother Samuel saying "Tell Almira that I should be very happy to receive her into my school next term which commences on the 11th of next Sepetember. The tuition shall cost her nothing and a term of fourteen weeks will be only 20 dollars expense to her but more of this another time" Mother says that she supposes that it will be considered the same as a withdrawal as it will be the very time of year that they will want me the most—the commencement of the realing business.[37] I had a letter from the Martins the other day and they write that Lincoln is but just alive, and would not live but a very few days in all probability Write by the people from the Convention. your sixteen years old daughter

Almira B Stetson—

Addressed: James A. Stetson. / Boston. / Mass. /
Merchant Whasa St. // By Giles.

7. Dolly W. Stetson to James A. Stetson

Monday Morning June 3rd [1844]

My Dear

I hear that there is a box to go this morning to you so I haste to say a few things to thee—we have had quite an exciting time the past week—on Thursday George Was Sullivan fell from the belfrey on the front side of the factory struck upon his feet and we all thought he would die—but by plentiful application of cold water and a cold water sweat he walked down stairs in six hours and remains quite [s]mart a little lame in one foot—[38]

Saturday afternoon Uncle George[39] and mother arrived—I was very glad to see them I can assure—I hope I shall be able to make Mother happy here—I think I shall not have so/// many lonesome hours as I have had—I know/// [y]ou will laugh to hear me tell of lonesome hours/// [bu]t James cries so much that I cannot take/// [hi]m out any where and no one wishes to///[?] with me—Yesterday at five oclock Mr/// [Ashley] was married under the pine tree the/// [name?] of the Lady I do not know—the novelty/// [of the] thing was rather damped by a shower/// [Mr. Warner jus]tice from town was the legal representative/// [George?] Benson I understood addressed them[40]

Rufus Lee has been here a week—I believe that the suit between him and Lucy is quashed as the lawyers say[41]—I think you may make the most of your being a "Boston Marchant" while your present stock of silk lasts as I [think?] the prospect is that you will have but little more/// [. . .] Mary Ann Smith says tell Uncle James that three of us can wind five ounces per Day day with Mr Havens help—The silk that Georg///[e] got in Boston they cannot work at any rate—[42]

There seems to be a fatality attending our silk/// [. . .] There has been a German here that professes to/// [. . .] the art of Dying silk in the Italian manner/// [. . .] weighting it more than James has done with/// [. . .] less expense—James has been to Conn with hi///[m?] and had him dye a few pounds of silk—he/// [is?] satisfied that he possesses the true Italian/// [. . .] the man understands dying silks and woolen/// [. . .] and talks of comeing here to join[43]—Enough/// [ ]

When I read your kind and affectionate/// [letter?] I felt humbled and grieved that I had not/// [. . .] deseved thy love and contributed more to thy ha///[ppiness?] but I hope and pray that our last days may be///[. . .] and happyest—

When do you intend to co///[me home?] if you dont come soon you will not/// [know your?] own children—Uncle George Mother and Ch/// [?] in love truly yours. DW Stetson

8. Almira B. Stetson and Mary Stetson to James A. Stetson

Monday Evening. [June 3, 1844]

To my father,

The bundle of silk has not gone yet and so I thought that I must acknowledge the receipt of your short letters today by Giles.[44] We of course were very glad to have them. I trust that in your excitement of Temperance processions Antislavery meetings and shop keeping, you will not forget our little festiveitis

Yesterday George Ashley was married up under the "pine tree". Uncle George Benson, got up and said some few things among others that Mr Warner's the justice of peace that he considered it an emblem of a corrupt state of public opinion that he was present and that his presence was necessary in order to have this brother and sister married. Tuesday Uncle George[45] came with Grandmother Saturday night and he staid untill Monday morning He seemed to like the place very well, and seemed entertained at the meetings, and wedding. I believe that all the people are well in Brooklyn. Lincoln Martin is dead. died about 10 days ago. We had quite an arrival last night only ~~evl~~ eleven, to be accomidated. It is astonishing how this factory streches. we were crouding full before last night, and we took in 6 strangers and might have accomidated 12 more just as well as not But this is not a <u>priming</u> to the Convention I suppose but if all the Convention people come to stay a fortnight as some have I shall give up.[46]

We are trying as hard as we can to get things put up and get to looking neater. they are painting the old boarding house inside and white washing it out side so there is a new house. I am in the cocoonery to work I like it very well this crop of worms ~~are~~ will be off in about three weeks. and then I am going to reeling I think it will be a very pleasant part to reel, (compared to what it was last summer) as the warter to be heated by steam so no heat will be in the room. Lorenso Nickerson has come and says he must return this week so that wedding will come off this week.[47] Oh did you ever see such a time Mr Wells has gone to Conneticut to be married.[48] Oh———————
I can not possibly write more of this stuff so as I have nothing else to write I may as well stop. All send love to you from your <u>daftur,</u>

    Almira

PS

    Among the comers last night were Mr Gillett and wife little boy and Frank Brown. Mr Gillette is the third party candidate for Governor in Conneticut— Roxys friends.

I am really ashamed of my letter when I see Marys. but she has not writen at snaches and in a hurry, as I have

My Dear Father

We have just received your letters, you do not know how glad it makes us to have a letter from you, without you are just as glad to have a letter from us and I guess you are, at least I hope you are. George was very much pleased with the picture that you sent him, I should think it would be a beautiful sight to see so many people together but I should think ones eyes would get tired if they looked at them long. I suppose mother has told you about George Washington's Sam Patch jump I guess he wont go out on so dangerous a place for a little stone again. Sojourner says that if it was the Devil that made him fall it was the Lord that prepared a place for him to fall upon for he came right between a large rock and the platform and on the softest place that side of the factory.[49] Uncle George Sharpe went back to Brooklyn this morning. Mr Ashley was married last night his wife was a very pretty looking woman. Mr Nickerson has come tonight & I suppose that we shall have annother community marrage. You must not think that our little baby crye's all the time for when I kissed him and told him that Father sent it to him he laugh as hard as any baby a month old could laugh. I suppose Almira wants to write and as Sarah is tired and wants that I should go to bed with her I must close my letter.   from your ~~friend~~ daughter
    Mary

Almira says that I have begun the letter on the wrong page but I guess you will find the place to begin,

we have only 13 strangers to lodge here in the factory to night

Addressed: For our Father Stetson. / Boston / Mass /
A Merchant there in N⁰ 2½ Hanover Street.

9. Dolly W. Stetson to James A. Stetson

Saturday Morning[50]

[I]'ll just say that we are all well///[disa]ppointed that you do not think///
[to come hom]e untill July—We thought you/// [would come?]home to the
Convention—///[ ]t had the marriage of Mr Nickerson/// [sol]emnized by
the legal authority—/// [They were?] married at the breakfast table///[. . .]

39

new brown bread instead of wedding/// [cake? w]ater instead of wine—I almost wanted to be married again it was done up in so simple a manner— No I dont either for I do not think that any one can do any thing better than S. J May[51]—

Lucy says that she wants to see Father berry much—I think James is getting to be a better boy he does not cry <u>more</u> than half of the time—we thank you for your fine discription of the temperance Jubilee—I read it to David Ruggles he said it was <u>rich</u> When you have "nothing eslse to do" you had better write "letters from" <u>Boston</u>[52] for some of the papers you excell so much in discription But unless you can get well paid you had better send them to me yours truly D.W. Stetson

Addressed: James A Stetson / 2½ Hanover St / Boston // By Mr & Mrs Nickerson

10. Dolly W. Stetson to James A. Stetson

Northampton June 16th [1844]

My Dear Husband

As I now am indebted to you two letters I think I will commese a letter in season to fill a sheet with something before Mr Garrison returns[53]—and first of all our "Convention" is a small affair in point of numbers to what was anticipated, and those that are here are more Abolitionists than Associationist and if I could judge by the meeting I attended this morning Association will have the go by.—the principle matter of debate this morning was the slavery of the north and south compared—Garrison objected to the term slave being applied to us at the north—N. P. Rodgers contended that we were are all slaves and that we must emancipate ourselves before we could do any thing efficiently for them of the south[54]

I have attended but one meeting they have been holden in the hall of Mr Hills house it was filled to a jam this morning this afternoon they ajourned to the pine tree—Mr Garrison will tell you much more than I can—Wm Adams of Pautucket exorted us to come out entirely from all connexion with church and state and acknowledge no Goverment but the goverment of God. he said we could not obey the command to love our enemies and feed and

Northampton June 16th

My Dear Husband

As I now am indebted to you two letters
I think I will commence a letter in season to fill
a sheet with something before Mr Garrison returns —
and first of all our "Convention" is a small affair
in point of numbers to what was anticipated, and
those that are here are more Abolitionists than Associationists
and if I could judge by the meeting I attended this
morning Association will have the go by — the principle
matter of debate this morning was the slavery of the north
and south compared — Garrison objected to the term
slave being applied to us at the north — N.P. Rodgers
contended that we were are all slaves and that
we must emancipate ourselves before we could
do any thing efficiently for them of the south.
I have attended but one meeting they have been holden
in the hall of Mr Hills house it was filled to a
jam this morning this afternoon they adjourned
to the pine tree — Mr Garrison will tell you much
more than I can — Wm Adams of Pawtucket exorted
us to come out entirely from all connexion with
church and state and acknowledge no Government
but the government of God. he said we could not
obey the command to love our enemies and feed
and cloathe them without being hung as traitors
by the Government if they were at war —

Dolly Witter Stetson was an active participant in the life of the Northampton Association. In this letter to her husband dated June 16, 1844, she relates the community's deliberations on the issues discussed by the leading abolitionists of the day. ". . . the principle matter of debate this morning," she wrote, "was the slavery of the north and south compared—Garrison objected to the term slave being applied to us at the north—N.P. Rodgers contended that we were . . . all slaves and that we could do any thing efficiently for them of the south." (Courtesy, Historic Northampton) cloathe them without being hung as traitors by the Goverment if they were at war—[55]

I have had Calvin Stebbins and wife as guests they were very sorry not to find you at home[56]—I have not seen Mother Stetson but once she has not come down to the factory yet—I intend to go to see her again tonight[57]

I have just had a letter from Anna Jackson enquiring the best way to come here—Perhaps you had better write to her when you are comeing home and have her come on to Boston and come with you if you think best[58] Direct to the care of N.[T?] Morse

¼ before 11 sunday Evening

We have had a meeting in the dining room this evening Mr Boyle and Mr Hayward have had a real fight of words it appears by Mr Boyles statement that when Mr Hayward went to Hopedale and other places he visited he indulged his fault finding disposition to its fullest extent implicatin the moral honesty of the leading men of the association and by his influence hindering those from assisting us that otherwise would Mrs Bassett told me that Chrystopher Robinson of Lynn was comeing here to place a daughter in the educational department but had been prevented by his representation of us[59]— Mr Hayward says that James Boyle has called him a liar and a cut throat of the Association before his family and he stands so accused in the minds of his own children—I can give you no idea of the scene you must witness it to conceive of it Hayward raved like a mad man Boyle cool and severe letting of his red hot thunder bolts—I was frightend grieved and ashamed to have such a demonstration of brotherly love made to strangers the Association hold a private meeting tomorrow morning to have a full hearing of the whole affair

Monday Afternoon

I have attended the meetings all day to day—Mr Boyle and Hayward settled their difficulty last night at least there has been nothing said today

We had a statement to day of our pecuniary concerns very much like what was made at our annual meeting—it seems that in consequence of the sickness of his wives sister last winter he was prevented from getting the subscription of twenty five thousand dollars filled up they have got 16 thousand dollars subscribed two thousand of which the Stebbins deny their intention to give theirs—

To induce the friends of Association to come together and make up the deficiency of the subscription was the object of this convention but few came and that few were of those mostly that had not much of the needfull—the whole therefore seemed to be a failure George stated that 12 thousand Dollars was nessesary to meet our liabilities and go on with our business and unless some way could be devised beside haveing him travel from one end one of the country to the other to obtain loans in one place to make payments in another he cannot do—he says it is a burden that he cannot bear—he would make two propositions, he would if they would take some of the responsibilities off his shoulders and try to get on with their business, he would relinquish his stock to the association, or he would purchase the property of the association and pledge himself to pay the deb[t]s and stock in four years—he would leave it for them to decide—Mr Sanger offered to loan them 4000 Dollars if they would go on.[60] I was not at the meetings all the forenoon but I believe they all had one general cry at the thoughts of breaking up. some say they will not go at any rate—I believe, the Executive the Stockholders and the visitors the men I mean are holding a meeting this evening in the office what the result will be I know not—I see by your last letter that your mind is much excercised about the stand this Association intend to take upon the marriage question I have heard but little said upon the subject they had a discussion one sunday afternoon but I was not present I questioned Sydney about his views understanding that he took what they called the no marriage side. he said that he did consider marriage a sacred institution that a man or woman could not be marrid but once, that those that were holden together merely by fear of legal punishment were not married in the highest sense—but he considered legal restraint nessesary for those who knew no higher bond of union—[61]

I expect to send this by Mr Swasey who goes tomorrow—When Mr Garrison gets home he will tell you more than I can write—

I have made up the purses that were knit last winter they are mostly poor silk and many of them poorly knit I thought it better to make tassils than to sew on the drops that would do for the better ones that the girls are now making—I will send the few they have done—Mr Mack says that a new kind of purse was introduced at a fair in Boston made small and attached to a clasp and selling for 2 or 3 dollars apiece—he thinks that you had better look about and obtain one as a sample if there can be so much profit on them—I will write again by Garrison if I can or any thing transpires that is of importance from your Affectionate, Wife D. W. Stetson

Addressed: James A Stetson / 2½ Hanover St / Boston // By Mr Swazey

11. Almira Stetson, Mary Ann Smith, and Mary Stetson to James A. Stetson

June 19.th 1844.

Dearest Father,

I was very glad indeed to receive your letter as I had indulged myself in feeling quite hurt that you said nothing about the reception of mine in either of yours letters to Mother. Father I do not feel one bit like writing to you or any one else to night for I have the blues as bad as ever a person can have them.

I suppose that Mother told you about our meetings and about the talk of giving up the Association so you must know with my love for this Community I am almost as unhappy as I can comfortably be. There cannot be any thing connected with my life here that will throw a gloom over my spirits as much as talking of this dear community going to break up. But if I cannot tell you something more interesting than this I will not trouble you with it. Most of the people here are strong in the faith of sucess and think that it is almost an imposibility for it [to] sepprate, but Uncle George's faith seems shaken and I cannot have one bit of hope. If every one else had have given up but him I could have beleived all would have been well but now it is all all gone. Uncle seems rather more hopeful now I believe, but my feelings are not at all changed. Oh you will say I wish such stuff might be kept at home so good bye from your daughter Almira

There has $5000 been subscribed now th[r]ough the convention I will endeavour to write a fit answer for you kind letter soon

Well Father the Convention is over, the Community allmost "bust up", Roxey married and gone off, the old cracked bell sold, and a new one in its place, the old bridge painted, the brown boarding house whitewashed on on the out side, the wood all sawed & piled, a new hog pen built and an addition made to your family of an 18 year old daughter since you left. Think you not tis time to come home and see to bussiness. The world will say "I knew 'twould be so." Nothing more of importance has occured, therefore I subscribe myself your daughter. Mary Ann Smith.[62]

My Dear Father

As Almira and Mary Ann have written to you I thought that I would write too we have had a convention that lasted 3 days and two evenings Parker Pillsbury was here and he spoke a few times but what he said was first rate,[63] Mr Garrison s[p]oke several times they have talked about the community's breaking up I do not bleave that it will, Sojourner says that she does not bleave that that it will 'go down" as they call it and as the Lord reveals every thing to her I guess she knows I must draw my note to a close as it is nearly school time but one thing I want that you should tell us if Mr May is sick or why he does not come back

do come yourself as soon as you possibly can.

From your most affectionate

daughter

Mary

Addressed: James A Stetson / 2½ Hanover St / Boston

12. David Ruggles to James A. Stetson

Northampton June the 20th 1844.

My Esteemed Friend Stetson:-

I send this to say that I addressed a letter to Thos Hill, containing an order on you from J. Bradbury, for $21,00; and a request that you or Thomas would oblige me by purchasing an India-rubber syringe, and send it by the earliest opportunity. If T. is not in town please read his letter, and should it be convenient send the article as it is indispensible to my progress in the "Water Cure".[64] You will of course hear from us all by your better-half.

Accept my best wishes for yourself and present my respects to Thomas Hill.

Yours truly,

D. Ruggles.

(By an amanuensis)

Addressed: James Stetson / 2½ Hanover St. / Boston. // By W. L. Garrison

13. Dolly W. Stetson to James A. Stetson

Friday Evening July 26th [1844]

My Dear Husband—I have a few moments of leisure and commence a letter hoping to get a sheet full before Mr Bassett sends a box to you—

I hardly know where to commence a diary of affairs that have occured here since you left as I do not know how or what the girls wrote to you.

The first thing that occurs to me is the fall that Almira had last Saturday. She was feeding in the upper story of the cocoonery and fell down backword to the ground her head and one shoulder striking a beam. She was brought home insensible and remained so nearly two hours—I had no idea but that she had injured her head so that she would never recover—and my first thought was to send for you but by the use of cold water she soon began to recover and was next day able to go down stairs and is now quite well except a lameness across her back and shoulders—she goes to school and work now She said that allmost the first thing she thought was I am glad Father was not here he would have sufferd so much on my account—I was very much alarmed myself but perfectly self-possessed—Mr Boyle saw her fall and thought from the manner that she fell she must have been faint She thinks so herself as she has no recollection of any sensation that she was about to fall—we received the attention and sympathy of all the people of the Association—The next thing of importance was the reception of your letters which afforded us a great deal of pleasure altho rather of a melancholly sort— we were glad to hear that you were well and to hear from so many of our Brooklyn friends ~~were well~~—but joy and sorrow seems mingled in their cup as well as in ours—It is and must be so with every place and every person and they who expect to be exsempt from sorrows will find themselves bitterly disappointed———I sometimes feel that I want to go to Brooklyn myself but I do not know but a visit there would give me more pain than pleasure—I think it has been so with your visits there—I wish you would tell us how Angeline Smith is——Mother returned from Hadley on Wednesday She has got thro with her services at Mr H—[65] She says your letter has rather discouraged her from thinking of fixing up the house not so much that Uncle George[66] does not think of going as that you think that there is no inducement to go there yourself—with regard to going onto the farm—it seems to me that the time for our going there under the most favourable circumstances has passed had we gone there when Father was alive or soon after his discease when the farm was in good repair and stocked it would have been much better for us than now when there is neither stock or tools or any conveniencies for doing the work in doors or out—[67]

On Thursday Mr Hammonds little child passed to the spirit land—It has been a great sufferer a long time it flesh was all wasted off its body the funeral was Thursday 4 oclock P.M. Mary Bryant composed a hymn which was ~~one~~ sung by the young people at the funerall another hymn selected by Mrs Hammond was sung[68] Remarks were made by Mr Boyle Mack and Bassett Sojourn[69] also spoke with much feeling and sang something on the death of an infant—The services were said to be very solemn and impressive—it rained very fast and I did not go over—Each of the children belonging to the Junior and Infant class had boquets of evergreen and flowers mingled which they intended to have thrown into the grave upon the coffin but as it rained they put them into the coffin as they went to look at the corpse—Last evening after the funeral two of Sojourners daughters came from New York— their meeting was very affecting one of them came like the prodigals son— haveing disobayed her mother and gone to live with a man who is a widower and under promise of marrying her kept her to take care of his family and I do not know what more untill she became afraid of him and he abused her shamefilly some friends of Sojourners rescued her from his grasp and wrote up to see if she could come here they said she could and her sister came to accompany her they are two fine looking negresses as you ever saw and are energetic like their mother[70]

Louisa Rosebrook has another severe attack of lung complaint Doct Barratt from town is attending her—her case I should think doubtfull—[71]

And now with regard to your questions and first, "do you have all the work to do." I can tell you how we proceed Stephen getts up in the morning makes the fire, puts over the kettles, cuts the bread, stirs the pudding, etc while I excercise a general supervision of affairs, the Hayden girls you know set the tables and wash the dishes—After breakfast David Ruggles gets in the wood shells peas strings beans or prepares potatoes as the case may be with the assistance of Mrs Bradbury I make the bread gingerbread pies etc when we have any—I cook the dinner and Mrs Bradbury gets the tea[72] Aunt Mary takes care of James makes my beds and keeps my rooms in order—so you see that my task is not very hard—second—"how have you settled the marriage question!?—I dont know as it has been settled in any way or even discussed. I have not attended any meeting since you left and if it has been brot up I do not know it—Lucy Hayden returned from Bath the day you left—She sayed that she had felt very unhappy ever since she had received Harriets letter and did not know what to make of it—but when she returned home and found how the matter was she sayed that she considered them engaged and nothing more—she says that as long as they do not live together as man and wife they have not sinned but she thinks they have acted foolishly—Lucy is not willing to go to Ohio with them so it was indefinitely postponed. David Ruggles told them the other day that he knew from the opinions he had heard expressed by a great many that they never could be admitd here as members and they had better go while the weather was warm than to wait untill fall when Sydneys year was up. that set them in motion again to go but about this time Harriet was taken raising blood from her lungs and has raised more or less every day since—I do not know how the matter will end I think Lucy does not like Sydney much they often have long and warm discussions in their room————[73]

With regard to our staying in the Association with an Accumilating debt[74]—I can only say that if we have not full confidence that this will be a pleasant home for us and our children it cannot be right for us to stay long in this way—but I do not know how we can know whether or not we are accumuleting a debt untill the end of the year—business at present seems looking up Lumber sells well and they have a lot of very good stock for the silk factory on hand—the silk growing is doing well and Pain[75] has got his reeling opperations started reeling onto bobbins or little reels about the size of bobbins whether it answers his expectations or not I do not know—your question with regard to the paying of debts would depend upon the other if we stay here I should prefer that this money we should receive for the place should go to pay debts as far as it would than any other way[76]————If Almira stays here I think she must with the advantigies she receives here (altho they are not all we wish) in two years more pick up a much better education than we ever received or than we should ever be able to give our other children if we went on to the farm—

With regard to you feelings toward this Associaton you aught to know their origin much better than I do but I tell you frankly that I think you have embibid a very bitter feeling toward///[. . .][77]/// and you consider him as the associat///[ion . . .]///id and in disliking him you dislike the whole altho you may not have the same feeling toward another member of the Association—Your business too has been very perplexing ever since you came here and that has still farther embittered your feelings.—I hope your business in Boston will be better now that they have started up the manufactoring with new life—

With regard to your being a Jonah I dont know—but it would seem rather hazardous for a Jonah to put to sea alone—There are things here that I do not like myself, but I do not know where we could go in this world and find every thing to our minds but it does seem to me that if you could be at home with us we might be happyer here than we could be to return to Brooklyn— but if you cannot stay connected with the Association and feel differently from what you have for some months past if you cannot be happy I think we had better go I will say as Ruth sayd to her Mother in law, "Whither thou goest I will go—where there lodgest I will lodge thy people shall be my people and thy God my God. Where thou diest I will die and there will I be buried—The Lord do so to me and more also if aught but death part thee and me[78]————

They are to have a conference of the three communites in this state and another convention the last of August I hope you [mean to be?][he]re at that time.[79]

I had a very pleasant call from David Reed and an invitation to make his house my home if I went to Boston—but Mother says—"I dont think you will go" which in other words means I think I dont want you to go. I hardly think I shall myself

Charles May wishes you to ask the Father of Ch^s Haslett if he ever received a letter which he wrote him and say that he had heard from Ch^s Haslett and he had arived safe at Chicago————

David Ruggles wishes me to warn you agains trusting George W. Sullivan about your store or recommending him any where as a trusty Servant he said he was going to Boston when he left.

Many of our people are suffering with bad colds amounting to influenza—I have had it but not to make me really sick—the children are all well I presume they would send love and kisses if they were awake but they and all the rest in the house are fast asleep and nothing is heard but the snore of the sleepers—I cannot flatter myself that this long scroll can give you one half the pleasure that your letters do us if it does I am fully recompenced for writing—This is a spendid evening—the moon looks so bright and beautiful contrasted with the dark trees down the lawn—I fancy you have been taking a walk on the common thinking of home and us, or what would be worse thinking over the difficulties that exist with regard to the Association—I do hope you will not worry any more flesh off—for do remember that it does no good to the Association or ourselves

Octavia tells me that she has had a letter from a brother of James and that you have got you a new coat.[80] I am glad of it—Theodore and family leave in a few days for Brooklyn—they do not withdraw as member of the A neither do they take their furniture and they may possibly return in the fall if Herbert gets more cheerfull and Theodore gets better.[81] they are going a trip to the ocean

Good night—I wish you pleasant dreams and a happy waking—truly thine, D. W. Stetson

Addressed: James A. Stetson

14. Almira Stetson to James A. Stetson

<u>Saturday</u>. [July 27, 1844]

Father Here I am it is almost breakfast time and a box of silk is to be sent today so I understood last night after bed time and I must write to you. therefore if this is not as good and perfect as you would wish you must excuse it. for it will have to be an excuse, as you say you do not overlook any faults in your children.

I suppose of course you will read Mothers letter first and hear of my over throw. so I will not tell you any thing about except that I am getting along very well indeed and there is no serious injury, so please dont alow yourself to worry about that atall, will you?

You enquired about the report I suppose mother has told you about I was not present at the reading of ~~them~~ it so I cannot tell you any thing. We had 25 bushels of cocoons of the first best quality they came off very well indeed much better than we feared having so much unfavorable weather and new hands put on to feed, and all other things considered we went beyond of best expectations. We have a larger crop on now and very ~~unfa~~ bad weather indeed I do not know what will be the effect but we are rather fearful that they will not do as well as the first crop.

My eyes ache badly now from writing this having nearly ~~knock~~ knocked them out of my head by falling.

But I must tell you about the school Miss Gove the widow that is with Mr. Bassets family has taken our class and makes it very pleasant and useful[82] Mr Mack was very much out of health and not very energetic and did not make it useful. I have not attended this week but shall commence again Monday. Mr Hammonds child is dead and we had a very interesting funeral on Thursday afternoon, but I must stop.

If you do not find worse mistakes than making n's for w's ~~then~~ in this note I am very much mistaken.

The book was very nice indeed next time I will write longer and better farewell from your daughter

Almira

Addressed: The earnest gase of / Father Stetson / Boston / <u>Our</u> Store // By the politeness of the silk box

15. Mary Stetson to James A. Stetson

[probably July 29, 1844]

My Dear Father

As Mr Green was going to Boston this morning I thought I would write to you. we were very much disappointed not to have a letter from you but I hope you will not let annother oppertunity pass without a letter. I had a letter from Diantha yesterday and a note from cousin Martha she made me a preasent of a nedle book. the people in Brooklyn are all well, Diantha says that she goes round taking care of baby's. I did not think when I wrote about the letters that you had been to Brooklyn. ~~but~~ and I hope you will tell about your visit in your next letter. Mr Ruggles says that I am getting strength the fastest of any one he ever <u>saw</u>. I thought I would tell you so that you might expect to see me when you come back a great fat girl almost as large a Almira If getting stength will make me ~~large~~ fat

    from Mary

Mother says that she did not know that there was any oppertunity to send to Boston until this morning and she is busy in the kitchin and cannot write but she hopes you will write a long letter an tell all about your visit in Brooklyn. George & Sarah send there love. Lucy talks about you most all the time

    Mother and I send our best love

    from Mary

    Addressed: Mr James A Stetson / Boston / Mass // By Mr Green

16. Almira Stetson to James A. Stetson

Northampton. [probably July 29, 1844]

Dearest Father

Mr Green is going to Boston at nine it is now seven aclock but we could not let him go away without saying a word or two. We were very much disapointed not to have a few words from you to tell us about your visit

Last night the quartely report was read but I was so tiered I could not attend Mary Ann said that it was the most encouraging report we had ever had all the departments are in a better train for business and there is a prospect that all the expectations of the members at the annual meeting will be fully realised

We have just got off our first crop of worms they have come off first rate, excellent cocoons and very few sickly worms. David Reed the publisher of the Register was out here the other day and gave Mother a very urgent invatation to come to Boston and stay at his house You know that Mother was an intimate friend of his wife He also urged me to come and spend several weeks with them. I think Mother will be down in October if possible. you must back her as much as you can. I can not write any more now so good bye,

Almira

Broken hearts are bad things.

Addressed: James A Stetson // By Mr Green

17. Almira Stetson and Dolly W. Stetson to James A. Stetson

Northampton Sunday August 4th 1844.

Dear Father

According to your request I now have sit down to write to you. But I donot know what to write. I hoped when I sent the last letter I should be entirely well and be able to write more encouragingly about my self but I cannot. My back is still lame and painful and I cannot do scarcely any thing that is atall laborious without being entirely tired out. Dr Walker was out here yesterday and I saw him. He gave me some directions, and is to send some medicine out to me, which I <u>hope</u> by care on my part will cure me before long. My head and shoulder do not trouble me atall now I do not think the fall affected them much. The pain I used to have in my hip has entirely gone. I have not felt any inconvenience from it this some time.

Well I think I have talked enough about my self, and will try a say a word about some thing else. We were all very glad to hear ~~about~~ from you by Thomas and to see him too. Sidney and Harriet and Lucy Hayden are going to Ohio week after next. Sidney is going to Brooklyn this week. I thought you were going to Hingham Friday, why didnt you go?. After supper Friday, the people went to Paradise,[83] and had a very good time, untill dark, and then the[y] went to the hall, on the second flour in the Factory, where they danced. Sorjourner's daughters waltz[d] and it was quite a wonder to the people here. I did not attend. I think the cause of Humanity must have been helped along so[?] much, by the meeting here!![84] I shall leave the rest of the letter for Mother,

From your daughter Almira Stetson,,

My Dear Husband. I am as much troubled to know upon what subject to write as Almira said she was—the news of community that has transpired since I wrote the long epistle, she has summed up in what she has written and the monotinous round of the kitchen is not much calculated to cultivate or enliven the intellectual facultes But I will tell you here lest you should think that my labours are wearing upon me that I was yesterday weighed and I was not "found wanting" in flesh for I weighed 152 lbs, about twenty pounds more than I usually weigh in the summer especially when I nurse[85]—But enough of this

I am troubled about Almira—Doct Walker was here yesterday and I happened to see him and had him see Almira he says she must practice cold bathing followed by a great deal of friction on the skin and by no means use violent exercise like running up stairs taking long walks etc He says it is not a difficulty of the spine but of the junction of the hip bone and the lower part of the back bone called the sancrum—I would sugjest whether she had not better go to Boston this fall and I stay at home I think it would be good for her to have a change of scene and air for a while—I have thaught of proposing to have her return with Thomas[86] but have said nothing about the matter to her and shall not untill I know your mind and I think she is not strong enough to go now—Mother goes to Hartford this week with Mr Huntington she will not probably make a long visit there—I read the part of the letter you wrote about going to Brooklyn if she prefered it She says that if we were contented and happy here she should be as happy here as any where—She thinks that I was more anxious to come here than you—have liked better and am less inclined to go onto the farm than you are—this may all be true—but I think that I know better than either of you the difficulties attendent upon going there with our numerous family and getting along with any degree of comfort—I believe that mother could not be placed in circumstances more unfavourable to her happiness than to have us go there and attempt to carry on the farm it would be such a trial to her to have things go on so differently from what they used to when Father was alive—But setting all this aside if you wish to go there and try farming I will go and do my best—I have no doubt tha[t] I can be happy there and should rather go than have you unhappy here or to have you permenantly located in Boston

Have you seen the call in the Liberator for the convention—it reads quite flattering—but I think it true to Mr Macks idea of what we are to become—I have heard nothing about the subsciption but I should infer from the language of the call that they had got it filled up[87]—We have not heard a word from Nancy for allmost 3 weeks she had then been sick with the Dysentary at Elizabeths and had not been to Lowell or Nashua We expected her home last night but were disappointed.[88] Mother Stetson is very much afflicted with lameness across the chest and in her knees Catharine has been quite unwell and Tommy and Mary both sick with summer complaint Our children have colds except this they are well and James grows finely—he is going to look like George—Aunt Mary thinks she has hard times taking care of him

I believe the silk growing business is quite lively they have a large crop just ready to wind one day last week they cut 200 bushells of foilage before tea and all hands turned out after tea they were in such a drive—The silk manufactory I think is looking up—two new winders are comeing tomorrow Abner Sanger has assisted them to purchase 34 cases some one told it cost 7000 $

You have a good deal of leisure in the store I suppose and I hope you will write often if you do not have private opportunities the postage is so little now. You need not fear that your letters will be unacceptable—Mary says that they are so much engaged feeding the worms that they have no time to knit purses but in school and they are tierd then and dont wish too knit— the school increases continually. Mr Parkers family I understand have got to move to accomodate the shollars[89]

Good bye for to night—May Heavn bless you
 D.W. Stetson

Addressed: To James A. Stetson / 2½ Hanover Street / Boston / Mass // Endorsed: Forwarded By Hale & Co. From Northampton.

18. Giles B. Stebbins to James A. Stetson

Northampton Ms Aug 7[h] 1844

Friend Stetson

I have thought of writing you a letter for some time supposing that any thing from one who every day sees your wife and children would be welcome to you; and in regard to the said wife and children I will now say that they are well except Almira, who has not yet quite recovered from the effects of her fall, although she is less hurt than I apprehended, and in an improving condition toward full recovery with proper care,

Your little boy grows "like a weed,, and is getting to be a sort of prodigy, having even so far shown the action of his <u>inner light</u>, as to have smiled repeatedly, and performed sundry other prodigies which I have no room to mention. All is going on here as usual-you have doubtless seen the call in the Liberator for a convention the 31st of this month; in regard to building a tenement for 100 families it seems to me that unless those families are to be the very <u>salt of the earth</u> it would be an injury to the Association to recieve so large an accession, as I can see every day that it is difficult to bring those now here into that order and appreciation of the great end for which they come together which are indispensable to success. However I have but little idea they will succeed in getting the necessary means for building so large a house; and probably, one that should accommodate in addition to their present number some fifteen or twenty families, <u>at most</u> would be much better for the present. I want to see none come here, rich or poor, humble or learned, except those who are by being <u>reformed themselves,</u> fitted to reform others: those who shall be ready to every good work, and gifted with wisdom and zeal to repel the approaches of evil habits and wrong principles, and make this a "city set on a hill,, to give light to all around.

I am more and more satisfied that those who engage in this Association reform must be possessed of rare purity, wisdom & truth, combined with practical knowledge and a large share of that indefinable regulator of strange vagaries which we call <u>common sense</u>.[90]

S Southworth is now gone to Connecticut, he returns in one fortnight and will then leave for J O Wattles community in Ohio. I think the marriage discussion has <u>done good</u>, and will put a stop to any farther proceedings like those of Sydney & Harriet.[91] On the whole I <u>do</u> think your people here are growing more rational, and nearer what <u>I</u> think right. I can see tendencies which I do not like, influences which are not what they should be (as one can every where) but on the contrary much that is good, although there is great need of improvement and want of wisdom to guide and elevate. Our friends here eschew physical power, and penal restraint, but they <u>must</u> be willing to bow to the power of superior wisdom, and enlightened self-restraint, or no reform will be accomplished; this they are seeing more and more, and if the wisdom is now, or <u>will be</u> here, and the ~~restraints are~~ necessity of mutual concession for the common good and earnest diligence be felt all will be well. Your wife says you wish to have her visit you in Boston this fall. If she does not go as she seems not inclined to, let me intercede with you for Almira to take her place—it will do her a great deal of good to spend a few weeks in B under your care, and I do think that a change of the kind would be highly beneficial both to her physical and moral health; think of it, and if Mrs S does not go, let Almira if possible be the substitute—

And let me ask how do you prosper in the city? I would like much to drop in of an evening, and have a good chat with you, but cannot just at present. You continue of course at your old boarding place which must be very pleasant, as you feel more <u>at home</u> than you would among those who took no interest in <u>you</u> or <u>yours</u> beyond that of a common place friendship. I have w[r]itten you these two pages and no chit-chat news in regard to what is going on here, in fact I am a poor vender of news, and I suppose too you get all that from your own folks. I shall leave here in a few weeks, and now intend to start for N York immediately after the convention—where I shall be I cannot tell having no particular place in view. Let me hear from you in answer to this pr private mail which costs next to nothing, and which I like to help break down the government monopoly. I have a favour to ask of you which is that you will get for me Miss Martineau s <u>"Martyr Age in America</u>,, being a review of Right & Wrong in Boston and the early days of Anti Slavery—also <u>"Right and Wrong in Boston</u>,, both of the above in a pamphlet form if possible as they will be cheaper. I want very much to get the Reports of the Board of Education by Horace Mann, for 1843 & 44, if they can be had of <u>Marsh Capen & Lyon</u> (who are the printers I think) or any other booksellers please get me one or both. the Minor[ity] report of the Legislative Committee last winter on Capital Punishment I want very much, will you get me a copy if one can be found?[92] I send a note to Miss Peabody N° 13 West St for some books, will you hand it to her, get the books, and pay for them, and also pay for those you may get for me, do up the whole in a secure bundle, and send to Wm Bassett by the Package express? If you will enclose a bill of the Am<u>n</u>t paid I will pay him here. Am obliged to you for getting Spear's work which I rec^d in due time, do not delay to send by private opportunity but forward pr Express—

I shall be much obliged to you for the trouble you may take for me. Please write if possible when you send the books, accept my best wishes for your welfare & happiness

Your Sincere friend

G B Stebbins

Addressed: . . . tetson / . . . anover St / Boston / Mass
Endorsed: . . . orwarded by . . . ale & Co. from Northampton.

19. Almira Stetson to James A. Stetson

Dear Father   August 8th 44.

I have just this moment been informed that a box of silk is to be closed to you in about five minutes and Mother says Almira go and write a few words. And I am very glad so to do. I feel more encouraged about myself than I have for a long time my back is some better not so much as I wish, but enough to give me encouragement. Dr Walker's medicen has done me a great deal of good I think, and with care I shall get along Do not worry about me any more than you can help. Thomas seems to be enjoying himself much (though he is with Mary Ann so much I donot see much of him). they have gone to commencement to Amherst to day I should have gone if I had felt able to ride so far. Grandmother and Mary are to start for Hartford tomorrow morning Mr Theophilus Huntington is to carry them down. Mary is very much elated and as Grandmother is to pay the expense I am very glad to have her go, it is a very sudden start as Mary did not think of going untill Tuesday night, they are to be gone a fortnight. O what a horrid pen I cant write any more with it if I try

So farewell from   Almira.

Addressed: Father Stetson / Boston / Mass // Care of Silk box.

20. Almira Stetson and Dolly W. Stetson to James A. Stetson

Edendale August 25th [1844] Sabbath.

I was informed at the dinner by Mr Chamberlain that he would carry any letters to Boston if we wished and so I thought I would give a letter of introduction for him. I hope that you will have some opportunity to writ converse with him as I think him a very intellectual good man, and if you ask about the country he has staid so long he will give you a very interesting account of it if he has time.[93]

Aunt Nancy arrived home safely on Saturday and we were of course very glad to see her after an absence of eight weeks, she is almost eaten up we are so rejoiced. Mother thanks you much for the long letter you wrote her if she ever finds time she will answer it. Those plumbs were beautiful to look at I presume they were very good. I wish if you come up to Convention you would bring some with you. Grandmother and Mary came home on Tuesday they had a very pleasant visit ~~stay~~ and Mary has her head as full of all the fine things she has seen as it can well hold. I would not have her go to Uncle's to live for any thing she would fall so easily into all the fashion and foolery of society she has a taste for it and would soon be a devoted worshipper at that shrine where so many have sacrificed every good and moral principle of their ~~souls~~ natures. Uncles people are all well and sent much love to you, and they send some very valuable presents to you also. By this time I suppose you want to know how I do Well I am better than I have been the past week[s?] I have not been able to do any thing this week of any consequence, but I think now I shall get well soon I wished you had come up with Aunt Nancy. The rest is for Mother so good bye Almira.

Monday Evening

My Dear, I suppose I cannot make you sensible how much I was disappointed that you did not come home with Nancy, Saturday for Swazy[94] had said that you wanted to come very much and I applied the old proverb "where the is a will there is always a way" and thought you would bring it about somehow I am very anxious that you should come up to conventon On Friday we are to have a conferense of the three Associations in this state and we hope to have Mr Ripley and Mr Balou here and who else I know not—Chales May thinks Samuel J. will be here, I hope he will I wish that he could be happy to live here I know he might be very usefull in the Educationl Dp[t95]

And now why cannot you remove your silk to your new place and come up on Thursday and stay a week at least they have got a beautiful lot of sewing and saddlers silk ready for you but they would like to keep it to show to the people that may be here—James Atkins thinks that the castele soap[96] is a great improvement in point of softness and lustre. I wish more over you to come and see Almira. I fear that the realing is not agoing to agree with her better than it did last year. Doct Walker advises her to go a journey and

Charles Richardson is going in a few weeks on a cousining tour and has asked her to go with him[97]—now I do not know what to do she of course is anxious to go—I want your direction as I very often do in our family matter—

Mother has had a letter from Emily Witter in which she mentions the death of Mr Adin Carter his second daughter and that Ebenezer Carter was very sick if living—She says that she heard that Mr Palmer had purchased our place in the villiage[98]—I suppose that Mary has given you an account of her visit to Hartford—I was happy to have her go and was glad that she had a cordial welcome—we have received some very good presants among which are two good winter vests for you next winter—James has interupted my writing so much this evening that I have not time to fill the sheet without encroaching on the hours of sleep

I wish you pleasant dreams of home,

I thank you for your <u>long letter</u> by sister Nancy. if you do not come this week I hope you will write a longer one, but I had much rather talk with you than write for my gift of the gab is much greater than my talents at writing

Almira says that she is much obliged by the musick you sent upon those papers—I suppose she hopes to be able to play it on the piano some time as she has commenced taking lessons of Mrs Hammond

Good night

DWStetson

Addressed: James A. Stetson / 2½ Hanover or 228 Washington St / Boston / Mass // Favourd by Mr Chamberlain

21. Mary Stetson to James A. Stetson

Aug 25th 1844

My Dear Father

I have a long story to tell about my visit to Hartford It was a pretty sudden start as I did not think of going until two day's before, I went. We went with Mr Huntington a man that lives in Hadᵉly we had a very pleasent ride indeed When we got to Springfield we met the whig convention in a prossesion marching to the grove where they were going to have several addresses. we could not get along and Mr Huntington stopt the Horse. there was a great many bands of Music & some beautiful banners. I never saw so many people in my life before. It made me think of the discription that you sent in your letter about the Temperance Convention. The Music appeared to frighten the horse and Mrs Huntington was in a great hurry to get ahead so that we did not stay quite as long as I wanted to. we never should have got through the crowd as I know of if we had not followed a stage and people did not appear to like it very well that the stage should break through the prossesion it took us half an hour to get through the prossesion. we went past the Armary but Mr Huntington did not tell us wath it what it was when we were near it so that we did not see it, we did not ride on the river excepting to cross on the ferry boat once. and over that great long bridge at Hadly. when I got to Hartford we found that Aunt Tyler[99] had gone to Saratogia but she was going to return. the next day Mr Cowan was very unwell and Aunt Tyler had gone to get his two daughters but he would not let but one of them come when Aunt came she appeared to be very glad that we had come she said that Mr Cowan was some better than he was when she went there but they did not think that he would live. She brought Mr Cowans oldest daughter to live with her she was 3 years old and her name is Catherine she is a very pretty girl and she sings beautifully and she dances when any one will play for her she keeps time very well but she does not know any of the steps. I found cousine Mary Stimpson there she is a very pretty girl her hair curls all over her head she has not very good health she says that she has sudied so much that it has made her unwell. she is ten years old. She made my visit much more pleasant than it would have been if she had not been there I went into the city several times which is only a little ways from uncle Tylers there house and I went to the deaf and dumb Asylum and I have learned all the letters so that I can talk some with them. Cousine Ogden goes to a Boarding school and only comes home Saturdays so that I did not get much acquainted with him he is going to be ready for collage in two years or at least is going to try to be. Cousin Edwin was to school most of the time and I did not see much of him I got acquainted with one two girls that lives in Hartford and that is all

Aunt Tyler has got a beautiful place. her house is very pretty and her garden is very pretty we stayed in Hartford 11 or 12 days and then we come home Aunt Tyler filled the carpet bag for us to bring home and gave us several little thing's beside I enjoyed myself very much while I was there and did not feal home sick once. when we came away Aunt Tyler said that she hoped that some of us would come again. I hope if you go the we came as far as Springfield in the Steamboat and we had pretty funny times the boat got aground twice and I was afraid that we should not get off but we did. they stopped before they got to Springfield and we all got out and took a stage and rode 6 miles and then we took a boat again and went as far as Springfield we staid over night to Mr William Chace's a nephew of grandmothers and the next morning we started for home I was as glad to get home as if I had been gone a year. the only thing I wanted was to see you and I was very sorry indeed not to have you come with Aunt Nancy but I hope you will come as soon as you can we all wants to see you very much.

from your affectionate daughter
Mary S Stetson

22. Dolly W. Stetson to James A. Stetson

Northampton Sep.[t] 1.st—1844

My Dear Husband—While the most of the people have gone up to the hall to meeting I will sit down to tell you some of my impressions concerning the convention—

Perhaps you may not know that a conferance of delegates from the different Associations in this state were to meet here on Friday or the day previous to the convention Mr Ballou and Mr Draper from Hopedale and Mr Wrightman from Brookfarm[100]

We hoped to have had the pleasure of seeing and hearing Mr Ripley and Dana[101] but I suppose they did not think it worth their time—I went up on Friday evening to hear their reports or conversations—Mr Wrightman appears like a thorough practical man—one who has seen much of the world as it is—and has long had a desire to make it better—he is a thorough Fourriaite[102] and most he had to say was upon the advantagies found in their present arrangement of their labourers into Groups and series over their former disultory mode: he holds it a primary truth that all the oppression and suffering and wrong under the sun is oweing to repulsive labour when labor is made attractive by a propper division and succession of employments when each is left to choose his or her work every person will fall into their right place and perfect harmony will be the result as certainly as from an instrument perfectly tuned in the hands of a skillfull musician—He said much of the advantages of a unitary building for the accomodation of a large number over isolated houses and thinks it not best to commence with less than 15000[103] persons—I should call his talk the poetry of Association Mr Ballou talked more of Association as it <u>is</u> and many things they have experianced we could likewise attest too he goes for single dwellings for families. I should think they were getting along slowly and surely—Mr Ballou is a fine speaker and I doubt not an excellent man and some of our people are quite captivated with him and his Association. I wish you had been here to see and hear for yourself. I suppose a report of the sayings and doings of the convention will be printed as it was voted to have a reporter that they might be— the more I hear of the sacrfices that are required and the labors to be performend in this cause I can but say "who is sufficient for these things, my conscience tells me that my motive in entering association was to better my own condition and that of my children and not the elevation of the race—

Monday Morn

The convention is over—I have not attended all the sittings of the meeting—I cannot take care of children and go to meeting at the same time—a great deal of discussion on the test question—our preamble was construed into a creed and we were attempted to be used up for haveing a creed Henry Clapp was the principle opposer of tests—He is a transcendentelest and would not bind himself much less a fellow man to a fixed and unmovable standerd hoping as he says under God to grow wiser every day.[104]

I think that as far as our association is concerned it will prove to have been "all talk and no cider" but perhaps it will prove vinegar as I think it will ~~widen~~ rather strengthen the impression in the mind of Mr Rosebrook and some others that the decleration of sentiments is a creed[105] Doct Jocelyn who came here with a view to join goes away saying that he will never join a Non Resista[nt] Community[106]—The convention was very respectable in point of numbers—the men looked like hard working Farmers and mechanics— There were none of the stars of Association here such as Channing Greely &c &c[107]

After reading the call at the opening of the convention . . .[108] stated that some explanation was nessesary to prevent a missunderstanding of it—He said that at the time of the issueing of the call they supposed that the 25000 $ that was nessesary to put us in easy circumstances was actually subscribed— but circumstances had arisse[n] that had wholey changed the affair—I suppose that as it was not filled up before the 1 July that some of the subscribers refuse to pay—but I have not authority for saying this—I have been told that Auth Ruths heirs intend to contest the 1000 $ she gave us—[109]

Mother,s Stetson and Witter are both well. Mother Stetson is comeing down here to spend the week after we get settled from Convention—I have had an attack of Dysentary and was very sick one night—and was cured as by a charm by a few doses of homopathic medicine—If I had 5$ to spend I think I would sooner by a box of that medicine and a book of Directions for its use than allmost any thing else

Almira has made acquantance with a daughter of Francis Jackson[110] who has been here and would like to go to Boston with her but she cannot start on a journey at a moments notice—Every moment of my time has been so occupied that I have not had time to come to any conclusion about either her or myself making a visit to ~~Boston~~ you but it takes no time at all for me to conclude that you had better come hom as soon as you can—you have money in your hands that you can use and I have not———

Last week we had a regular blow up from Sojourn and Boyle[111] about the young people—Thomas Hill and Mary Ann Smith had to take the most of the cursing for being together so much—Swazy and Lucy R came in for a small share—Boyle used most unjust language and prodused a great deal of disgust W. Basset says if he and his children have got to hear such language here he shall go some where else

you see that I have written things just as they occur to my mind and as fast as I could write you DWStetson

Addressed: J. A. Stetson / 228 Washinton St / Boston

23. Dolly W. Stetson to Anna Jackson

Northampton Sep[t] 8th 1844

My Dear Friend Anna

George Benson told me that you wished me to write when I intended to go to Brooklyn and I write to say that I have given up going this fall—

Almira has been quite out of health for some months past and I thought it better for me to stay at home and let her go a journey this month—she has gone to Boston to stop a while with her father and will then visit Lowell and

Nashua friends I think she will probably be gone about all of this month and I hope she will return with her health improved—I hope this will not effect your visit here for Mother myself and the children have looked forward with a great deal of pleasure to seeing you and haveing you make us a good long visit—I think you had better come by the way of Boston where you will find husband at 228 Washington St—I think it not impossible that he will come home with Almira and if you could all come together it would be all the better

I will write to him to let you know about it

We have lately had a letter from Brooklyn it seem that death had been doing its strange work among our friends in B—blasting the hopes of parents and removing the protectors of childhood—Alass! how wretched would be our lives here without the hopes of immortality inspired by the Religion of Jesus. That its hopes and blessings may be your is the sincere wish of

your friend <u>D.W.Stetson</u>

Addressed: Miss Anna Jackson / Providence / R.I. //
To the care of Nathan Morse Esqr / [37?] Pine St.
Endorsed: Forwarded by Hale & Co. from Northampton /
Collect six cents for Hale & Co.

24. Dolly W. Stetson to James A. Stetson and Almira Stetson

Thursday Morning Sept 19th [1844]

My Dear Husband and Daughter

I have only time to say that we our family are all well, that Lucy Richardson is quite sick but is better this morning somewhat—that mother Stetson is spending sometime with us now—that I have expected a letter from Almira telling me something of her journey and her first impressions of the city of the manner of spending her time and more than all of her health that I hope when you come home you will write to Anna Jackson and let her know that she may come up to Boston and come home with <u>you</u> as I have again heard from her saying that she wished to meet me in Brooklyn and come home with me from there—that I think if you do not come home soon you will neither know or love our little Jamie he grows

so fast—that Lucy and all the rest wish very much to see both of you—
that Frank Fuller has been rejected by a small majority and that it was
nearly a paralell case with Larnards[112] there was so strong sides taken and
warm speeking I was told—I was not there—that the carriage is at the
door—and that you have my best love

DWStetson

I think that I would try a plaster for Almira before consulting any physician

25. Dolly W. Stetson to James A. Stetson

Friday Morning

My Dear Husband

As you are comeing home so soon I think it unnessesary to write a long
letter not that I have not enough to say to thee but that I had rather see thee
face to face and and converse with thee by the tongue and the eye.

Now do not disappoint us I shall look for you every day untill you come
after this week—I suppose Almira will be gone before you receive this if she
is not give my love to her tell her to make good use of this visit let it not be
to show herself off but to observe the persons and things that pass under her
eyes—let her observe the manners and customs of such as have had advantages superior to her own—but above all try to regain her health and
strength—I think you will not receive much silk at present Lucy is sick but
we hope a little better she sat up a little yesterday Mary Cone has gone to
Springfield and I do not know when she is to return[113] Mary Ann Smith is in
very miserable health and is going to Hartford tomorrow So you see that
skeining is left to Susanna Bassett I believe however that they have hired Mrs
Bottom to help[114] If you should change your mind about comeing home next
week I hope you will write Sunday Our Family are all well—Little Tommy
Benson[115] has been sick with the Dysentary but is better All send love truly
thine

DWStetson

Please tell Isaac Swazy that Lucy Richardson is not able to write an answer
to his letters she has been scarcely able to read them

[Postscript by George W. Benson]

Dear James,

I have waited as long as I can to see you—Sophia Foord also waited some time—There is a Box of silk at 451 Washington Street directed to you. Send these letters to Northampton if you dont go, by first private opportunity—the letter to Mr Chamberlain ought to be put into his hands to night. G.W.B.

Addressed: James A. Stetson / 228 Washington St. / Boston // [by] Miss Ford

26. Almira Stetson to James W. Stetson

Nashville Oct. 3[d] 44, Central H[116]

Dear Father.

I received your (well I hardly know to call it, it was so short.) note by Thomas. I was very glad to receive it and I was glad it was so short for it showed that at you was very much hurried with business I feel quite encouraged on your account. Charles has gone to Manchester, and Thomas only stayed one day (but he did very well I believe) so I feel alone—[117]

Though I do not have a great deal of time to be homesick Aunt Betsey was taken Monday with a fever and I take care of her day times She has been and still is very sick. Her fever has settled in her throat and that has ulcerated She has suffered a great deal of pain, and has not been able to sit up to have her bed made I do not lift much as there are so many in the house who I can call upon. I am very glad I happened to be here for there is so much to do that they I cannot possibly take care of her properly—and it saves hireing a nurse. Uncle takes care of her nights—Her physician is a regurlar calomel doctor and he has salivated her I expect [118]

George has been sick but he is out now though not well. he lost about 30 pounds of flesh so he is quite decent now. all the rest of the folks are well. I have not been to Aunt Almira's to stay much but shall go as soon Aunt B— gets well.[119]

All of the friends here seem to insist on my staying all winter or at any rate untill thanksgiving they say that you said that when I came I might stay two or three months. They want you to come up very much and why cant you?

I want you to write and tell me how the Ass-[120] affairs are going on and how you enjoyed your visit? You did not stay long!

I wrote to Mother Sunday and asked her to send up my cloak and a few other things thinking you had not returned. prehaps she will send them by Isaac Swasey—or some one else, if she does you bring them up when you come will you?

I suppose that Isaac has not got back yet? famous for making long visits.

Saturday night just as I was getting into bed Uncle came to the door and said I have got something for you Almira! I asked him if it was a letter and he said yes O I was so glad for I had been real homesick. But what was my surprise and almost dissapointment when I found that it was a most splendid boquet from Cousin Waldo Fisher who brought it from New York.

I never saw any thing so splendidly arranged in my life, and they were not injured at all There were almost all kinds of dahlias. I wish you could have seen them.

My back is about the same some days I think it is a good deal better and some I think it is worse. I dont know what to think hardly.

Write soon I give love to Mr Atkins people especially———and Nancy— and Mrs Swaseys people. I hope she is more contented as business increases.

Good bye ever your affectionate but some times undutiful child

Almira B Stetson.

I received Mothers letter just as I was getting into the cars for Nashua the penny post left it just as I turned the corner in the coach—John brought it down.

Almira

Addressed: Mr James A Stetson / Boston / 228 Washington St. / Mass //
By politeness of Mr Lovejoy.

27. Dolly W. Stetson to James A. Stetson

Sunday Oct 6th—44

My Dear Husband

I am happy to seat myself to talk to you thro my pen for a few moments— and first to thank you for your leangthy epistles by Anna—the news commuctd. concerning the addition to Mr Mays family I heard of soon after it transpired thro Charles May and I was fully prepared to have you crow and of course was not disappointed—but what you will think quite as strange is that Samuel J May writes to Charles that he is strongly thinking of comeing here to live he is undecided whether to come here or go to Syracuse I know not what to think of this—Is George reall honest in ~~believing that~~ representing to such men that this is or will be such an home as they desire—it is true that the Association will be just what it is made by those that compose it and if we had enough such men as Mr May and were out of debt it would be a desirable home.[121] I think the tendencies are to improvement Our Sunday meetings are more interesting and they have commenced the formation of Voluntary classes for every evening in the week—Sunday Evening Bible Class, Monday Evening Singing, Tuesday Evening Grammer, Wednsday Lyceum, Thursday Mathamatics, Frday Readings, Saturday I have forgotten I wish you were here to help to sustain them and keep alive a spirit of improvement among us I think that Instruction and Amusements in their proper places would save our young people from the follies that have been so much complained of—I cannot oppose innocent amusements for the young for I do not believe that utility in a sense confined to the making of money ought ever to be the governing principle or even the acquireing of knowledge without relaxation

I think I can look back to my past life and see where I may have been saved from what might have been far worse by a game of whist—and I had much rather my daughters should be dancing or playing cards (as wicked as that sounds, in a mixed company of boys and girls than in the language of Sojourner to be lolling on each other squeezing each others hands or sitting in each others laps—Now mind I do not say that Dancing and cards are the best way that young people can spend their time but I say that where they are often together they will be apt to spend it much worse—

Mr Bassett has come home quite in love with the Roxbury community[122] the principle advantage of that over this that I ha[ve] heard him speak of is that they have a change of plates & knive[s] at the dinner table some times three changes—this is a great matter truely—he says while our women are so much occupied in manufactoring we can never have proper domestic arangements for ease and comfort—this is somewhat true—

I have had a letter from Almira this week I fear she is not so much benefited by her journey as I had hoped—

I want to see her very much and if she is not likely to be help^d by any new course of treatment she had better come home Mr Bassett would be very glad of her help in the finishing room and if she is not able to work there, she can sew or do something else for help is needed in every department—I dont know but we shall have to keep Anna if she will stay thro the winter[123]—Our pleasure to see see her was only equaled by that we feel when you come home

Lucy Richardson still remains quite sick altho they think her better—She has had a very severe attack of inflamitory rheumatz and has suffered a great deal—Isaac I think has proved himself to be that friend that sticketh closer than a brother—I presume he has endeared himself very much to all the family by his unweried attentions. Mary Ann Smith has returned from Hartford much improved in health—J. D. Atkins was married last Monday Morning at the clergymans house in Chesterfield—he was married by a minister to please his mother—After the ceremony was performed he came home and left his wife, yesterday he went to bring her over here they are going to board at G.B.s untill some place can be assigned them[124]—He would be glad to know if the Swazeys intend to come if they do not he can go into the rooms that have been left for them in the Hayward house—Ploughcut[125] the new dyer has come and has gone into the rooms that Preston used to occupy there Parkers family have moved there so that the Grahamites or rather Sophia Ford has got her will by haveing the whole house under the controll of the Grahamites[126]—Last week there were two fires in town on Wednsday and Thursday evening a barn was burned on each evening about 8 o,clock it was no doubt the work of an incendiary—I believe they have arrested some on suspicion—Our people have become somewhat alarmed and have instituted a watch beginning tonight—you say your cold has left you. I do not know but you gave it to me as a parting blessing as I have had a very bad cold almost ever since you left—but it does not make me sick or take away my appitite—Anna Jackson took a very bad cold on her way here—Sojourner has not yet returned but is expected soon—I do not think of any thing else that has transpired since you left—Robert Owens Address to the people of the United States was read to day in the meeting by Mr Kerr and the relations that should be sustained between Parents and Children and the relation in which children were to stand to this Association is to be discussed—Mr Mack opend the discussion by saying that the relation between parents and children was a divine institution and that Parents were instituted by God as the protectors Guardians and Governors of their children untill they were capable of reasoning judging and acting for themselves and any institution that intefered with this relation whether Associat[ion] or any think else must be contrary to the divine law and deserved only to come to naught—I suppose you will see Owens address as it is in the Daily Mail his ideas upon Marriage are not so bad as have been represented[127]

Almira wished me to send her cloak and a winter dress but Caroline Robinson thinks she cannot take it and I should almost fear that she would loose it too—I will try and send it by George Benson who I understand is to go to B. this week[128] She writes that Aunt Betsey is very anxious that she should spend the winter—Poor Child she does not know that all is not gold that glistens. I want you to write me a good long letter soon. I am so disappointed if you do not write every time any one comes I have not had any thing done to my teeth yet I can hardly muster courage to bear the pain and I sometimes think as age is laying its hand upon me I may as well not try to avoid the sighns of its approach—

Yours Truely   D. W. Stetson

Addressed: James A. Stetson / 228 Washington Street / Boston //
By Miss C. Robinson

28. Dolly W. Stetson to James A. Stetson

Saturday Evening Oct 12th—44

My Dear Husband

I find myself again drawn up to the secretary to write to the absent ones I love—I felt quite sorry to hear that you had given up the store in Boston. I liked to feel that I knew something where you were and not that you were driving about pedling silk—I do not understand how you have given up the business of retailing to Mrs Swazey—Is she to have the p[r]ofits of the trade, for the privilege of putting your silk in the store.—I must say that I fear if she does not keep her own things in good order she will certainly not do well by yours—As for her being a friend to the Association I do not believe it, and I think she would as soon make money out of us as any body even if we supported her husband and the children that cannot take care of themselves.—Isaac says that she will never come here herself or allow her property to be put here—and moreover that his father is a mere non entity in the family—I hope you will keep a good look out for her trading Alas! for these smart women.—I suppose that the attentions of Isaac to Lucy by day and by night, has so knit their hearts together that "no knives can cut their loves in tu" as John Grey used to say, but there is may a slip between the cup and lip as I suppose Rufus Lee could testify—Lucy is some what better and can walk across the room—but her leg is swoolen yet and I think it will be a great while before she will be well again—it is now 10 o,clock so good night

Again it is a most delightful Sunday Mother Witter and Anna Jackson have walked into town to attend Church the children have gone to meeting and I sit beside the cradle to write to you—I feel so much disposed to grumble that you are obliged to be away that I had almost forgotten to be thankfull that I could write to you untill Nancy said to me that I ought to glad that my husband was where I could write to him and the tear that trembled in her eye told me that her mind followed him that had gone to that land from which no messinger returns Let us be thankfull that while death has entered our family and taken some of our brightest gems we are yet spared to each other and to those children that remain and may we be induced better to fulfill our duties to each other and to them that when we shall be seperated from each other and them it may not be embittered by the recollection of neglected duties[129]—

Affairs jog on here in the usual way nothing particular haveing occured since I last wrote—It seems quite like olden time to have Anna here again. I do not know but she will stay thro the winter and take care of the dining room I think that Sophia Sojourner is clearly "encienta" and will be obliged to give up the work which by the way she has done poorly enough[130]—Anna says that she had an application in Boston to cook for a boarding house. I think at any rate if you feel that you cannot be happy here it would be well for her to stay and help us away—but I think if you lived here all the time you would be much more happy—but I do not see how we are to do any thing at boarding in Boston with out money or friends I hoped that if you continued in the store and we left here it might lead to a business that would help us to live that is if the Association were obliged to break up.—I have written to Almira that I wish her to come home. I have felt very anxious about her ever since she wrote me that she was taking care of Aunt Betsey—A public house is not the place for her to stay and nursing is not the employment for her as she must of necessity go up and down stairs a great deal which must be bad for her back—she says to[o] that she suffers much with pain in her head—if she should get a fever and be sick there I should be very miserable indeed I fear too that as she has been most of the time with Betsey she will imbibe a prejudice against the family of her Uncle Winch that will lead her to treat them rudely.[131] I have written to her that if she has not all ready made them [a] good visit to go there and then return to Boston to you.

I think if she does not seem much better when she returns you had better have Dr Wesselhorf see her for I fear that the pain in her head indicates a diseased spine[132]—It was Walkers opinion that it was not the spine that was affected but the jucture of the hip and spine I dont know what big name he called it,—I have got well of the bad cold I had when last I wrote—Anna too has been almost sick of cold and Mary has a bad one now—Lucy says Father must come home and see her—James is gaining streangth daily sits alone upon the floor and has cut two teeth—Sarah and George are the same as usual—Mary wishes me to say that Mrs Mack commences a bible class this afternoon for reading and committing to memory passages of scripture—James D. Atkins and wife board at George Bensons. Mr Kerr and wife are going to occupy the rooms left by Thodore Scarboro—James would be glad to know whether Mr Swazy intends to come with a family to occupy the rooms left by Mr Boyle if not he wants them himself—Isaac goes a ded set against the Association and says that his mother will never come here if he can prevent it—If he does not intend to come he ought to write—it is said that Mr Boyle says that he has outlived his usefullness here there is so much prejudice against him

I shall expect a long letter from you the first opportunity and if you send a bundle of papers I will try and make better use of them

I hope you have ere this got you a new coat if you have not I hope you will get you a good one—I have begun about your pants and will try to get them done by the next chance to send but I do not get much time to sew now Sojourner is gone Anna takes right hold of the work with me which makes it much easier than when you was here—

Charles Richardson has concluded to lieve the Association and live in Manchester with his Uncle Charles[133] Nancy has had a letter from Elizabeth that Little Willie was very sick I hope you will have your silk more to your mind I think what they have on hand now looks nice—

I would send your drawers if I supposed you would need them but Isaac will have a large bundle—I hope you can come home before the weather becomes very cold from your
　Wife

Addressed: Mr. James A Stetson / Boston // by Mr Swazy

29. Mary Stetson to James A. Stetson

Northampton Oct 13th 1844,

My Dear Father.

As Mr Swazer[134] is going to Boston tomorrow I thought that I would write you a short letter. though I hoped that you would write to me first. We are all very well except that I have got a bad cold. We have beautiful schools now. we have Geography and Grammer to learn out of School. Mrs Mack began to have Bible classes now for those in my class we began today and intend to have one an hour every Sunday we had a very interresting one to day.[135] We are going to read the Old and New Testament and compare the Jewish Religion to the Christian. I have knit a purse for Aunt Tyler and had it carried into the fair in town but I did n[ot] get it in early eneough to get the prize. James Atkins is married and has brought home his wife, he has got some very pretty furniture. Anna[136] came here a few days ago we were all very glad indeed to see her she says that Jamy does not seem like any of the Stetson children but he loves her almost as well as any of us. I work in the Silk Room now every day. Anna says that she is homesick and that she wants to go home this week. but she cannot get ready. I am very sory that she is homesick I would give a good deal if I had it to give if she would stay here this Winter, it is almost time for you to come home again is it not: I would write you a longer letter but I have got to write a composition. Do answer this letter if it is short and hardly worth reading
　From your affetionate daughter
　M. S Stetson

Addressed: Mr James. A. Stetson. / Boston / Mass

30. Almira Stetson to James A. Stetson

Nashville[137] October 24th 1844,

Dearest Father,

I received your letter yesterday, I am very glad you are coming up here Saturday for all the friends seem to want to have you come very much

I am glad too because I feel that I had better be getting <u>home</u>. though they want I should stay very much untill after thanksgiving I feel that it would be impossible and as I feel better and able to do <u>something</u> I ought to be at home. My back is better, but my head troubles me considerable and as I ~~am inheriet~~ inherit the propensity of looking on the dark side of things I get low spirited and think I never shall be well, again, I think that plaster has helped me. I should have written to you before if I had not gone to Milford I went up Friday and stayed untill Tuesday with the "Hutchinsons" I had a beautiful ~~day~~ time.[138] I wish when you come up you will come so that you can do some business in Lowell if you want to going back as I promised to stop ~~over~~ when I went back, prehaps we had better not ~~spo~~ stop over night ~~and~~ as they have but little room, and cousin John is down again I feel afraid if I do not see him now I shall never see him again. they want to see you

All the folks want some silk so you had better bring up some

Do excuse mistakes for I shall be late to send it to day. Do come as soon as Saturday. I am very much obliged for the cloak I should not have been able to do without it.

I shall always try to be your
dutiful daughter
Almira Stetson
   Almira B Stetson

31. Dolly W. Stetson to James A. Stetson

Saturday October 26th [1844]

My Dear

I send your pants how they will fit or how they will do I know not they are some of Anna,s handy work but I think they will not last very long they

seem more worn than I thought—I suppose Almira is with you by this time—
it seems to me that she has been gone a long time and I cannot help looking
for her home some to day I wish you would come with her if it were practi-
cable but I do not suppose you can

Sojourner her [has?] returned so that I have got a discharge from the
washing room—We had a very interesting Lyceum last Wednesday Evening

The order of exercises are first a choice of a chairman for the evening—
second declaimation by some of the young people—third reading the Pic
Nic which is a paper not printed but contributed by different members Wm
Bassett Editor—the articles are put into a box for the purpose he selects
those he thinks most suitable for publication pastes them onto a large sheet
and that with a good deal of Editorial makes up our paper we have a colum
of items embracing all the news that interests us as communitists—(I think
you might occasionally send us "Letters from Boston" that would be very
interesting and acceptable.[139] you must write only on one side of the [s]heet,
ask Thomas to write for the Pic Nic) fourthly debate upon some subject
agreed upon at a previous meeting. The subject debated last evening and it
is continued is this "can we adopt the systim of Fourier in the arangement of
our Industry with advantage" Mr Mack Bassett Rosebrook are in the affirmative and I think Parker Hammond and Mrs Mack will take the negative—I
wish you were here to help the cause along. I believe the classes get along
very well alltho I do not attend and know but a little about them Anna talks
of going to Providence next week—and Mother talks some of going to
Brooklyn this Fall—There is some fuss about Isaacks being here—there is a
strong prejudice here against him and I wish he had gone to Brook Farm
if they were so anxious to have him[140]—we are all well the children all
send love and wish you to come home in all of which I most cordiall
join   Written in haste
     DW Stetson

Addressed: J. A Stetson

32. Dolly W. Stetson to James A. Stetson

Tuesday Morning 19th Nov [1844]

My Dear Husband

I cannot fobear taking a few moments to tell you some of the passing news of the Community

And first of all news has arived that the community at Prairie Home is blown up entirely—they found themselves unable to meet their payments and the former proprieters would not trust them

Sydney Southworth and Harriet have obtained a situation as teachers in a family and Bradbury and wife have got a shelter somewhere—the family that went from Lynn did not arrive untill after they had disbanded[141]

Isaac Swazey and Lucy Richardson are posted as intending marriage so I suppose you will see them in Boston as Mr and Mrs Swazey as soon as the usual forms can be gone thro with—I presume that this is quite a sacrifice for Isaac[142]—

Mr Bassett has decided to lieve and commences packing up to day—I consider this as the death blow to our association. What will reformers think of a band of reformers that William Bassett cannot live among—He says he has for some time intended to lieve in the spring but he goes now in conciquence of some things that were said to him in a meeting holden at Samul Hills last sunday—Sojourner commenced upon Mr May for leaveing the children to play cards—Mr Bassett defended him and Mr Mack said that he did hope that that was one thing that would not be intefered that Mr May loved children and loved to make them happy that the game that he taught them was a mathamatical game and taught them to reckon numbers with ease and combined instruction with amusement he should wish his children to learn it and his pupils likewise—Mr Bassit was censured as haveing introduced cards and as haveing a bad influence—He said in reply that if after performing the labour that was required of him by the association, he could not seek relaxation of mind in his own room in the manner his conscience did not disprove he wished to know it that he might go away before winter set in

Samul Hill told him he did not hesetate to tell him he had better go— Hall Judd said he could not feel to one that would play cards as he would if they did not—Sophia Foord did not think it worse to play cards than to eat meat and that we could not establish any such test [143]—

I heard the story pretty much in this way—I was not at the meeting—Mr Bassett will leave a vacancy in this establishment that they will never fill.

Lucy and James continue to be rather unwell yet and cough a good deal, but I cannot decide whether or no it is the whooping cough the rest are well—I hope to hear from you soon

thine forever

33. Mary, Sarah, and Almira Stetson to James A. Stetson

N. Hampton Mass Dec 1ˢᵗ 1844.

My Dear Father

As Mr Swazer and his wife are going to Boston in a few days I thought I would write you a short letter but it is so long since I have written a letter that I shall make blundering work of it but I know you will excuse me if I do.—

I wish that you could have time to write to us more than you do we have had only one letter since you went away the last time—and it is always such a treat to have a letter from you that we miss them very much.

Isaac and Lucy were married last Friday by Mr Warner there was only 8 that saw them married. During ther marrage ceramony Edwin caused a great deal of mirth by going into the garret kept dropping little sticks on Isaac's and Lucy's head, Mr Warner went away without pronouncing them man and wife and they would not have been married if he had not given them a certificate.[144] Thanksgiving we had quite a good time in the evening all the Junior and Senior class and a great many others was invited to Mr Macks to supper and to spend the evening the dining room was full with the people all standing in the evening we had a very good time. in I forgot to tell you that we had a snow storm thanksgiving that lasted all day. There is not any more news as I know of to tell you. from

All send love to you. come home as soon as possable

from your daughter Mary.

My Dear father

I have now thought I would write you, Mary has begun you a letter, and she wants we should all write in it. I now remember that you told me to write to you when a box went. our friend miss Gove is going to her home in three weeks from next Wednesday and mr May our greatest friend is going a few days before Christmas,[145] and does not think he shall be back again till next summer and then ~~he~~ we does not know that he will live till then, for dont you know that any body does not know all things that might come before next summer. Lucy and Isaac was married last friday by mr warner. Charles has taken Lucy's and Isaac's and Aunt nancy's profield[146] Edwin's is not very natural but all the rest are as that they were taken as I think. I have been taking some fancy portraits and I am agoing to send you one of the prettiest men and one of the prettiest ~~men~~ women they are [most?] very handsome but you will judge for yourself because you will ~~never~~ know that they all are humbler than these. I want you should come home very soon because that you donot write. you must come back next week or I shall write a scolding letter, but I suppose I need not write my name you will know the writing

From your daughter sarah

Dear Father   The box is about being closed to send to you, and I must say a few words I think you will find the silk superior to any thing yet from Northampton especially the hundred skeins of <u>blue black</u>. we compared it with the Italian and could scarcely tell the difference (Oh what a lie) We are getting off 50 pounds, like what you told James you wanted so that you could take it and throw it across the room and have it ~~lay~~ lye as ~~y~~ it fell. We might throw it to Boston and ha[ve?] it land safely at 228 Wash—St. and not a skein would be tangled. It is exactly like the Italian in this respect. The silk is done up nicely. I shall write a good long letter by Isaac and Lucy and so will Mother. I wish you could witness the connubial bliss that is enjoyed so there—it is enough to—make me wish my self in the same place bah—

I expect the six dollar silk velvet bonnet from Mother Swazey will cut a dash in Boston through Winter and Wash—Sts—I wish I was going to spend the winter in the city. Consider my case yours ever for I do not see much prospect of ever being any bodies else—Pray excuse mistakes for I am almost to late Almira.

Addressed: Our Father Stetson / Boston. / some where // By silk box

34. Dolly W. Stetson to James A. Stetson

Northampton Thursday Morn Dec 5th [1844]

My Dear Husband,

I use the last moment before the box is closed to say to you that we are all well as usual and to give you some idea of how we get on here There have been several meetings holden here to see what is to be done next year—before Mr Bassett left and after I wrote you there was a meeting of some of the elder members of the Association before which Mr Bassett stated the reasons for which he at first became dissatisfied with the management here or rather with the way that the financial affairs of the Association were conducted—this implicated the integrity of G.W.B.[147] and he defended himself as best he could. some thought he got himself deeper in the mire for he lost his temper and talked badly to Mr Bassett—but perhaps you have ere this seen him as he thought he should see you in Boston—George at the next meeting said many hard things of Mr Bassett—brought up all the ill things he could of his father &c[148]—this looks something like the feelings towards one that leaves an Orthodox Church— Mr Bassett was defended by Mr Mack Sophia Ford—this consumed the time of the second meeting—Last Sunday they came on to something to the point and appointed a committee consisting of Rosebrook Hammond and Martin[149] to take into consideration the condition of the community and report at the Annual meeting what is best to be done under all the circumstances of our condition—

If the adage is true that "rats lieve a falling house" I should think that this was about to fall for many are lieving particularly the "young people" Fowler Hudson has gone Martha Brigham Morgan Lydia Pierce and Sarah Brigham are going next week to Dedham Silk Factory haveing obtained places there— Frank Rosebrook is going to[o.] George Hill and I know not what more changes as "every day brings something new"[150] Mr Havens family are comeing into the rooms occupied by Mr Bassett

Isaac and Lucy are going as soon as the travelling will permit and Charles is hoping daily to recieve a letter from his Uncle Charles summoning him to Manchester—Macomber has been fitted out again pedling[151]—it seems to me that we must be doing a heavy business to employ four men in selling silk—I think they might let you come home and I do think you ought to be here to take part in the delibrations and know

what is going on. I hope you will come [soon?] I hope you will <u>write</u> immediately—in haste thine
 DW Stetson

35. Almira Stetson and Dolly W. Stetson to James A. Stetson

Northampton Dec 10th 1844.

Dear ~~but~~ neglected, <u>oft remembered</u> Father,

I am incited to write this letter by a multiplicity of reasons. partly from a
desire to counte[r]act the foolishness of my last letter, but mostly to show in
a small degree the love and gratitude I feel toward you as my Father and
Protector. Still I know that words or ~~charcters earach~~ characters are inadequate to this. When I think of the many girls who know nothing of a Fathers
love or a Fathers care I feel that I <u>do not</u> or cannot appreciate the blessing I
enjoy in having a watchful parent to look to for advice and counsel. One ~~who~~
"In whose voice to <u>bless</u> his child lay tones of <u>love</u> <u>so deep</u> Whose eye oer <u>all</u>
<u>my</u> youth has smiled" and placed perhaps his hopes of future pleasure in me
I feel as if a great responsibility rested upon me as being the first born. These
feelings received a new impetus from some letters Mother showed me ~~your~~
wrote to her when I was about two years old. in those you spoke of me with
such high hopes, that the questions instinctively arose. Have I done as I
should to help <u>you</u> to realise those fond hopes? Have I been the useful
obedient child I should have been? and have I carried out the ideal of a kind
fathers heart in my life? The answer comes back to my heart cheerless and
cold. No! I have been far from the child my <u>circumstances</u> could have made
me. I felt that my sin is all my own therefore the thought is harder to bear
than if it could be thrown off on others, Once my plans for the future were
high and the thoughts of raising my father and mother to renown through
the acts of their daughter were bright and happy. The idea of a second Abby
Kelly or Anglinea and Sarah Gramke was my model by which I shaped my
desires and [wims?] those were my every thought, and many an hour of
plasure have I listened (I[n] imagination) to the tones of applause you have
gained by being the father of such an illustreous personage I have seen myself
addressing halls filled with the intelligent and enterprising people of the
United States and even have I traversed the ocean and spoke words of reform
to Europeans.[152]

But these dreams of bliss are passed and I find myself nothing but Almira still. perhaps all these were pernicious, but I think they showed me better than any thing else the need of principles which are steadfast. But now I have dismissed all these, and feel that my life must be made up of small acts of virtue and I must characterise myself with doing the every day duties of life faithfully and truely, not by the great events of life. And what is a greater duty than being a "good child" I do not feel prepared to pass through the trials many are called to, and remain with there parents. But it is not my lot to pass through these. I had a letter from the girls Elisabeth and Sarepta telling of the inhuman conduct of their Father. He has stoped all their newspapers and seems determined to shut them away from all intellectual pleasures. I think I would require a greater a grea strength of principles than I now possess.. to submit as patiently as they do. I hope if you go to Brooklyn as T— says you think of you will carry them some papers. Give them much love from me I wrote them a long letter but it was before I received theres so I could not express my sympathies for their situation[153]

I have much more to say but Mother wants to say a few words and I presume they will be much more acceptable. Excuse all things that are wrong and believe me your affectionate daughter

Almira. B. Stetson.

My Dear I think you will like to hear a word from me too as well as from Almira. And I suppose I must begin with what is uppermost in my mind that is that I want you to come home as soon as you can—I know not at what time the Annual Meeting is to be holden but I think you should come and be prepared to act on the matters that will come up for consideration, for I suppose upon the doings of that meeting depend the existance of the Association—Thomas says that you talk of returning thro Providence and Brooklyn—I send you a letter to Anna if it be convenient I should like to have you see her Mother wishes you to ascertain the state of her affairs in Brooklyn—I presume you will look after ours too

Give my love to those that I do love in B— likewise in Abington if you go there. Mother too sends love—

The children are much better than when you were home the sores upon their faces are mostly well James has a new tooth and Lucy teases[?] continually to see her Father—I thank you for your last letter but am sorry that you seemed so depressed in spirit—Doubtless it is thro dissapointment and trial that we are to be perfected we should therefore take it patiently yea joyfully not expecting here any thing better

I shall expect a letter from you on your return from the east and if you return as soon as I expect I shall not write again if we are well

yours truly
DWStetson

Write soon.

Addressed: Mr. James. A. Stetson / Boston // By Lucy Swazey

36. Dolly W. Stetson to James A. Stetson

Sunday Febry 16ᵗʰ 1845

My Dear Husband

haveing an opportunity to write you by Mr Preston I gladly avail myself of it to inform you how we do &c

We are all quite well except Lucy and she is not realy sick but seems rather unwell I think it must be she has worms, and I hardly know what remady to use I am so much unacquainted with the disease—

I have been quite anxious about you since you left in consequence of the severe snow storm that occured the night you left and as I have not heard a word from you I did not know but you had run into a snow drift and there remained but Mr May told me yesterday that he saw you in Boston last Monday.

We hardly know what to make of his visit here he came yesterday morning haveing stayed in town all night picked up his things and was off I presume in 15 minutes. He said he would have a talk with us after he had picked up his things and Breakfast was prepared for him but he did not stop for either. I should think he did not dare to trust himself to stop or had done something he was ashamed of—he said he had come back an altered man—he also said that he was comeing here with his wife and Brother Sam to make a visit in a few weeks

The proposed alterations in the domestic arangements of the factory are going on rapidly there seems to be a general rush to get into the factory and those that cannot convinently come here are dissatisfied that they should be obliged by circumstances to pay 80 cts for board while those that live here live for 60—this is the burden of Mr Kerrs complaint he says he has to be the mouth piece for all dissatisfied ones

The present intention is to give up the hired houses accomodate what more we can in the factory and have George Bensons family and Whipple and Hammonds eat here the two last have commenced. Mrs Hammond is going into the finishing room tomorrow—Perrin and Theodore Scarboro are expected here this week—Theodore haveing written to Hall Judd to that effect Mother intends to return with them if they can take her

Mother Stetson seems quite well now the sweet oil haveing done wonders for her—Abner Mead has abandoned his cold water and is taking the oil with the same effect.[154] Mr Ruggles is taking it but I have not heard how it opperates on him—but it has not restored his sight at any rate

Mr Rosbrook and Milton and Mr Loomis and wife left last Monday[155] I think that Mr Rosbrook will probably return after he has been about awhile and gone down to Pennsylvania to see about his patent or rather to see the man that has taken a patent on the same kind of mill—but Mr Loomis and wife are probably gone forever—I am very sorry they could not have stayed for I consider them an ornament to any society they may choose to live in—Mr Loomis said that he never expected to live among a like number of people [that?] he loved and respected as much as he did the people here

Quite a number of applications from people in different parts of the country have been receivd but I believe that the mind of the people is made up not to receive any new members unless there is something <u>particular</u>ly in their favour—

Give love to Lucy and Isaac when you see them

Children all send love to you and want to know when you are comeing home—I wish it were so that you could be here all the time unless you are happier in Boston than you can be here—I am going to write to Aunt Mary which you will please to forward   truly thine

D. W. Stetson

Addressed: James A Stetson / 25 Cornhill / Boston

37. Sarah Stetson to James A. Stetson

Feb 17th 1845

My Dear Father

I have just thought I would I would write you a letter I am very much obliged for your box—this noon we received the valin tine[156] which come in the box there has been a freshet I will tell you what kind of a freshet it was to be sure it was water but the cakes of ice came so abundantly that it filled the river and this morning Mr Atkins and Mr Haven and some boys went on the cakes in the river and pushed them down so that the wheel could run I have had a new pair of boots since you went away they are very good except there is an iron-peg sticking through the sole of the boot and it makes my heels sore George wants that I should tell you that Miss Ford read a story about a man who was in pursuit of whales He took a cake of ice to be an island at first and afterwards for the whale he was in pursuit of at last he found out that it was a cake of ice and he thought he was very much deceived George sends his love to you. Grandmother and mother have got mary[157] quilt on the frame in aunt nancy's room and Mrs Paul and Mrs small is helping them Aunt nancy and Mrs Small & Grandmother send their love to you[158] Mr Ruggles sends his love and best respects to you Lucy sends her love and a kiss the second volume of Flowers for children has come George Thompson has got both volumes[159] My mother said before the annual meeting that perhaps I might have a doll after it was done I thought I wanted a doll but now my mind is changed for I see that I can spend my mind time in a better way We have established a new paper called the miniature where only the young people of the educational Department are to write We are going to have it every Saturday evening and up to Mr Mack's house and after the paper is read we are to have an hour of plays—I have often thought When I read over your letter that those boys who chewed tobacco must not have been brought up very well for most every good boy must know better than to do such a thing. if Miss Shackford is their now give my love to her and best respects to her and tell her I want she should come to the community and stay a few months here. For it is very long since I have seen her give my love to Lucy and Isaac and the boarder that sent me that duck that I am very much obliged to him for it the boarder that I mean is the one that lives at Mrs Atkins. I hope you Will correct my letter as I have yours In one place in your letter It says you went away and I did not with any very curious incident Now you left out a word you must begin When Writing to any person not to leave out words and then when you Write to [king?] George you will not leave out any words I expect the word you left out is meet, as, I did not meet with any very curious incident. Mrr May was here day before yesterday he had not had any breakfast but asked him to he did not take off his coat but got his trunks and his other things and went right a way he said he would be back with his Wife ~~was coming back~~ in a fort night[160] give my love to Mrs Garrison and wendy and and in the answer to this letter tell how the little Frances does[161] answer this letter when you send a box

Excuse the bad spelling and writing of the letter for I have a bad pen

From Your affectionate d[aughter] Sarah Frances Stetson

Anna Benson has got a box worked with beads on the top and in it is a green ship it is glass and it has a mast and all the rigging is glass

Addressed: To My Father

38. Dolly W. Stetson to James A. Stetson

Thursday Evening Febry 20th [1845]

My Dear Husband

the letters I sent you to day by Mr Preston I expected to have sent last Monday but he delayed going for one reason and another untill I wished I had my letters again to put into the box—I received your letter to day written the 18th—Mother is much obliged for the information therein contained she now intends to start on Monday or Tuesday Mother Stetson spent the day here the day before yesterday [and] is pretty smart she is comeing to stay with Nancy and me some time—

I write mostly to ~~exicute~~ communicate commissions The enclosed letter was written by James Willson to his mistress. I think there can no harm come of it to him—he wishes you to mail it in Boston[162]

Miss Sophia Foord wishes you to purchase Miss Margarett Fullars new work "Woman in the Nineteenth Century" and send it in the next Box—[163]

Mrs Rosbrook wishes to know if you have heard any thing from her sister whose name you took—

I am very glad to hear from Lucy Shackford and should be happy to have you assist her if you could without injury or perplexity to yourself but you thought you should not go into partnership with another woman—Alass for poor Mrs Swazey the elder and pray how does Mrs Swazey the junior get along with all the trouble—

Nancy was very much disappointed that she did not have a letter in the box for they have all written to her and hoped she would answer as punctually as they promised too

I am sorry that you have such unpleasant reflections upon your visit at home—I am sure I know not to what you allude when you speak of regreating that you said any think at the Annual Meeting—I am sure I know of nothing that you said that you need regreat—

I have just been reading Sarahs letter to you, I think it will amuse you very much—

Mary has been engaged writing for the "Miniature" the childrens paper of which Sarah wrote—George wants me to ask you if you suppose there is any Robinsons Crusoes in Boston he says he thinks he could read it—James has had a an ill turn occasioned by teething—

Since Mother has been prepareing to return to B—[164] I have had quite a desire to go too—I have some little desire to know what is to become of my patrimony there—If it is to run on without bringing us any rent it will soon eat up the small interest I have in it and bring us in debt every year and if Taylor has failed to get rent for it the two last years it will have cost us reckoning the onehundred and thirty dollars that Mother payed upon it all that it is considered worth above the morgage—of course we had better give it up to the society at once than to have this state of things continue[165] I suppose that if Taylor had a chance to sell it this spring he would have informed us of it before this

Give my love to Lucy Shackford and tell her that I should be very happy to see her again.

the arrival and dispatch of the box is quite a matter of interest here and is considered a capital idea but I think it may be something of a tax on your time to deliver letters and exicute commissions—dont forget Sophias—

I hope you will write long and often for we are probably quite as happy to get a letter from you as you are from us and you have material to make your letters much the most interesting

Yours DWStetson

We are all much obliged for the Valentine it was very pretty and pleased the Children very much—I never saw any thing of the kind myself

Addressed: To James A Stetson / Presant

39. Sophia Foord to James A. Stetson

[February 20, 1845]

Will Mr Stetson have the kindness to purchase for me Margaret Fuller's late publication entitled "Woman in the Nineteenth Century" and charge it to my account[166]—thus obliging his friend & Serv[t]

Sophia Foord
Northampton Feb[y]—20th

Addressed: Mr James Stetson / Boston

40. Almira Stetson to James A. Stetson

Father. You see I am very economical in paper and Mother is trying to write at the desk too and if you have a very uncomely sort of a letter please excuse me. But I must proceed to business, and as Mr Hill[167] is gone away I must try to do my best, It is the last time I shall have an opportunity for Mrs Hammond came into the finishing room to work on Monday, and has been put in overseer. So now you may expect to have the silk come about right. Oh, she is ~~as~~ so nervous, worse than Lucy ever was, and she is so anxious to learn in order to direct, that I have almost flown out of my skin several times today, for she did not know untill last night "her horror" But this is not what business men call buisness and I want as I am going to close up buisness to do it up right.

You will probably see if you open the box that there are several kinds of silk. Well I suppose you want to know what it is. The first lot begining with [the?] bottom is a lot of 50 lbs which came up from the dye room last week, we think that it is pretty nice good lustre, and with the exception of consid- erable second quality we think it pretty sleek, but every lot that comes from the dye room is the kind most like Italian &c,, There are 20 lbs 1 oz. the rest is reserved for Mr Powers.[168] Next to that is 5 lbs oz of American There are two shades of that. It was considered "pretty fair" when it came up but so many more splendid lots since it has got to be quite an old story. Then there are 2^{lbs} 5$^{1/2oz}$ of Green I guess I wont say much about this, it will speak for itself. Then in the quarter pound papers there is 1 lb 6 oz marked F on the wrapper, that is fine that we considered very handsome, and Uncle G[169] wanted it put up so. And then to cap the climax there is <u>the</u> lot that came up last one of the most beautiful colors and lustres that <u>ever was got up</u> so nearly resembling the Italian as to render it difficult to tell the one from the other and <u>more</u> specially ours! This is short skeins. There is 1. 6. in quarter lbs papers. Dont laugh at the way they are done up for I did them and there is no one else that knows any thing about it to teach me. If we are to do up our silk so, I think I shall <u>have</u> to go to Boston to learn or else have very explicit instruction by letter. The other strings I presume you can find out what they mean without my ~~righting~~ writing. Father you know when I was in Boston I got some purse silk and had it charged to you, with the idea of selling them and paying some of my expenses, but as the year has gone and all is well as far as money goes, I have got the silk, and being in need of some little things which I do not like to call on the Association to get for me and I think I shall finish them and [have?] you sell them for me and return the money to me. If you have any of those rings and tassels left that you had in the store I wish you would send them up. and if you have not and can get them cheap I think you had better for the purses sell much better with them on. I hope you will get tassels of beads instead of the drops for they set off the purse so much better. pleas send them up by the first opportunity Has Nancy said any thing about the edging yet

I hope she will conclude to have some. Have the boys said any thing about receiving the letters—I dont feel very anxious about there getting the letters, but do not know but they would feel that I did wrong to neglect them if they have not.

How does Lucy get along through all the trouble of Mrs Swazey? Tell her to write give love to all and yourself Almira.

41. George R. Stetson to James A. Stetson

March 2nd 1845

Dear Father I ~~geo~~ get along very well with reading and am going to try to write to you I was very much pleased with my present but I was disapointed when I found that it was an imperfect ~~one~~ copy the first seventeen pages was Esops Fables and when it ought to be Providence, it was Vidence I braid ~~an~~ palme leaf an hour every day which I like to do very much indeed[170] I think the men in Boston that ride on horseback throwing up iron balls better be at work than rideing around there, I was very glad to see Sarah feel so happy at ~~the~~ receiving her present Sarah gets out of humour quicker than I do Mother said that I did not use to cry so much as she did when I was a little child. (George began the letter himself but getting discouraged he got Sarah to write and she not haveing written all he wishes, I am engaged as his amenuensis, Mother)

I have just come up from Lyceum and have just spoken a dialouge with David Mack,[171] we did not either of us miss the dialouge was between a poor and rich mans child—Our plants grow very well and the Egyptian Calla has got two little ones.—I wish I could go to Boston and go to the Museums and see skeletans and other things that are there

Roxy Brown told me that the man that stuffed her owls had allmost a house full of all kind of things stuffed such as toads frogs pollywogs &c &c I did think of sending the book back, and I believe I will and perhaps the man will give you a good one if he will not you can send it back again, in the box— I think the book binder was very careless and you ought to have looked at it before you bought it—I hope you will come home by May Day that is the first day of May for I expect we shall have a good time I cant think of any thing more from George

Addressed: James A Stetson / Boston / 25 Cornhill

42. Almira Stetson to James A. Stetson

Northampton March 4th 45.

Ever dear Father.

There is a box to go to you day after to morrow and I thought I would commence at this early period to be sure of having something for you for I can scarcely make any calculation of my time so I have found it best to take time when it is going and for another reason I write too. I feel, yes know that I ought to disclose all my plans of life to those who have thus far been one of the means of keepin life in me. You know that it has always been m the greatest wish of my existence to be a thouroughly and highly educated girl, to this purpose have I laid all my plans of life and my hopes for the future have been to this purpose end. I never have said a great deal about it but enough as I thought to have those around me know what my dearest wishes were. I have said little but thought all the more.

I have from a life necessity for a while past given up all hopes of pursuing such a course of study, but I have been reading and hearing a good deal within a few days of Margret Fuller the author of "Woman in the Nine-theenth century," (which is a very superior work) She is an almost entirely a self educated woman. her father was once a wealthy man but failed in business and being honest he gave up almost every thing, but Margret was very ambitious and she went on her with education alone, and it is the opinion of all who are acquainted with her that she is a very superior woman. Mr Mack knows her and he says that he "never saw a woman with such a mind and so complete an education". I do not <u>expect</u> to come up to her however in talents but I can do my best for it. I can attain as near as possible to my ideal. But I find that as a general thing those that educate themselves, and are obliged to make some sacrifice (if you please to call it so, no sacrifice to me) to attain to a thourough education are generally the best <u>learned</u> and use their learning to the best advantage.

But it makes no difference to me what such persons have done or are doing. I want a good education and I think I can have it by improving every moment. and I really did not know how much time I had untill I tried to im-prove every moment of it. My plan is this, and I go to Mr Mack for his opin-ion of the authors and works. The following are are the branches A thour-ough course of ancient and modern History. Latin. Phylosophy Astronomy Chemistry. Algebra—Geometry. Physiologs and Botany. Geography as a distinct from history I think I have a pretty good knowledge of. Grammar I am going through with now minutely. These are the principle ones. there are others which would come in incidentally. I hope Mr Mack will be able soon to teach me in Latin. this study may seem to you as rather foolish for me but it has always been my wish to be a good Latin scholar, and I hope to go through with it. I shall expect to work my regular number of hours, and improving diligently every moment I think it will take me four or five years to do what I have stated. I think I have duly weighed all things (I think) and feel convinced that I _can_ and ought to do it, and if I meet no opposition from you I shall commenc immediately. I had hoped to go to some seminary for a year or two and devote my whole time to study, but if I cant do so I must do the best way I can, and this is the best I can think of. I hope you will think favorable of this proposition, and will give your opinion of it as soon as possible, for I feel that every moment that is lost now is of great importance to me.

But enough of this for the present. You said something to me in your last letter about some ¼ lb papers. now I am very sorry that they did not meet your mind but I really felt ashamed to send them and such a time _I_ never had, Mrs Hammond on one side trying to learn and mixing all the kinds together and James A—[172] thinking that his way was best (when in reality he had no way) and Mr Haven trying to do the best he could with Uncle George[173] hurrying me for fear I should not get ready and every one handling the silk and misplaceing it. I think I ought to have some praise for ever getting it in to the box in any shape whatever. You wanted to know about the weight I will send it as I have it—but _I_ cannot ~~vough~~ vouch for its correctness. I packed the box Thursday afternoon and Friday morning when I got there I found James A— had been to it, and how or what he did with it I do not know. I had a really crying spell about the silk and the box after it ~~wh~~ went away but it did no good. I wish if you have a correct account of it you would send it up. For it has not been entered on the books, yet. send it immediately. There was of the silk according ~~with~~ to my account

Fine Black—20 lbs 1 oz—   Greens—5 lbs 5 oz ¾

American—5 lbs 8 oz—   That in ¼ lb papers.—1 lb in one paper and
                                          1lb 6 oz in another.

I want you to thank John as politely as possible for those cards—I have been very neglectful indeed to not have mentioned it before—ask him to excuse me for my neglect as it was unmeaning in me. also tell George I shall write him by the next box for I had not time to write by this one. Give love to all and believing myself to be your loving child I close this epistle which I hope you will answer soon.

Almira B Stetson—

Why dont I hear something from that purse I knit for Mrs A Appleton? dont she like it?

Addressed: Mr James. A. Stetson. / Boston. / Mass. // Box.

43. Dolly W. Stetson to James A. Stetson

Thursday Evening March 6th [1845]

I intended to have written you a long letter this evening but I have been up to spend the day with Catharine[174] and taken Lucy and James and they with her children have kept me in a continual fuss all day and since I have got home I have been trying nearly two hours in vain to get James to sleep and I am quite out of patience if not temper and dont think I could get up much of a letter any way—I have not been out before since you went away and think I shall not go out again for some time to come—past eight—

Well James is at last asleep—and if the beauty of letter-writing consists in writing just as one feels or just as one would talk if the other were presant I am quite sure my introductory remarks are quite beautiful——

You ask if Sojourner has returned—she was absent two weeks in which two Stephen[175] Mrs Small and myself did the washing easily in one day each week. Mrs Haven doing her own families washing but she has now return the washing room is a seperate department Sojourner Director and Mr Fitch[176] assistant and they wash for all the community that choose to send their washing—You say there was a button gone off your shirt and I can tell you that the shirt is gone too—I suppose that it has got among some ones clothes out of the house but as it is marked I presume it will be returned

Lucy had got quite well before your box arrived of course I have not administered any of the medicine you sent and I am so much afraid of these patent Nostrums that I should hardly dare too even if all her worm symptoms returned—perhaps their virtues will kill worms by keeping them in the house—James walks much better and has got two new teeth—

93

Mother Stetson is still staying with Nancy and me—she is not very well just now—she thinks she shall have to take another course of sweet oil—Nancy has been quite comfortably sick nearly two weeks she has taken a few doses of the oil without any apparen[t] benefit—but she is nearly well now and intends to put the new kitchen into opperation next week—Stephen is to be her right hand man and George B talks some of sending to Providense for Anna Jackson to take care of the dining room. Stephen and Mrs Rosbrook and sometimes one of her girls have done the work in the kitchen since Nancy has been unwell—My work is the same as when you was here making beds and sweeping I have to get thro before Sarah goes to school as she sees to James—Mother is very anxious that you should write if you know any thing of Joseph—Lucy Swazey wrote that Joseph was in Boston looking for a house and that he was to give up the Centrel House the first of April—I think she is very much troubled about them[177]—Almira I suppose has written you a letter divulging her plans for the future—well I am glad to have her have something to aim at, something to live for, and altho I think she will find herself obliged to abandon some part of her plan I will not say one word to discourage her Mary is quite engaged in her studies and is making good progress

The principle item of community news is that Mr Selliway and family are going to lieve and probably Mr Carr[178]

Mr Selliway goes to work for Mr Conant in the brick business, into which he is going—at 23$ pr month Mrs Selliway is going to work by the week for Mr Bottom who has purchased Mr Valentines house and [20?] acres of land and Mrs Bottom, skeines silk for Valentine[179]

I suppose that G. W. B. has written to you that Mr Conant has contracted with the firm of Edwards and Stoddard to make silk for them they finding the stock at so much pr pound—and he starts another mill in Conn—he does not tell how much he is to receive—Mr Conant likewise offered himself to Caroline Williams his wives niece, in less than a week after his wife was buried—and the preliminaries are arranged and they are to be married soon!!!!![180]

Louisa Rosbrook is sick again but Prindle is urging her by letter to name an early day for their wedding if possible this month[181]—so the world goes—

Remember my love to Lucy and Isaac and thank Mr Garrison for the report sent by box—likewise give my love to Sarah Benson I hope she will come up here this summer—Catharine Sayd she tried to arrange a visit here with Sarah and Olive Gilbert together but that Olive was going to Kentucky to see George S— I hope she will keep clear of the penitentiary[182]

I have nothing more to say so good night

D.W. Stetson

44. Mary W. Bryant to James A. Stetson

Northampton March. 6th

My Kind Friend,

The bundle I sent by you to Boston. my brother—says, he has called twice to Mr—Garrison's office, but no bundle was there, if it is at the house will you please leave it at the office.

Mary W. Bryant.

Addressed: Mr—James Stetson. / Boston. / Mass

45. Dolly W. Stetson to James A. Stetson

Tuesday Evening 18th March—45

Dear Husband

I suppose you would be as much disappointed to open the box and not find a letter, as I should be to have it return without one for me—so alltho I have nothing more to say than how much we love you and how much we wish you could be home with us, all of which you know without its being repeated; still I will write. Ah! I have some news to tell you.

Our new kitchen and dining room are completed the latter of which was formily dedicated last Tuesday Evening we had a Pic Nic to which all of the Association were invited and most of them came After supper we had a speech from Sojourney[183] on the beauties of the room—and truly it did look beautifully decorated with evergreens and brilliantly illuminated with hanging lamps borrowed for the occasion from the silk room. the room extends across the entire east end of the factory and is large enough to seat the whole community comfortably at table—next a speach from G.W.B. upon ingratitude and complaining when we were surrounded by so many comforts and luxuries next followed Mr Mack upon order in all things and temperance in eating—next Mr Hill upon rational enjoyments and occupations that became rational beings Mr Kerr closed by hoping that the hall would be dedicated to free speech and that it might never be disgraced by chairmen and secretaraies to keep folks in order—Mrs Hammond had her piano removed to the hall with the intention to have dancing but as it was understood that Mr Hill intended to bear his testimony against it there seemed a general reluctance to commence but at last Mrs Mack Mrs Whipple Sophia Ford and a few other independent ones danced a figure and were just forming another set among which was your wife when Mr Hill entered and anounced the astounding fact that it was 9 oclock and asked who would act like reasonable beings and go home and go to bed?—Mr Hammond perswaded his wife to lock the piano—and thus ended the matter not so either because there was a great deal of grumbling that they were not permited to dance—

I wonder if it is like rational beings to be up poreing over account books till 1 or 2 oclock at night? or to be so driven for money as to have girls set up till that time skeining silk and have to suffer months and perhaps loose her sight like Marion Smith[184] Oh! ye Scribes and Pharisees hypocrites who strain at a gnat and swallow a Camel[185]—Mr Hammond Whipple and Bensons families all board here—Nancy has got well and has Stephen to help in the kitchen—Mrs Rosbrook and Susan Byrne have the care of the dining room at presant—George has talked some of sending to Providence for Anna to take that place[186]—You dont know how much I miss Mother I am shut up in my rooms from morning till night and night to morning—except that Sarah takes care of James while I do my work in the morning before school—I have not been outside the walls of the Factory half a dozen times since you went away and have only been up to Catharines twice since I went there with you and have not been into any other house in the association this winter—

but I dont care much about that if my health does not suffer—James walks finely has two new teeth and is getting to be quite a pretty baby but his fretfullness is much the same—Lucy wants me to say to you that she thinks you ought to send [her?] a book—George[187] send his love and thanks you for getting him a good Robinson Crusoe—he left all play untill he had carefully read the whole of it which took him about two days—he is improving in his reading and begins to have a taste for it—

Sarah has commenced a watch guard for Atkins but she has but little time to work on it between her lessons her straw braiding and her school—as for Almira and Mary they are so occupied in their work and studies that I should seldom see them if I did not meet them at table and if they did not come home to sleep—I have not head a word from Mother since she left neither from Taylor to whom I wrote requesting to know the situation of the place in the villiage whether there was any prospect of selling it and whether there had been any rent collected to pay the interest on the morgage

I wish you would call on David Reed and settle the long bill with him in some manner and stop the paper I am sick of the long Parker controversy and do not think the paper improved under the new Editor Mr Upam[188]

I forgot to say that tenements have been made of the old dining room and kitchen for Mr Martins and Ashleys families and they are comeing in soon— Mrs Ashley has a daughter a few days old all well[189]

I hope to have a good long letter from you soon

your collars and bosoms do not look very nice but I believe Mrs Small tries to do them the best she can and it not possible for me to attend to ironing now

Yours DW Stetson

Mother is gone

I hope when you write again you will tell us if you intend to come home and when

Forgive me for not writing but I have not time—Love to all Almira

Addressed: James A Stetson / Boston // Box

46. Dolly W. Stetson to James A. Stetson

[April 3, 1845][190]
Thursday Evening

Dearest Huz

I just write a line to tell you that the health of the family is improved since you left. Lucy seems rather fretfull but I do not see but she is well—those of us that had colds are better—I should like to know whether you are in

Brooklyn or Boston or to which place your steps are tending—I hope you will write immediately and report your journey—

It was announced in the pic nic of last evening that next Monday would be the third Anniversary of the formation of the Association and that ~~the~~ all persons connected in any way with the Association were invited to meet and have a social time and supper at the factory dining room on that evening— wonder if we shall dance

Yours

D. W. Stetson

It seems as if I had had a dream that you were at home sometime lately

Addressed: James A. Stetson / Boston / Mass // BOX

47. Dolly W. Stetson to James A. Stetson

Sunday Evening April 13th—45

My Dear Husband

While most of the family have gone into town to listen to the "<u>eloquent fugitive</u>" I sit down between the cradle and the secretary to talk with you[191]— And in the first place your letter made me quite sad—I fear you are acting rashly in making up your mind to lieve the Association I have always noticed when you came home the longer you stayed the better you liked, and you certainly was very happy the summer that you lived at home all the time— now it seems to me that you had better come home and stay a few months before you decide to lieve and <u>perhaps</u> you may feel differently—I think I <u>know</u> that if we were to go to the farm our situation would be far less desirable than here—We should look in vain for society for ourselves and children such as we enjoy here—we could never place our children under the care of such accomplished teachers as they are now under—I say accomplished because I think Mrs Mack one of the most accomplished women I ever met and one whose influence over girls as far as education and manners is concerned is most salutary—But we ought not to be looking for our own good alone Can we do as much good to our race to return to our isolated condition where whatever of moral power we may possess will be rendered powerless because we have not the wealth and station to render us worthy of notice.

I know that many things here are not right but where shall we go where they are all right—I know not—

But I will not write any more upon this matter as you have not explained to me your views I cannot write understandingly—I hope you will not act rashly in this matter or from prejudice—but haveing once made up your mind I shall make it <u>mine</u> and endeavour to make the best of our lot whatever it may be. this has alway been my duty and that for which I have laboured with how much success is better known to you than to myself—

Mr Hill and family have just returned from their visit to R.I. and Conn. they stayed to Mr Scarboroughs the next night after you did. I am exceedingly sorry to hear that the health of Theodore and Herbert is so poor—Mrs Hill told me that Theodore told her that he had often been sorry that he ever left here and still looked forward to the time that he should return—

Mrs Hill says that they thought I would have come down last week[192]—but I did not understand you that you thought it nessesary or that I had better go—I think that the <u>pleasure</u> of the <u>visit</u> if I went for that would be more than counterbalanced by the fatigue of taking James around with me—I did at one time last week make up my mind to wean him this month and go down to Boston to attend the Antislavery meeting, but upon more mature reflection I thought as you had so often expressed a wish to have my teeth replaced I would spend whatever I might feel that I could afford this year for that object—I accordingly went into town to Doct Smith last Wednesday morning and had three front teeth and one back one removed including the stump of the one that was broken—the other two were mere out side shells—I shall be obliged to have them set on a plate and that together with haveing a few decayed ones filled will cost me more than 20 dollars—but if I had nothing done to them they would in a short time have broken off and I should be obliged to go the rest of my life the horrid looking object I now am unable to sing or speak plainly. I shall probably have to wait 6 weeks or two months before my gums will be healed solid so as to admit of the plate being fitted to my mouth[193]—We have all been suffering with colds since you were here mine is not much better now than when you left and altho it does not make me sick I am far from well—

Our celebration of the third Anniversary of the formation of the Association came off on the 8th very well we had talking, singing &c this afternoon Frederick Douglass talked to us upon prejudice against color—this is an old subject but one upon which I never heard a colored person speak in public—

he did very well—Mr Mack made some very good remarks and the meeting was closed by singing[194]—

I wish you had given me a more full account of your visit to Brooklyn who you saw &c but perhaps it is as well defered untill you come home—

I send this by Mr Clark whome I like much—I should think him a man of sterling worth—yours DWStetson

Addressed: To James A. Stetson / 25 Cornhill / Boston //
Politeness of Mr Clark

48. Dolly W. Stetson to James A. Stetson

Tuesday Evening April 15th [1845]

Well My Dear Huz

I think you cannot complain of me as a correspondant if I write you every other evening nevertheless I thought I must tell you that we are haveing great things on the tapis here now—

It appears that Trusdell has offered the Association assistance to go into the manafacture of cotton for their own profit paying him interest—or he will hire the factory or purchase it[195]—the matter is still in the hands of the Executive and a few of the directors and will probably be brought before the Association at the quaterly meeting—

I obtained these facts by pumping David Ruggles who I suppose is in Halls confidence[196]—there is he says a differance of opinion among the Counsil which to accept—Some think it best to sell out the vally about the factory with the exception of the saw mill and purchase the lot that Mr Hill is building upon and put up cottages and become an Agricultural and mechanical community

I overheard Saml Hill tell Hall Judd yesterday that it was probable that Mr Stetsons family would go away, so I suppose you have written to him to that effect or you told Theodore Scarboro so in Brooklyn

So now that the fiat has gone forth nothing remains but for you to make up your mind what to do and where to go for we shall be looked upon as alians now that it is known that we think of going away—

I have not heard any thing from Brooklyn yet and you did not write whether Mother was comeing up this spring or not—I hope you will write soon I think you will owe me a good long letter

I send this by Frederic Douglass—he has not enjoyed his visit here much he has been so much unwell—Mr Hammond has been very successfull in his portrait if I am a judge[197]

Frederick Douglass, c. 1845, attributed to Northampton Association member Elisha Hammond. As Dolly Stetson's letter of April 15 suggests, this was probably painted during Douglass's visit to Northampton. Oil on canvas, 26 × 17½ in. (Courtesy, National Portrait Gallery, Smithsonian Institution, Washington, D.C.)

We are all recovering from our colds alltho my head still aches most of the time.

Good night

D. W. Stetson

Nancy desires love to Isaac and Lucy and says that she aught to write but she cannot get time to write by day and her eyes will not permit her to write by night. She too has had the prevailing influenza and is quite unweell

The box I believe is not yet ready to be sent

Addressed: James A. Stetson / 25 Cornhill / Boston //
By Frederick Douglass

49. Mary Stetson to James A. Stetson

Northampton April 25th 1845.

My dear Father

I wonder what you will think of me because that I have not written to you before, I am afraid that you will think that I have not thought of you much since you went away but I can assure that I do think of you ~~almost~~ every day. I am almost ashamed of myself for not writing to you more I would say almost every Sunday "now I must write to Father today" but something would happen to prevent me from writing and so I would let the letter go until the next Sunday until all this time has gone and you have not had a letter from me yet. and I am affraid that you will not have but part of one now for I am so sleepy but a little is better than none you know. Yesterday all of the girls in the junior class had a letter from Mrs Loomis,[198] the letter was all in one sheet it was directed to Harriet Hubbard & co. it was a beautiful letter. I have had a letter from Miss Lucy and from Diantha Harding since you have been away Miss Lucys letter was as good as they always are Dianthas was good too, they were both short. I suppose that you know that Mr Douglass has been here, his portrait looks very natural. I am getting on in my lessons first rate no not first rate but very well we have got almost through the Grammer. Father do excuse this short letter and all the mistakes in it. Please to tell Mr May that I have sent all the books that I could find and tell Mrs May that we have been expecting her letter ever since she went away. From your affectionate daughter

Mary

[Octavia reques]ted me to ask you to tell Mr Atkins family that she or james have not had time to write to them but they will in the next box.

Addressed: Mr James A Stetson / Boston / Mass

50. Dolly W. Stetson and Almira Stetson to James A. Stetson

Friday Evening April 25th—45

Well Husband

You shall not say the box came and no letter for <u>me</u>—to <u>morrow</u>. and really I do not think you had much reason to complain as you had two letters from me last week well—but I suppose you would have liked another—but I had exhausted myself and had nothing more to say.

Geo W Benson has been absent a week to Providence, New York and returned by the way of Boston. I suppose he has been out on a cotton mission. The result is not known to me.

S. L. Hill has been out to Palmyra N.Y. to transfer the silk from Miller to Hartwell[199]—what a pity to loose a pedlar that can sell 2d qlty silk for more than you can 1st qlty—It is said that you have a most splendid lot of silk sent to day—I hope you will like it—Almost one month of your three that you were going to peddle is over and I am heartily glad of it and I cannot doubt that you are too, tho I fear you will find community life rather dull and monotinous—Louisa Rosbrook was married to Geo Prindle Wednesday Afternoon 5 oclock at Geo Bensons by Mr Warner the Rosbrook family and Mr Mack and wife were the privileged few

thus endith community news—

I have had a letter from Mother this week what she said about the place in the villiage I will transfer to this she says "As for your place in the villiage it is not settled yet. upon examineation we find ~~think~~ that Mr Taylor has not the power to sell the place or you either thro the misswording of the instrument but it must go to court to get liberty to sell—Capt Taylor came home according to agreement but could not do any thing about it—There is to be an adjourned court in Brooklyn the last week in April and he hope it will be done. But Palmer is off about it. I think the society will take it into there hands and make what use they can of it. Mr Searls told Brother George that he thought Walter Webb would ~~take~~ buy it. Mr Searls is the societys committee to take care of the fund—you will see by this that there is no hurry for you to come this cold weather and I do not know as it will be nessesary for you to sign the writings."

So you see that this little last hope will probably by entirely cut off. and if it were the first disappointment we ever met it is probable we should be quite disheartned. I could not help feeling quite down a few hours but I have made up my mind to care nothing for it—I hope I shall always have what is nessesary and haveing that I aught to be not only contented but thankfull I have written to Mother concerning the insurances and likewise that she had better come up here as it seemed to be her wish. All well. Thine truly D. W. Stetson

Father Stetson.

I have not two minutes to write in as my time has all been taken up in preparing the box—which I have taken more interest in than any one box since I have had the charge of them for I thought you would like it so much— there are an assortment of beautiful colors for spring—and is the handsomest lot of silk I have sent away. I hope it will help to counterbalance the miserableness of the last one—for I should think by the tell that the top of the box was filled with something that would give you a broad hint of their intention of manufacturing "cotton"—I had nothing to do with that—I am authorised to write to you by "the directors" of the finishing room—the trinity which co[n]sist of James 1st 2nd Octavia and 3rd Mrs Hammond "to get some Otto of Rose and put into the silk that smells so bad and make it smell better nor matter if it is [dearly?] sold for it is too bad to lose such a good lot of silk"!!! Now dont dare to disobey for if you do!! You buy some and recollect when the silk is gone ~~to~~ that Almira Stetson is extravgantly fond of it—I presume there are others too that like it—but never mind—Dont you think we have done pretty well to skein all that silk in a week—"But Octavia helped"

"Those gloves fit to a T—but why under the sun did not Nancy write and tell me the price and how she liked the edgeing—Oh Father I want to come down to Boston to the anniversarrys dreadfully—but good bye

Almira

If too many cooks spoil the broth I wonder how many directors it will take to spoil silk—I guess the echo answers—Not many

Mr Hill found Mr Miller had been butchering of late That is the pedlers that sells second quality silk so well!!!!!! Dont say a word it is one of "the directors secrets"

Addressed: Mr James A Stetson— / Boston / Mass— / Cornhill—

51. Mary W. Bryant to James A. Stetson

Dear—Friend Stetson,

If you will please carry this box to Thomas F.[?] Norris's I shall be ever indebted to you and do as soon as possible, and if you think the flowers have withered do not send them they were put in saturday, I think they will be fresh please put these two letters in Boston Post office

Yours In Friendship

Mary W Bryant,

Addressed: Mr—James stetson / Boston / Mass.

52. Dolly W. Stetson to James A. Stetson

Sunday Evening May 4th 1845

Dear Husband—I think I will follow your example and write this evening lest I should not find any other time to write all I wish. And first I wish to beg pardon for not acknowleding the fruit received by the former box. Itt came safely and was a most delicious treat and while we enjoyed the gift we did not forget the giver, altho we did forget the thanks that were due.

Mother Stetson wishes me to request you to call at the office of the attorney that settled Aunt Betseys estate (Wm Bemis will tell you where) and see if there is any thing more comeing to her likewise who the two heirs are that have lately been payed off—she says if there is but one dollar comeing she would like to have it. Robert Small wishes me to thank you for the trouble of selecting the vest you sent and he is much pleased with it.[200] thus much for messages—

I had been expecting your letter very anxiously for several days and was very glad to receive it altho sorry to hear that you were not well and suffering from depression of spirits. I think it the natural consequences of the scenes you passed thro the previous week. I feel sorry for our Nashua friends but poor sister Eliza my heart bleeds for her. I feel with all the grief that I have suffered in parting with my children that I hardly should know how to sympathize with her—just as she might expect to reap the reward of her toils and labours in seeing them usefull men in society to see them languish month after month and have the dread uncertainty at leangth settle into the giving up of all hope and the waiting to see the last struggle and gasp

Oh! this is more than human nature can sustain unadid by that religion that sheds light even on the darkness of the tomb—

And here is my objection to Parkers theory[201]—If he denies to Christ all <u>authority</u> except what belongs to any true man (and he says that Christ was sometimes mistaken) and also if he deny the resurection of Christ, I know not on what he would base a hope of immortality—surely not on the almost universal desire for it, for all desire happiness <u>here</u> but they do not obtain it.— I sometimes doubt whether any do.

Well you say you have been unusually depressed—so have I—but from a different cause Change Change is the order of things here Mr Kerr and family have gone. two families from Chaplin Ct by the name of Ross have come[202]—Mr Fitch left a few weeks ago in a state of mind bordering on insanity—he has probably been insane—I should like to have you ascertain of his Brother in B. if you could without too much trouble whether he arrived there and what has been his state of mind hithertoo[203]—Sojourner has gone to N.Y. on a visit but previously to her going she turned Johnson the old colored man out of doors—James Willson lieves this week because he is not a good workman. Brigham has now gone to find a place for himself and family—[204] the Rosbrook family have all gone except the old lady and two girls that are at work for wages—

There were two private meetings of adult members of the Association holden last week the first on Monday evening to consider some propositions of G. W. Benson which were first to fill the factory with cotton machinery and go into manufactoring cotton as an association. Many object to this Mr

Hill Hall Judd and others think it would be morally wrong to increase our debt to 70 or 75,000$—Next he GWB proposes to hire the factory of the A[205] they erecting buildings for the oporitives to live in at a cost not exceeding 5000$ he paying 2000$ pr year for ten years and they agreeing to take the property at the expiration of the time—this was opposed—It would increase our debt to erect building for the factory and for the association lessen our means and take George from our business without whom our financial affairs would suffer[.] another proposition is that George and others of course that have offered to assist him buy the factory and a few acres of land adjoining and a privilege to take water from the canal to run another factory the size of this which they propose to erect by the side of this for which they will pay 20,000,$ this was objected too by many—A proposition was then made by Hall Judd seconded by Hill Mack and others that the whole estate be sold and the debts paid and the associatio[n] disband or some spoke of forming again some where else this was carried but two votes dissenting altho some did not vote. George was not present at the meeting but it was stated as his reasons for urging a change at this time when we have been so often assured that all things were never in so good a train and business going on so prosperously is that the [pressure?] from without is increasing that it is more difficult to obtain money because we are not doing more business that we are not using the water privilige &c that our credit is declin[in]g but if as an Association we would go into the cotton he could get money to any amount—Georg did not like or did not choose to appear to like the decision of the meeting. he says that just as we have the means in our grasp of getting rich and paying our debt we throw them away—but one thing I think is certain Hill, Judd, Mack, Foord and others will never go into cotton—Last evening there was another meeting A proposition was submited by Mr Mack to sell the factory and two thirds of the water and a certain portion of land and retaining enough for the Association to live upon the Grist Mill and Saw Mill and have those that wished go on together this gave rise to a dissussion upon our affinities and differences—religious opinions diet amusements and many other things came up the question was then put—Is it the opinion of the meeting that we are by our principles and habits fetted to live happily together and cary out true Associational principles the no[s] had it the question was again put whether it be the opinion of the meeting that we had better sell a part or the whole—the whole was the voice tho some dissented—

These have been informal meetings nothing binding the Executive have-ing the power to do what they please—All the things are kept secret untill something defenite is known—George is off looking up capitalists I sup-pose—he is determined to have the factory filled with cotton machinery at any rate this fall—Perhap you will see George in Boston this week—Well you are going away has been said to me several times—I have expected Mother Witter this past week but have been disappointed I hope she will come soon if she intends to come this summer Good night

  D. W. Stetson

I have filled my sheet and will send it perhaps I shall have something more to write when the box goes—Thomas Hill has decided to go down with you in a few weeks he has now gone to R.I. to carry his mother

  Addressed: James A Stetson / 25 Cornhill / Boston / Mass

53. Almira Stetson to James A. Stetson

[May 4, 1845][206]
Broughton Meadows
Sunday night 11 o'clock.

Dear Father.

  I do think it was to bad to have you go off so and never bid me good bye—next time it shall take it before hand—but I will send it in this letter—so it will do just as well. I am real glad you went to Mt Holyoke when you came home—but dont you candidly think it was a most magnificent sight? Perhaps you may have the same idea that a Gentleman had—who said to Eliza Walls brother—"This is a beautiful sight—but how much better it would be if the Conneticut ran st[r]ait!!!." Now I would like to ask you if you ever in all the days of you life heard a greener speech than that! Who would not see that the principle beauty consists in those long and graceful curves—~~to~~ which the magnificent river makes through the meadows.

  But I must close by telling you that I guess you will like the silk—and that I am real glad I did not go to Boston—Give my love to all the folks and tell them they all are indebted to me for letters—and believe me [when?] I superscribe myself your aff daughter

Almira Stetson

I wish you would send me some thing by the box if it is nothing more than a sugar plum. for Mr Parker came and brought me not the sign of any thing

A B S

Father I wish you would enquire at the bookstores the price of an "Herber-amium," for pressing flowers.

Addressed: Mr James A Stetson. / Boston / 25 Cornhill.

54. Dolly W. Stetson to James A. Stetson

Sunday Evening May 11th—.45

Dear Husband

The box goes tomorrow and I would fain say a few words to thee tho I might have to steal a little time from sleep. How I wish you could have been here to have enjoyed this beautifull day in wandering about in the shade, hearing the birds and admireing the flowers. Nature is putting on her beautifull garments and calling upon Man and all that is within him to bless her God

Mother Witter arrived here Friday afternoon by the way of Worcester she is well and brought word that you had been there and were well likewise—I wonder that you did not just run home when you were so near dont you intend to come home before the first of July—

Mother says that Capt Taylor had left the care of our place in B.[207] with Sept Davison with direction to advertise and sell. S. Webb thinks he would give 650$ for it—I am very sorry that we did not accept his offer which he made the first summer we were here which was 900 A great falling off truly in two years. One reason why B Palmer would not buy the place was that he could not raise the money on land in Abington. Another probable reason was that the society were unwilling to have any thing to do with him and would have the Morgage foreclosed Bowers family were still there

I heard this last week that you had written to Mr Mack that you should provide for your family some[w]here else than here after the first of July. I could not think this was so, for I thought that if you had decided what to do or where to go you would have told me as soon as Mr Mack and moreover you would not write so untill you had some idea of what we were to do. I have said repeatedly that I did not know or believe that you expected to remove from here the first of July—but enough of this

There has been a meeting of the members of the Association to decide upon the affairs in the prsent crisis—

I think that George Benson will take the factory at about twenty thousand dollars and those of the Association that can agree go on with the rest—The subject of Amusements is the great matter that seems to devide the members. Hall says that there are many here that he cannot go on with—he told Eliza Wall this afternoon that if she were not a member he would not vote for her that he considered her influence worse than a common Drunkard and so of ma[n]y other members here—that he was willing to withdraw if he was the only one that stood in the way &c[208]—S. L. Hill, Wells Bumstead[209] and Hammon[d] and Benson to a certain extent take the same ground against games or sports of all kinds for children even playing ball &c

So we go

James has woke up so I can write no more

Good night

    DWStetson

     Addressed: James A. Stetson / Boston / Mass // BOX

55. Almira Stetson to James A. Stetson

Monday Morning 12th of May—[1845]

Dear Father

I thought that I should write you a great long letter by this box but I have not had the time, so a short one must answer. I guess you will laugh when you open the <u>box</u> at the <u>bottom</u> of the <u>box</u>, and find what is in it. I would just say that they are my present exclusively for nobody knew any thing about it. but I thought when you sent that fruit up, that perhaps you would like something that came from home as well as I used to what came from Grand-mothers—I hope they will taste good—and you may carry one of them to

Lucy, and tell there is no butter or grease about them—(which news I guess will be as acceptable to you who eat so much). I was reall sad to think about that concert and now that other ticket was meant for me—if it wasent who was it meant for?. Oh! how much I would have given to have staid of been there to hear those unrivalled songsters (unless they are rivalled by those I hear now out of doors—I wish you would send your ears up here in a letter and I would fill them with such harmony, and send them back—Well you suppose I have first rate times in the finishing room—with Mrs H[210] and company. there you suppose entirely wrong, for I am so sick of that work—that I dread it like going to prison. I have sat there now every day some sundays not excepted over six months, and then to have such a lot set up their opinion about the silk, when they dont know any thing about it—I[t] raises my dislike as "much as a feet." I would give any thing to get away a week or so—but I suppose I must work on—it is making labor to me very disagreeable and a task to perform which effect I do not want to produce—but I am stringing out this matter longer than I meant to, for what is the use of troubling you with such things—you have enough of your own—

The Assn is getting a long bravely (I suppose) they hold meetings enough to—that is a good sign I believe in churches and I dont know why not here—

I am requested to ask you how much it would cost to go from Springfield to Boston in the second rate cars. the fare from Northampton to Springfield is ,25, cents—will you write in the next letter—

I suppose you will send the box this week—will you send back the little box in it—?

But I must bid you farewell for the present—from your affec daughter
     Almira

That affec means affectionate not affected—

Love to all the folks. Why don[t] Nancy write—Give her a "blowing up"

I should wonder if something should happen to that silk for I packed it Sunday—

Addressed: Mr James A Stetson / Boston / Mass // By Box.

56. Almira Stetson to James A. Stetson

[May 22, 1845][211]

Dear Father

It is quite late and my eyes ache so badly I shall not attempt a long epistle. The box is packed once more—but I shall remain very quiet about its contents thinking that it will speak for itself. Do you know that seventeen years ago to day I became your child—a squalling ugly fat homely youngone—and that through all these long and yet short years—I have remained about the same in charater only gained strength to carry out that character—Where and what do you suppose I shall be seventeen years from this time? Nothing worse than I have been I hope. I send you in the box some flowers One bunch is my birthday present to you—and two to the Jacksons—one for Harriette and one Mary Lincoln—if there. leave it if she is not—and one for 'The Atkins, I hope they will not get ~~wilted~~ damaged or crushed entirely and that you will deliver them with my best wishes I would write notes but they all are indebted to me for letters. the two nearest the bottom were for the Jacksons if they are not more jamed more than the rest—

I would send some to Lucy but hear she is out of the city—-I send some edgeing to Nancy A. 5 yards that come to 60 cts the same as the other—which makes it 1.20—the price of the gloves out—I do not know but Nancy is put out for she does not write—

I am very much obliged to you for my dress and think it very pretty. Mother is making hers—I tried to have Mother go to Boston offered to wean James and take care of him. But she has concluded not to go—I suppose she will give her reasons. Those oranges were very acceptable—and I was glad the cakes were so to you. But I must close—after wishing you a pleasant night's rest—it is raining like every thing here—your daughter who is just sweet seventeen

Almira Stetson

Addressed: James A Stetson— / Boston / Mass.

57. Dolly W. Stetson to James A. Stetson

Thursday Evening May 22^{d}—45

My Dear Husband

I seat myself to answer your letters by the box and the one by mail of Monday—it was but a poor substitute for the visit we were led to anticipate by ~~the~~ those letters that came by the box for altho you did not write positively we expected you untill Sunday night—and I think you will be somewhat disappointed when I tell you that I am not comeing to Boston—You do not know how much I did wish to go but you know that I wrote you sometime ago that I had decided to spend what money I felt I ought too this summer upon my teeth. this was before you had decided to lieve the Association. And now I feel the greater need of Economy—But there were various reasons I had not weaned James and altho Almira was willing to take care of him day and night and wean him yet it would produce serious inconvenience in the finishing room for her to lieve—I had not got my teeth set and more than all Mother did not seem at all to encourage my going and I supposed she had a right to dictate as we shall be obliged to come to her for funds in case we go away from here

Here seem to be an array of reasons sufficient to satisfy any reasonable being but I must confess I have been a little or a good deal unreasonable and have felt quite unhappy to day because I could not go.

Seventeen years ago to-day we commenced the responsible duties of Parents. The insufficiency I felt for the duties of Mother has ever since troubled me and probably always will but if my capacity had equaled my desires I should have been <u>such</u> a mother and my children oh! what children they would be

I feel at any rate that I have exhausted all my energies in the care of children and I hope "the time past of our our lives will suffice us to have worked the works of the flesh,"[212] but we may devote the remainder of our time to the children we have and to each other—

With regard to your questions about the place in Brooklyn—I can say— that if we are to lieve here I know of no place that I should prefer to go myself provided there was a prospect of business, but I do not like the idea of haveing you go pedling there any better than here

Mother says she is willing to do what you may think best and if you had encouraged her doing it last summer she could have saved a good deal of expense in the way of timber lumber &c. She wants if she has any thing to do with it to pay the morgage and in that case she would have no money left to repair with—I do not see why the mortgage cannot remain as it is—I do not understand what you mean by paying interest semiannually I am sure we never have. If it is your mind to return to B. I think you had better go there and see how much it would cost to repair it and return this way next week.

On Saturday evening of next week there is to be the first quarterly report of the Executive and Directers for the year 45—and probably other matters will come up for consideration

What ever we do we must do or decide to do soon—it is said that the factory must be emptied by the first Sept—Mr Macks family lieve in July we are to have no more schools after June—Sophia Foord Eliza Wall probably John Prouty[213] and I know not but all in the house lieve with Mr Mack or before Sydney and Harriet have returned right glad I think to find a shelter for their heads. Harriet is very low in consumption and Sydney has had the chlls and fever hold of him and looks misserably. they are at Mr Macks. Sydney dined here the other day and went into the consumption of Fish grease and butter at a great rate[214]—

I would thank you for the very pretty present of calico the very good one of Oranges and best of all Mrs Childs letters[215]—I wish you could have stood an unseen spectator when the box bundles were opened I think it would have paid you. David Ruggles thinks he will be obliged to give up his trip to Boston his eyes have become so sensative to the light that it is exceedingly painful for him to be out in the sun Mr and Mrs Parker are going on Monday[216] I presume you will see them and hear from them of the affairs here— I believe that Mr Parker as well as others here think that if the Association sell the factory and personal property to the amount of 30 thousand dollars they can erect a small silk factory and fund the debt which they think will not exceed 15,000 after erecting such buildings as are nessesary and be placed on a better foundation than ever—Mr Hill I suppose will have to be President as George will have to withdraw in order to carry on the cotton business. I hope you will write soon and let us know if you conclude to go to B and come here next week, yours D.W.S.

Mrs Paul desires her most respectful regards to you and says that she is exceedingly happy to hear that you are to return to your family so soon—

It is reported here that you have withdrawn from the Association, but I understand George contradicts the report and thinks you wrote to Mr Mack in a fit of despondency—I wish you had not written any thing about it untill you knew something what we were to do.

Addressed: James A. Stetson Esqr / Boston / Mass

58. Dolly W. Stetson to James A. Stetson

Northampton May 29th—45

Dear Huz

Mr Ruggles wishes me to say to you that he thinks he will have his sack of some dark color—he wishes me to remind you that he is 4 inches taller than yourself and just your size about the chest but smaller at the bottom of the waist. he wishes you to procure for him 6 ~~Venetian window blinds~~ window curtains or blinds of the following dimensions 4 ft 4½ in long by 2 ft 6 in wide provided they can be obtained for 2 dollars or less They may be sent by Mr Parker on saturday

I suppose you understand what they are they are made of small splits of wood woven like the rush curtains—Mr Ruggles says they are sometimes sold for a shilling apiece

We are all well this morning and I hope you are well and safely landed at your home in Boston—Mr Brighams family including Mrs Small remove to George Hills house to day—

Mr Ruggles says you can find the blinds at the wooden ware stores or furnishing stores

Truly thine

DW Stetson

Addressed: James A. Stetson Esqr / 25 Cornhill / Boston / Mass
Endorsed: Hale & Co.

59. Dolly W. Stetson to James A. Stetson

Sunday Evening June 1st [1845]

Dear Husband

this has been a most delightfull day in the outward world but my mind has not been in harmony with the external, I know not when my spirits have been so depressed. I fear I have lost all confidence in God and man—

The quaterly meeting was holden last evening the quaterly report was very indefinite nothing of interest transpired except that Geo W Benson and David Mack gave notice of their intention to resign their offises and a meeting is call[d] to elect their successors.

Sophia Foord has left the Educational Department and Marion Smith[217] takes the class while Mr Mack remains director that is till the first of July.

Mrs Rosbrook wishes you to get her a ninepenny calico of the style of mine but darker and send it by the next box—[9?] yds is sufficient.

James is quite unwell. I think it is his teeth I wish I had the time and spirits to write you a cheerfull letter and one that would make you more happy but lest it should have the contrary effect I will close by wishing you good night

yours

D.W. Stetson

Addressed: James A. Stetson / Boston

60. Dolly W. Stetson to James A. Stetson

Thursday Evening June 12th—45

Dear Husband

I am glad to have an hour to sit down and write to you and tell you of matters and things at home—And first we are all pretty well. James got well soon after I wrote and has improved so much in the use of his limbs that I have been obliged to have slats put at all my windows to keep him from going out.

We are enjoying a visit from Theodore Scarborough wife and son, Olive Gilbert, and Sarah Benson. Theodore is very much out of health he has come to the conclusion that his disease is a spinal affection. Olive Gilbert has gone to Brattleboro to day with Mr Mack and Theodore would have gone but he is so much fatigued with his journey here that he does not feel able to ride so far. I believe he has sent a disciption of his symptoms to Wessellhoft with a request for advice if he thinks he ~~thinks~~ can cure him.[218] I do hope he will get relief for it seem too bad to see a young man so feeble and dying or draging out a miserable existance—he says that he can never make Brooklyn seem like home to him and hopes to come back in a year, but I guess his wife is not of that opinion. It really seems like olden time to see them and talk over Brooklyn affairs.

We have had an election of officers of the Association Joseph C. Martin President Hall Judd Secretary Samuel Hill Treasurer.—I believe that most of the people are satisfied with the choice but I "guess" Mr and Mrs Hammond are somewhat disappointed that he is not president—but the new house is going on notwithstanding. Mother Witter is going to Brattleboro next week in company with Sarah Benson. She sends love to you. I wish you would purchase the song sung by the Hutchinsons entitled "My Mothers Bible" I want to send it to Uncle George

Almira says tell Father that I shall not write to him because he did not send her a sugar plumb but she hopes to have a dozen letters and a sugar plumb by the next box. Sarah says tell Father I have got a new doll—Grandmother Stetson gave it to her—Nancy says tell James I am not half so blue as she was when you was home and she hopes you are not—She says tell Lucy that she hopes she will finish the letter that she commenced to send by Sarah Benson so as to send it by the box.—I understand the beautifall poem entitled the Bustle was written by Doct Graham I think it a vulgar affair alltogether.

I hardly know how or what I have written for there have been severall talking in the room all the time one saying write this and another that—

I hope I shall have a long letter by the box

Good night DW Stetson

Addressed: James A. Stetson / Boston / Mass // Box

61. Dolly W. Stetson to James A. Stetson

Thursday Evening June 19th [1845]

Dear Husband

Again the word is given that the box goes tomorrow and again I seat myself to inform you of our welfare we are all well Mother Witter has gone to Brattleboro to day in company with Sarah Benson She expects to be gone a fortnight—Harriet Hayden died last Saturday and was buried the night before last by moonlight I did not go to the funeral myself but those that were there said the servercis at the house were very appropriate and the burial very solem and impressive. they had singing reading from the New Testament and talking by several—Sydney is very much out of health and looks as if he would follow her to the spirit land soon[219]—

I am disappointed that you are not comeing home as soon as the first of July I thought you would come next week Saturday but I suppose you will have business to settle before you can return. I do not know what I said against lieveing the Association but I certainly do not wish to stay if you cannot see things here in a more favourable light than you have for sometime past I am sure I could never be happy where you were so wretched and where every thing seemed wrong to you

Mr Ruggles was very much disappointed that he did not receive 1½ doz more of F Duglass Narritive by the box he said he had written both to you and Douglass for them and had engaged many of them to people out of the Association.[220] Nancy and the children were disappointed also that they did not have one word from Lucy and Isaac Edwin walked into town monday just at night and found the box there and then came back and ran all around to find a horse and went in again and got the box and opend it and rumaged all the waste papers boxes and all but nothing could be found[.] Edwin declaired that he would never write a word again to them in the world &c[221]

The fruit came very well and was very accepable the children send thanks for it as well as myself—the tab for my Bonnett is very pretty and as I suppose it was a hint for me to get my Bonnet altered I have sent it to day to the milliner—

I am going into town to morrow and hope to have my teeth compleeted— but I do not suppose that they will make me feel any younger if I look a little more so—I am glad to see by Marys letter that you had a pleasant time at Scituate I presume the place had changed as much as your friends thought you had—

I have not been able to do up your clothes in season to send but I think you will not need them this week

Mr Hammonds new house has been raised to day and I suppose that Mr Hills will go up soon

If you go to Brooklyn before you return give my love to all friends there I wish you had kept the song I had you purchase for Uncle George and his girls—as I know of no opportunity to send it untill Mother goes—I hope you will be home as soon as convenient

Yours

D.W.Stetson

Addressed: James A Stetson / Boston

62. Almira Stetson to James A. Stetson

Friday Morning,[222]

Now Dear Father I intended to have written by this box a good long letter to you—in answer to your very kind one. But I cannot, for last night Dr Graham lectured in town against "Odd Fellowship" and the team went in so I thought I would go not expecting much but the ride to be pleasant, I was however very pleasantly dissapointed and enjoyed the lecture highly. Graham out did himself. But I must let these things go and touch on something else. I thank you for the discription of the Swedenborgens Chapel, it was interesting to me to know such things.[223]

I should like to go there, for I very much admire Gothic architecture and should like to see it where there is attention paid s[t]rictly to the archtecture. I have never seen only here and there a pointed window or some thing of that kind I guess I inherit some of your love of seeing things complete and handsome and a taste for that that is beautiful. I thank you too for that for it makes me enjoy much in the view of such things. Mrs Candles lectures were kindly received they seem to please many, and Mother the other night was having a good laugh over them, but I have not much taste for such things and if I had I have no time but I am just as much obliged.[224] I suppose Mother will tell you all the news and some you will find very sad indeed (Mr Parkers).

I hope you will be at home before long—so I shall not be prescribed to paper for a conversation

But this was intended for a businis note when I commenced and I must go on. I want before you come home (or if you send another box) to get me "Emerson's Third Part" which is an Arithmetic with a key or supplement.[225] I have been using John Hurts but he ~~has~~ is going away next week. ~~Perhaps he is going to~~ Perhaps you can get it at the [book?] stores where they keep second hand books I had just as lief have it—and economy is necessary. I am out of pens almost and should like some more, and if you want to write comfortably when you get home you must bring some. These are my "must haves" for the pesent. I must bid you good bye. Almira.

"I dont like to have you plague me about eagles and owls."

That fruit was beautiful and it is so rare here that it was all the better. [Adieu?]

Addressed: Mr James A. Stetson / Boston. / Mass. // By box.

63. Mary Stetson to James A. Stetson

Northampton, June 26th 1845.

My Dear Father,

I am writing you this letter in the belfry of the factory there is a beautiful view of the river and meadows, but it does not begin to equal the view from Mt Sugar-Loaf I wonder that this mountain is not more celebrated than it is I think it suppasses Mt Holyoak in the beauty of the view there is a most beautiful curve in the Connecticut and the plains looked more splended than any carpet I have ever seen. We could see the ranges of Holyoak and Tom they looked beautifuly at the distance and the villages looked like little play houses among little trees.[226] Now I have told you about the view from Sugar Loaf I think that I had better tell you how I got there thought I have got the cart before the horse (I guess that you will excuse it.) We started Sundy morning about five O'clock there was ten or elevn of ~~them~~ us ~~and~~ we went in a two horse team it looked like rain we hardly knew whether we had better go or not but we at last decided to, and after we had gone a few miles it cleared up as bright as it could be, we passed through Hatfield and saw the tree that is 30 feet in circumfrance it is a very large tree but is not of a handsome form. There are some beautiful trees in Hatfield and it is a very pretty village indeed (I think) after we had passed through Hatfield we saw sugar loaf it looked so steep that we thought we never climb it but we thought we would try and see what Perseverance would do. When we got to the foot of Sugar Loaf we decided to go to the Bloody Brook monument which was two miles from there when we got there we all got out of the waggon to see the monument it is a very pretty monument it is made of marble one side is covered with a discription of the battle the monument was erected on the spot where the battle was fought and the grave was about 20 feet of the monument the only thing that marked the grave was a stone laid even with the ground with a few words on it but it had got so worn that we could not read it, we went back to the mountain after we had seen as much as we wanted to. The mountain was very hard to climb but when we got to the top of the mountain we were more than paid for our trouble we staid on the top of the mountain to dinner and started for home about 4 O'clock, and got home after 6.

Now for the news all I know is that Mr Parker has sawed his hand in the circular saw and had to have his first finger on the right cut off near the hand he bore it very well indeed and sung or whistled wile they were takeing it off. His wife is in Nantucket and knows nothing about it mother thinks that if you see her in Boston when she is comeing home that you had better not tell her of it. Grandmother Witter has gone to Burlington and Grandmother Stetson is here on a visit she sends her love to you and to every one there that knows her. Aunt Nancy sends a note to Isaac and Lucy and wants that you should give it to them. Lastly but the most pe important we shall all expect you next week now do not disappoint us.

from your affectionate daughter
   Mary.

Grandmother Stetson wants that if you go to Nashua you would give her love to Aunt Sally Ann and tell her that she must come up here berfore she goes away that if she will grandmother will go home with her. Grandmother wants that she should write and tell in what month she can come. all send love to you. I changed my location from the belfry to our sitting room before I finished the letter

Addressed: Mr James A. Stetson. / Boston. / Mass.

64. Thomas Hill to James A. Stetson

Northampton July 1ˢᵗ 1845

My Friend Stetson,

I write you at this time to request that you will call at Mr. Leach's & obtain for me a pair of pants which I left there.

They are those dark gray cassimere which I have worn most all summer. You will please go up into No 9. or No 5. with Mr Leach, & get them. If you have any doubt about the right ones get Mr. Leach to ask Mr Sawin or Gregory, what belongs to them in the closet. They have no linings.

Give my love to Mr & Mrs Leach & the friends generally.

I arrived in Northampton 5 minutes [b]efore three the afternoon ~~you~~ I left you.

Mr. S. I will not attempt to describe to you the pleasures of meeting with those loved ones. You know too well the joy that comes with a sight of your dear, family & friends. Great changes are taking place among us. To day most of the scholars leave us, & part of the remainder of our family go this noon to commence boarding at the factory. What I shall do I have not yet determined Marian[227] is so much unwell that we are trying to make some arrangements to carry her [to] Brattleboro to go through the Water Cure. Her lungs are very weak & have been so ever since my absence. You family, I believe are all well, & I hope you will soon be blessed, as you so much desire, with a sight of them. I think some of going to Springfield to day

Uncle thought as I did so well that I was more profitable than I could have been else where but I told him not to think of my going again.

Farewell friend S. In the hope that you too will be permitted to enjoy with me the face of your beloved̲s̲.   Your friend Thomas Hill

Addressed: James A. Stetson / 25 Cornhill / Boston.

65. Dolly Sharpe Witter to Dolly W. Stetson and James A. Stetson

Brooklyn [Conn.] August 28 1845

Dear Children

I have just made up my mind to write to you to inform you of my journey and arrival at home Indeed I have not had time to write before I found so much to do My House was out of place every where but found nothing damaged I have been all this time puting things in there proper place I suppose that James informed you that he saw me in Worcster and that I was going to see Hariot and staid with her all night found her pritty well They are going to remove to a smaller teniment and do not intend to keep Boarders—I found Mr & Mrs Allin there and it seamed that I had almost got home

I Purchased me alpacker for a cloak and cotton carpiting enough to cover the bedroom floor and you cannot imagine how smart I look I wish that you could just step in and Behold I got to Capt Taylors to dinner and after dinner Mrs Taylor carried me home baggage and all but first furnished me with Poark Chease and indian meal and I caled as I came along at Robinsons and got me tea and sugar so I lived like pigs in the clover—

I have got before my story When I got to Danalsons Vil[228] who should I see but Bengamin Cross & we gave a hearty good shake of the hands and he was glad to hear from community and promised to come and see me this day but has not He said that he was going to write to some of you the next day. I asked him to mention that he saw me safe at the depot

I have received a very Friendly reception from all the Neighbors that I have seen I have only been to Mr Howels & Capt Taylors I have seen all of Cousin Nathans family and he shoed his joy by bringing me a very nice peace of Lamb & the next day Lemuel Cady sent me an other—I Had an opportunity to send to brother Georges the next day after I arrived home & Mariah came down laden with my beads and provision that lasted me allmost a weak & fruit grapes pears peaches & George & Lucreat[ia] came down thursday after and staid a litle while bringing butter and honey and soap which was a very nessesary ingredient—The Abington Friends are all will,[229] they appeard Disapointed that you did not call on them again Davis thought he saw you comeing down the hill & Cyrena got her dinner ready & waited ever so long.[230]

Capt Taylor is not athome and is not expected for a long time but I learned from his wife & William that your Teniment is removed about 10 feat from where it formely sood so that it ranges with the tavern and Palmirs hous—They are fixing it for two tenements with a suller the bigness of the house a well and an addition on the Wist—Palmer was at Taylors Sunday Night said that there would be two as plesent tenemen as any in the vilage About the money busenes I know nothing They have compleated the Old Meeting house and it is to be Didicated Wednesday 1 of October I suppose as great a bustle as possible for you must know that Fredrick Grey and A Mr Clark from Mass and others are expected I have had severel offers to be carried down and think that I shall go as I have not been to the vilage—I am ready to have Mary & Sarah come and visit me & if Olive Gilbert has not come home When she does I wish they might come with her I will help them home If you can spare Sarah lit her spend the winter and go to school I think they will try to have a good one

My mind is with you both Night and day I have wonce dreamed of seeing D & Almira I thaught I was in a room where they passed through Dolly said some joious thing about my gitting back so soon & Almira came to the door & laughed but said nothing soon I was left alone I thaught that I might as well be alone at home—

N P Rogers[231] sais it is in bad tast to go into paticulars thus but you know that I must write of what runs in my head—I saw Elisabeth Martin at Robinsons she said tha Sarepta[232] was very low has no appetite vomits a great part of the time and is actually failing her aunt Polly Williams died the weak before I came home

I am very desireous to hear from you all especially L & James and hope that you will write soon Sister Chase is not hear and my Friends have not heard from her I wish very much to here where she is and how she does I should like to have her come and stay with me a while all winter prehaps

I do not get any knowledg f[r]om Hartford except that Fredrick has been in N York a part of the time this summer with George and Lucretia thinks that Sophia has been with him some of the time

I do not think of any more items to write and therefore I will close by sending love & respects to all who may have any interest in my well-fare   D Witter

I hope that when you write you will [give?] all the paticulars of your affairs————I shall reserve the farm for you untill I am convinced that you do not intend to come and live with me I think the scenery in some parts of Brookly as pleasint as NH[233]

I hope one or both of the girls will com Martha is much dis appointed that they did not come

Lucrecia says that Hariot always thaught that she should like to keep Tavin or boarding house but thinks that she has got satisfied on that busines and I think you will by Spring Mrs Bakers little Boy has just came to the door and tried to come in he is 11 months old a great good naturd boy but does not walk yeat—looks like Nathan Weigh Mrs Baker possises a kind and generous spirit under an unpolished exterior Mr Baker has done all I have asked him to do with regard to wo[o]d works hard and to little profit I fear there is carcly a door shut in the Barns and outhouses every thing looks Baker fashion as Uncle Clement says

Addressed: James A Stetson / Northamton Mass
Postmarked: BROOKLYN CT

66. Joseph C. Martin, Hall Judd, and Samuel L. Hill to James A. Stetson

Northampton, Dec. 4. 1845

To James A. Stetson:

Having full confidence in your ability & willingness to manage the affairs of the Silk Manufacturing Department, we hereby reappoint you Director of the same.

Joseph C Martin
Hall Judd,
Samuel L. Hill[234]

Addressed: J. A. Stetson / Northampton.

67. Mary W. Bryant to James A. Stetson

Northampton Commity

My Kind Friend

As I wish for a discontinuanse of my paper—and feeling rather—penny-less, I have to troubl you again by leaving this letter—at [Nareiss?] office or

~~by~~ put it in the Post office if you mail it please pay the postage as he will not get it without, and charge the same to me,

Very Respectfully,

M.W. Bryant,

Mr—James Stetson;

Addressed: Mr—James Stetson / Boston / Mass

68. Dolly W. Stetson to James A. Stetson

Sunday April 12th 1846

Dear Husband

This is a dull rainy sunday and ~~and~~ between the community habits of the children and the sabbath notions of my neighbours I have a good deal to attend too[235]—

the transition from community life to life in the world is attended with no small inconvenience—Were it not for the hope that the children would be interested in their schools (I mean Sarah and George) and have something to occupy their minds I should give up in utter dispair—We have about completed our house cleaning and arrangeing our furniture—I like the house better than at first and think if the slabs and logs are removed it will be quite plesant—I have written to Mother and have not as yet heard from her. We have had calls from Hall and Francis and quite a number of community people[236]—Elizabeth Martin is spending Sunday with us—I have had an application to send the girls to a writing school—The teacher is a man that says he has taught here more or less for thirty years—As writing is not much attended to in the high schools he has a class during vacation his terms are 1.25 for 15 lessons he finding stationary I have about concluded to let Almira and Mary go

Monday Evening

We have done a large washing to day and I am quite tiered of course.

I can only say that we are well and getting along as well as could be expected. If you have not time to write just send us a paper now and then and write as often as you can.

I shall write you again when I hear from Mother——Yours in haste
D.W Stetson

Addressed: James A Stetson / Boston // By the Box

69. Samuel L. Hill to James A. Stetson

Northampton April 23. 1846

J. A.Stetson
Esteemed Friend

We enclose herein a check on New York for $870. ~ having borrowed it of George to take up your acceptance at the Globe Bank on Saturday You will please gather and send to us all you can so we may get it on monday. Hall is putting up silk to send you to day by express and will put a memo in box. We shall also put in box 2 circulars relating to the exhibition at Washington in may next, we have some mind to send on a case of col^d silk, please advise what you think about it. We hope you will have seen or heard from Macomber when you write again we are anxious to learn what he is doing—we must know something how to calculate for our payments next month.

Yours Truly
S L Hill

P.S.
Please acknowledge the rect. of Dft on New York and the box of silk

If possible wish you to find the poise belonging to the balance you used when in Boston last summer.

BB.[237]

70. Dolly W. Stetson to James A. Stetson

Wednesday April 23^d 1846

Dear Husband

We have received both of your letters in due time, and the contents thereof and should have written before but have been hoping to receive a letter from Mother before I wrote so that I might inform you of her decision with regard to comeing here and whether she wished you to come that way home—but as no such letter has arrived you must do as you think best about comeing through Brooklyn—We are all well and have got pretty nearly settled and I am quite sorry that you have suffered yourself to feel uneasy about us for we have got along quite well

You speak of going to Nashua and Lowell and I should like to have you go to Waltham and see Nancy—Mary has had a letter from Mary Richardson requesting us to board her this summer, and let her go to school with the girls—I should like to have you see her and tell her that we are not situated so that we can take her conveniently.—I am happy to say that the girls do not need new bonnets—Almira has sent hers to the Milleners to be new dressed—

I am sorry that you cannot find a cheap and decent carpet for our front room for these white floors are very hard to clean and require it very often to be desent—I wish if you return by the way of Brooklyn and bring Mother that she would bring her cotton carpet for her chamber

The writing school that I wrote you of ~~are~~ is I suppose blown over, as the Gent never calld again to inform me when the school commenced as he said he would if he had a school.

I hope you will show Aunt Alexanders letter to Aunt Bemis and see if something cannot be done to help her back. I do think it is too bad that a woman that has toiled as she has for her children should be so unhappy with them.

If I was rich I would (or I think now that I would) send her money to come on with and give her a home—Anson Martin has come on here and has placed himself under the care of Dr Gridley—He is boarding out at the Com Boarding [House?][238]

He brings no news from B. as he came from Norwich

I do not think of any thing more to say

so good bye

Yours

    D.W.Stetson

Addressed: James A. Stetson / No 9 Bulfinch St / Boston / Mass
Postmarked: NORTHAMPTON Ms. APR 23

71. Dolly W. Stetson to James A. Stetson

Northampton May 3^{d}—46

Dear Husband

As I think you might be somewhat disappointed, that you did not hear by the box; (which by the way I knew nothing of untill too late) I thought I would write to day.

I walked out to the Association yesterday afternoon made a few calls, bought a few things, drank tea at the boardinghouse, and rode home with Mr Snow haveing passed a very plesant afternoon. It is the first time I have been into a dwellinghouse except the one we inhabit since we left—the people all seemed glad to see me and the girls at the boarding house seemed allmost ready to eat me up.

This morning Thomas and Marian[239] came in as usual on Sunday morning and say that this morning about 5 oclock Mr Barron struck his wife on the forehead with a hammer probably while she slept ~~probably~~ with the intention to kill her and as it is supposed went to the river and threw himself in to drown himself for the girls were arroused by a call or noise from Mrs Barron Elizabith Martin looked out of window and saw mr Barron comeing to the house with his cloathes all dripping wet. he came in and went into their room and refused to let any one come in said it was his wife and they should not come. but the boarders got up some of the neighbours and went in found she had got of the bed onto the floor covered with blood and was not wholey insensible

They sent into town for Doct Walker and when he came he found it so critical a case ~~and~~ that he returned to the villiage for council and when Thomas and Marian came in they met Doctr,s Walker Barrett and Thomson and the Sherriff. I have since heard that Mr Barron was in jail. Poor Man, how much he must have suffered ere he arrived at such a dreadfull pitch of insanity. and his wife too if she has had any fear of this dread event what misery she must have lived in. I will not write any more about this now. I expect Martha Brigham here tonight to take the early cars for Worcester and I shall then hear more of this sad affair[240]

Hall and George Benson returned home last night

I hope you have sent some money to me by them for the money I had when you was at home was not sufficient to pay for the childrens books that they needed and my milk and butter bill were both due last week—Things do not come here without money. The three oldest girls commenced going to school last Monday. They seem quite pleased with their schools. The school is quite small this summer. More than 90 in the one that Mary and Sarah attend and about 30 in Almiras. Mr Snow has been here and says that the fracture on Mrs Barrons head is just above the temple on the right. they have removed the fractured pieces eleven in number lieveing an opening of about three inches square. She is very weak oweing to the loss of blood but bore the operation as well as could be expected. some hopes are entertained of her recovery. Mr Snow has little charity for him and says that this has all arisen from Mrs Barrons refusall to give up what little property she has which is a deed on some land in Ohio to him. His own daughter says this, and has as little charity for him as any one. he is in jail.

I have done nothing about a garden yet and do not know what to do. I do not know who to get to make it and I should have all my seeds to buy. both of the other families are going to buy their vegitables ~~both~~ Mother and myself are both so fond of them that it seems [as] if it would cost a good deel to buy them. I wish you would write and tell me what is best to do.

Slabs logs &c remain as they were. Mr Damon is too much engaged in making money to attend to the comfort of his tenants. The Anthony house that we talked of is about being vacated there was a sale of furniture Carpets &c there yesterday.

I suppose you have written to day if you did not write by Hall, and I hope if you have not written when you are comeing home you will in your next letter. Lucy has had a great crying spell to day because Father does not come home. your last visit was nothing but an aggravation

All send love yours <u>DWStetson</u>

Addressed: James A. Stetson / No 9 Bulfinch St / Boston / Mass
Postmarked: NORTHAMPTON Ms. MAY 4

72. James A. Stetson to Dolly W. Stetson

Boston July 2[d] 1846

My dear wife

I returned yesterday from Portsmouth N.H. and was glad to recieve your letter and glad that you have written to <u>Emeline</u> I am sorry you are not well.

if you put on a thin Feather bed I think you will get rid of the pain under your sholder. I have slept on boards but I think your straw bed was harder

you say I do not write long letters. one reason is the novelty of the scenes I meet with. [?] [passed off in a masure?] & more I have never been more ancious to sell silk than I have this season and I fear that I never have done so little and one man to whom I sold a large bill has not payed as he agreed to & altho I hope to get it all it has nevertheless given me much trouble the last month other business has hindered me at times doing as I would. howiver I have done the bist I could and all I could & can only leave the result to come out as it will

tell Mary I am much obliged to her for her letter should like to recieve another & from Almira You must make a visit among my friends it is now a long time since you have had any leisure or recreation you are intitled to all the pleasur the world can afford—you will get Mothers consent. She and Almira & Mary can take care of the rest

I think I shall not return to Northampton to stay long at presant cannot say however when I may return I must consult the Interest of the Association only in the case

I ment to have sent you twenty five dollars to day but I have taken so little since I sent home to Hall before that I can spare only twenty you can pay the rent & I will if I do not return next week send you more—you will want some clothes to make you comfortable neat & clean to visit your friends I want you to get what ever you want &c &c—Love to all

Yours Ever

J. A. Stetson

write so that I can get a letter monday or tuesday morning

Addressed: Mrs. D. W. Stetson / Northampton / Mass

73. Sophia (Sharpe) Tyler to Dolly W. Stetson

Hartford Sept 1846

My dear Neice

I have been thinking all summer of writing to you but the extreme heat has induced me defer every exertion that I could and keep cool I wish much to hear from you and your family, and your dear Mother I wish much to have your mother come and spend a week or two with us and your Aunt Chace also, I would write her but I have not known [where?] to direct a letter If you know where she is I wish you would write for me and tell her I wish very much to see her I feel now as if we could accomodate our friends ~~now~~ as we have been building an addition to our house and have now 3 spare rooms. Since Sarah came home we have been very much cramped for room, but now, our house is plenty large enough for all our friends and ourselves and why can you not come with your Mother and bring the traveling bag I think it time it was here, tho I have not many things to put into it yet but I think it would fill by degrees I think the silk you send us is worth more than the dudds you get from us we seldom use a skein of silk without speaking of the convenience it is to us and I assure you that I am greatly obliged to you for it I wish I could know what kind of clothing you most wished for I should not send so many useless things perhaps and those better adapted to your wants

Mr Tyler is again from home this summer as I suppose yours is, husband is and I need not tell you any of the inconvenien[ce] of living in such a way, I have little to complain of in comparison with those who are in a sad state of widowhood who never expect to be again united to those they have held so dear, but I often feel the need of an adviser and friend to assist me in my cares All our children and Grand childr[en] are with us now (except George) and are well and happy I expect Mary Stimson has a little infant by this time I had a letter from her some two monts since I think by her letter she is more happy in her husband than she has been she says her father is in comfortable health and the rest are well I have heard nothing from Abington lately I have written brother George last week and hope to get an answer soon

I hope you will write me soon and tell me how you get along and how your family are Sarah and Helen send love to your dear mother, and yourself and fami[ly (]In which I cordially join) Your aff Aunt S Tyler

74. James A. Stetson to Dolly W. Stetson

Boston Feby 8th 1847

Dear Wife

I received your letter on my return from Nashua, Concord, & Manchester Mrs. Winch went with Betsey (the day before I arrived in N) to Plymouth to spend a week, Betsey had ben up to see the new House in Manchester, but received a message from home that she was wanted to help Joseph make up his mind whether to accept an offer made by the Rail Road Company to continue there so I suppose by this time they have decided

I am pleased at the view you take of our return to Brooklyn that we ought to have learned some wisdom by what we have seen and Experianced is true and I trust we have and we must make use of all we have ever obtained for our own and neibours benefit, and we must dipend mainly upon our own resourses for Happiness and improvement after we are settled there, look at home and to the good we can do for all our injoyments—our hopes in having Mr May as a preacher are at an end. I understand he is appointed General agent of the M.A. Slavery Society for our sakes I am sorey for this but hope it is for the General good[241]—you say the general topic of conversation is our moving, & George wants to know what horse we are to have Mr Nathan Allen has a nice horse that I looked at when there & if he dont sell it before the first of April we probably shall have it if he does we can get some other— we must not expect to have every thing just right and all we want to begin with but must wait patiently for many things, and by striving we can get them and injoy them the better for striving after them,—we shall have a great many things to begin with so as with comon industry we can get a good living I hope without severe toil

as to making much progress in packing before I give up travelling and make a business of it, I dont expect you can—I intend to go home the last of this month and stay a few days—It is so very uncertain about hireing such a man as we can trust when I am absent, that I shall write to Samuel[242] to day that he must not depend upon me after about the first of April

I will endeavour to get the book you mention and should like to get a Book and Box of <u>Homeopathy</u> medic[ines] if you would like to have them and I find I can afford to do so, but I dont know where or how to procure them if you do let me know

There is nothing verey new or interesting in the city that I think of I attended an antiwar meeting Thursday evening but was too tiered to stand up all the evening and dislike too much to be in a crowd Especially so noisey a one to stay long, the volenteers leive this week, and the city will be restored to comparitive quiet,[243]

I heard Theodore Parker this forenoon preach another first rate sermon upon Mans Individuality—the house was crowded with hearers. I think they increase in numbers fast—but to day is a very plesant day and every body takes the oppertunity to go out[244]

I have ben as succesfull in business as I expected to be and perhaps more so,—I shall send tomorrow to Samuel about $400,, as the result since I left

I sent to you 5 Dol. last monday and send 5 Dol to day if I do not send enough you must let me know as I have a long letter to write to Samuel I must bid you good Bye Love to the children & yourself   yours

    Ja⁵ A. Stetson

Addressed: Mrs. D.W. Stetson / Northampton / Massachusetts
Postmarked: BOSTON MS 8 FEB

75. Dolly W. Stetson to James A. Stetson

Wednesday Evening May 12ᵗʰ—47

Dear Husband

I received yours of Sunday, Tuesday morning and was glad to hear that you were well and felt at home again, We are all well here and getting along as well I suppose as could be expected. John has planted he thinks about 1½ acres of potatoes on the hill and has got the field back of the woodhouse ploughed ready for planting. I suppose he will begin to plant tomorrow. George says that he wants me to tell you that planting is not like sowing three [twitshes?] and go on, but it is a long steady business. I think John is very faithfull and industrious but slow.[245]

The cows have been turned to pasture several days as you requested, the last cow has calved to day and has a nice heifer calf. I dont know of any thing more concerning the stock unless it be that Harris has mended the fence and the sheep are turned into the orchard and their corn is dispensed with.— The school has commenced and Sarah Lucy and James go. The teacher of course is boarding here and she says that James does very well, so we have quite quiet times when they are gone.

We have had no rain since you left and the ground is very dry, grass of course grows slowly and seeds do not vegitate.

Grandma says do not forget to say that we have got a hen setting and the pigs have been turned out to pasture and do better—likewise that the cherry trees are getting quite white with blossoms.

I had a long letter from Almira as you supposed Mary thinks it a great pity that she could not go up and be her assistant she thinks it would be more profitable than knitting socks or picking whortleberries

I am very sorry the[t] Almira has so large a school I fear it will be to hard for her—

We had a short visit from Geo W. B. and Mr Tarbox last Saturday. I was glad to see them especially George he seems to take a great interest in Almira, and says that he will look out that her health does not suffer He looks as if a wonderfull change had taken place in his health. By the way have you been to Garrisons yet and will you say something about the Liberator. the Chronotype I have not yet seen either, I should like to see some paper giving an account of Frederic Douglass treatment and the excitement in England arising therefrom.

You need not have sent me all the money you had—and I did not understand whether it was all that was due you from the Association or only you[r] last years wages—Should you go to Providence I should like to have you call and see Anna J.[246] as Mrs Kies says that she felt hurt that we did not send for her to come to Northampton. tell her we shall want her more this fall. D. Taylor can tell you wher to find her

Mr Wells that married Betsey Scarborough died sunday morning after a short illness and Harriet Scarborough wife of George Sharpe died a few days previous of the measles. there are six little children left 3 without a father and three without a mother grandchildren of Ebenezer Scarborough.

I somewhat expected from what John said that you told him that you would have written for us to meet you in Killingly next Saturday and shall expect you to write that you are comeing the next week.

Give my love to all friends in your travels. All send love to you—

Good night

Yours

   D.W.Stetson

I shall probably have no opportunity to send for Marys bonnet as I know no more who is going to Worcester than I do who is going to China

Addressed: James A. Stetson / No 9 Bulfinch St / Boston / Mass
Postmarked: BROOKLYN CT MAY 13

Notes

1. Fragments of an earlier letter from James A. Stetson to Dolly W. Stetson were published in Edward J. Lee, Jr., "The Old Letter," *Vermont History News* 33, no. 6 (November–December 1982): 88–90. The original of this, and other letters from which it was selected, have yet to be traced and the author's transcription has not been checked.

"... [Washington, Vermont, October 16, 1842]

"... It is with pleasure that I can now, after another weeks traveling inform you that I am rather improved—the pain in my back and foot that troubled me much the first week, have almost entirely left me. The only pain I now suffer is one I do not expect to get rid of, and that is of the heart at my absence from home—I last wrote you from Hartland, since which I have traveled 152 miles—I rode yesterday 12 miles in the rain, and it is some colder to-day threatening a storm. I am in an open wagon, and do not like to ride in the rain. However, I shall do the best I can.—

"This is an extremely bad time for business, as merchants have availed themselves of the pleasant weather to go to market and purchase their winters supplies. I have sold $86 worth since I left. I do not know that what I have done is what my employer expects, but I think, as they told me of other men's doings for them, that I have done quite as much. . . .

"... but in Hancock, I felt my spirits improved by the grandeur of the lofty, rough, and inaccessible mountains, the deep black and yawning chasms, the bumbling, rolling and mad career of this branch of the White River . . . , and as I approached nearer Burlington, there was added to the grandeur of the view a quiet lake, most perfect and enchanting. . . . then too, I add that there is the fine appearance of the town, handsomely laid off in squares, the streets being very spacious and some very handsome buildings. . . . But to me, the work of God in this region utterly excludes the consideration of the works of man—for after all . . . if we turn our minds inward and contemplate man in his wonderful formation, we are bound to say he is the most noble work of an all perfect Creator. I hope our dear children will never think meanly of all that demeans their natures (as some teach) but only think meanly of all that demeans their powers . . . God has given them, and seek to exalt them by adding virtue and increase in knowledge and excellence until they arrive at the perfect stature of men and women in Christ which lies in perfecting our mental, moral and religious abilities. . . .

"Now I want to say to my boys a little about hunting. I think it is very mean and wicked to kill little birds and animals that do us good—or if they do not directly serve us, they do not hurt us much. But when any animal destroys our sheep and corn and are dangerous to our persons, then it is right to kill them. They just had a hunt 5 miles from where I stayed in Rochester . . . they turned out from two or three towns and surrounded a mountain and closed up to the top driving the game before them until they all met. What do you suppose they hunted? little birds? no little squirrels? no, George, ask what they did kill then and I will tell . . . 7 bears and 12 foxes. . . .

"I think it is important for you to get down the big map of Vermont and lay it out on the floor to trace for the older children my route through the different towns so they may learn about this land of valleys, rivers and mountains which I have described. . . .

your affectionate husband—James A. Stetson."

2. Elizabeth and Sarepta Martin were Brooklyn, Conn., neighbors of the Stetsons. Elizabeth would later move to Northampton, and although there is no record that she became a member of the Northampton Association [hereafter referred to as the NAEI] she may have boarded there in its final months.

3. Sophia Foord (1802–1885), a teacher from Dedham, Mass., a nonresistant and acquaintance of the Garrison family, came to the NAEI in January 1843; she was admitted as a member in April 1843 and stayed until June 1845; she then went to Concord to teach Bronson and Abby Alcott's children; see Walter Harding, "Thoreau's Feminine Foe," *Publications of the Modern Language Association* 69 (1954): 110–116. In a memoir published in the *Woman's Journal* (April 11, 1885), Louisa May Alcott described Foord as "one of those who, by an upright life, an earnest sympathy in all great reforms and the influence of a fine character, made the world better. . . ."

4. The words "Mr Ruggles" were inserted, probably by James Stetson. David Ruggles (1810–1849), born in Norwich, Conn., had been a noted New York City abolitionist writer and activist in the 1830s. Heading the New York Committee of Vigilance to protect fugitive slaves and free blacks from kidnapping, he assisted hundreds of escaped slaves (including Frederick Douglass in 1838) and was subsequently publisher of the *Mirror of Liberty*, one of the first African American magazines. After disputes with other New York abolitionists, failing in health, and almost blind, Ruggles was helped by Boston abolitionists and at William Lloyd Garrison's urging accepted into the NAEI in November 1842.

5. Rev. William Coe (1804–1872) was minister of the Unitarian church in Brooklyn, Conn., from 1837 to the early 1840s. He assisted in the founding of the NAEI but sold his interest in it before it was fully organized and later took up farming in Worcester, Mass.

6. William Adam (1796–1881) and Erasmus D. Hudson (1805–1880) were among the NAEI's founders and prominent early participants; for details about them see Christopher Clark, *The Communitarian Moment: The Radical Challenge of the Northampton Association* (Ithaca, N.Y., 1995; Amherst, Mass., 2003), 25–29. They were attending an antislavery convention at Manchester, Conn.

7. This letter is written on a printed copy of the NAEI's 1843 constitution.

8. Daniel Tarbox was a Brooklyn, Conn., abolitionist.

George W. Benson (1808–1879) was one of the founders of the NAEI and probably its most influential leader during its early years. Benson had married James A. Stetson's sister Catharine (sometimes spelled "Catherine") in 1833, and the Bensons were among the Stetsons' closest neighbors and associates in Brooklyn. Already prominent abolitionists, the family had its position in the movement bolstered by the marriage of George's sister Helen to William Lloyd Garrison in 1834. See Clark, *The Communitarian Moment*, 18–20.

9. Josiah Hayward (1801–1874), a mason by trade, and his family were members of the NAEI from March 1843 to July 1844. They had been active abolitionists in Salem, Mass., and in the Massachusetts Anti-Slavery Society.

10. Brooklyn.

11. Theodore Scarborough (1814–1850) and his family were Brooklyn neighbors of the Stetsons, who had helped to found the NAEI in April 1842 and remained there until July or August 1844.

12. Theodore Scarborough's brother Herbert (b. 1820) had participated in events such as the Chardon Street (Boston) Church, Ministry and Sabbath Convention of November 1840 that had helped define nonresistants' and radical abolitionists' opposition to orthodox churches and ministers. He had come to the NAEI in November 1842 and left with other members of his family in the summer of 1844.

James Boyle (1803–c.1884) and Laura P. Boyle (1803–1852) were at the NAEI from June 1843 to October 1844. James Boyle had grown up in Canada and trained for the Catholic priesthood before becoming an evangelical Protestant and then a Perfectionist. He had been an active abolitionist lecturer in Ohio and New England before joining the NAEI.

13. Stetson is referring to changes in the organization of the Hopedale Community at Milford, Mass.

14. An advertisement in the *Liberator* on May 31, 1844 announced that the Northampton Association had its sewings and saddlers' silk and twist for sale at wholesale and retail at 2½ Hanover Street, Boston, by J. A. Stetson, "one of its members."

15. "Aunt Mary" may have been Mary Benson, George W. Benson's sister. "Aunt Ruth" was Ruth Stebbins, who was being nursed by friends at the NAEI through what would prove her final illness; see David Mack to Henry Douglas, March 9, 1844, Northampton Association of Education and Industry, Records, 1836–1853, American Antiquarian Society, Worcester, Mass. (hereafter cited as NAEI, Records), vol. 4, p. [46].

16. David Mack (1803?–1878) was a founding member of the NAEI and lived there with his family from May 1842 to July 1845; see Clark, *The Communitarian Moment*, 15, 17, 24–25.

17. Samuel Lapham Hill (1806–1882) was a founder of the NAEI. With his family, he was a member throughout the community's existence and would become its most

prominent leader during its latter years. See Clark, *The Communitarian Moment*, 20–21.

18. Catharine [or Catherine] K. Benson (1809–1890), James A. Stetson's sister, married George W. Benson in 1833.

19. Thomas Hill (b. 1827), probably a nephew of Samuel L. Hill and a member of the NAEI from 1842 to November 1845, was a well-regarded young abolitionist.

20. The Hutchinson family were popular singers, especially celebrated in abolitionist circles; see Dale Cockrell, *Excelsior: Journals of the Hutchinson Family Singers* (Stuyvesant, N.Y., 1989).

Sydney Howard Gay (1814–1848) was a lecturer for the Massachusetts Anti-Slavery Society from 1842 to 1844 and subsequently editor of the *National Anti-Slavery Standard* (New York).

Charles Lenox Remond (1810–1873) was an abolitionist lecturer whose moral-suasionist views would have been well received at the NAEI; he was probably the best-known black abolitionist before Frederick Douglass became famous.

The birth of James E. Stetson and James A. Stetson's consequent visit home meant that there were no more letters for another month, so there is no description of the Hutchinsons' visit. Entries in the Hutchinsons' journals (see Cockrell, *Excelsior*, 264–270) and an account in the *Liberator*, May 10, 1844, record the singers' stay at the NAEI and their performance at an antislavery meeting in Northampton Town Hall on April 29 before an audience of five or six hundred. The chief speaker at the meeting, it turned out, was not Gay or Remond but Frederick Douglass himself, who also stayed at the NAEI for a few days. Either at this meeting or at another one in 1845, a stone thrown at Douglass was collected and kept by young George R. Stetson as a souvenir.

21. Oliver D. Paine (b. 1819) was a member of the NAEI from April 1842 to June 1845. A machinist, he developed new silk-reeling apparatus and other equipment for the silk-manufacturing department.

22. Nancy Richardson (b. 1799) was James A. Stetson's widowed sister, and Mary Richardson (b. 1834) his niece; the Richardsons joined the NAEI in September 1842. James and Dolly Stetson's son Ebenezer had died in November 1843 at the age of ten.

23. Anna Jackson was an African American woman who had worked as a servant in the Stetsons' household in Brooklyn. The letter is addressed to her in Providence, R.I., where she was evidently living or working, and was to be carried to her by Catharine Benson, to whose family she was also well known.

24. John 14:2; Matthew 25:21.

25. William Bassett (1803–1871), a former shoe merchant and manufacturer from Lynn, Mass., belonged with his family to the NAEI from May to November 1844. His background as a Quaker, abolitionist, and nonresistant is discussed in Clark, *The Communitarian Moment*, 69–71. Bassett was director of the NAEI's silk department, and James Stetson will have corresponded with him on business.

26. Genesis 1:28; Genesis 9:1.

27. Probably B. F. Fuller; he would in July 1844 be formally invited to live in the

community for one month on a trial basis, but in September not accepted into full membership.

28. Elizabeth Bradbury (b. 1819) had moved to the NAEI from Boston in April or early May 1844 with her husband, Cyrus Bradbury (b. 1811), and their young daughter Sarah (b. 1839); Cyrus Bradbury was probably a carpenter or joiner.

Luther Brigham (1800–1887) from Worcester, Mass., was a draper and tailor with interests in community reform and was at the NAEI with his family from November 1843 until May 1845.

29. G. Gorton Loomis and his wife arrived from Cicero, N.Y., in May 1844 and were at the NAEI until February 1845. After visiting the NAEI in 1843, H. Jocelyn of Cicero published a favorable description of it in the Syracuse *Onondaga Standard*, August 16, 1843, and continued to correspond with NAEI officers. Writing to Jocelyn on February 10, 1844, NAEI Secretary David Mack had encouraged "Mr Gorton Loomis" to come to the community in May (NAEI, Records, vol. 4, p. [44]). "Theodore" was Theodore Scarborough who, as director of the community's agricultural department, was no doubt keen to elicit Gorton Loomis's assistance on the farm.

30. Elisha Livermore Hammond (1799–1882) and Eliza Preston Hammond (1804–1878) arrived in May 1844 from New Ipswich, N.H., and remained NAEI members for the rest of the community's existence. They occupied a house that had been vacated by William Adam and his family on May 16. Elisha Hammond had practical and artistic interests. In September 1843 the English communitist Charles Lane described visiting Hammond in New Ipswich: "he has built with his own hands a smart cottage, being an expert workman, and has moreover a respectable talent for portrait painting which he estimates humbly without a consciousness of humility." (See Clara Endicott Sears, *Bronson Alcott's Fruitlands* [Boston and New York, 1915], 115.) He had brought with him designs for a new community building which the NAEI executive had ambitions in the summer of 1844 to start constructing (see below, note 90) but which, like the landscaping plans he discussed with Almira Stetson, would never be executed.

Benjamin F. Whipple (d. 1870), formerly partner in a carpentry firm in Charlestown, Mass., was Eliza Hammond's brother-in-law. Whipple arrived at the NAEI in June 1844 and remained until August 1845, being mentioned in NAEI, Records, vol. 2, p. 80, as "our mechanic."

31. James Kerr and his family, from Pawtucket, R.I., were at the NAEI from May 1844 until March 1845. "Uncle George" was George W. Benson.

32. Hiram Wells (1811–1859), a blacksmith and machinist from Mansfield, Conn., had been among the founders of the NAEI and lived there throughout its existence; see Clark, *The Communitarian Moment*, 20.

33. George Ashley (1819–1879), a shoemaker from Chaplin, Conn., belonged to the NAEI from April 1843 until 1846.

Abigail Roxanna (Roxy or Roxcy) Brown (1816–1906) had joined the NAEI from Bloomfield, Conn., in December 1842; Lorenzo D. Nickerson (1811–1893) a tanner of Harwich, Mass., and Boston, had joined in April 1843. Brown and Nickerson were married in early June 1844 and moved to Harwich.

34. This was probably the James Wilson or Willson referred to in letters of February 20, 1845, and May 4, 1845 (nos. 38 and 52). This letter and that of February 1845 clearly imply that he was a fugitive slave.

35. This may have been John Ryle, an English silk weaver; he had made an earlier visit to Northampton, described in L. P. Brockett, *The Silk Industry in America: A History; Prepared for the Centennial Exposition* (n.p., 1876), 111–112, and was now establishing himself as a successful silk manufacturer in Paterson, N.J.

36. The sisters Lucy C. Hayden (b. 1812) and Harriet W. Hayden (1817–1845) were abolitionists from Bath, Maine, who had arrived at the NAEI in April 1844.

37. Charles May (1788–1856) had been a mariner and teacher before coming to the NAEI from a post in Alabama in November 1842. He continued to teach until he left the community at the end of 1844; young Sarah Stetson would call him "our greatest friend" at Northampton.

His brother, the Unitarian minister, abolitionist, and educational reformer Rev. Samuel Joseph May (1797–1871), had been a significant figure in James and Dolly Stetson's early married life; see the Introduction to this volume. After resigning as Unitarian minister in Brooklyn, Conn., in 1836, May moved to the church in South Scituate, Mass. From 1842 to 1844 he was principal of the state Normal School at Lexington, Mass., but at the time of this letter was apparently planning to start a school in Scituate, to which he invited Almira to come and study.

38. George Washington Sullivan (b. 1825), from Baltimore, who may have been a former slave, lived at the NAEI from November 1843 until about July 1844; see Dolly W. Stetson to James A. Stetson, July 26, 1844 (letter no. 13) for David Ruggles's comment on him. The *Hampshire Gazette* (Northampton), June 4, 1844, reported the "colored man" Sullivan's fall from the factory roof. An entry in NAEI Records, vol. 1, p. 78, gives Sullivan's birthdate as July 4, 1825; possibly he chose this date to symbolize his own new-found independence.

39. This is Dolly Stetson's uncle George Sharpe, of Abington, part of the town of Pomfret, Conn.

40. George Ashley (see note 33) married Eliza Forward (1821–1855) on Sunday, June 2, 1844.

Nonresistants, like Quakers before them, denied the necessity for a clergyman or civil officer to officiate at a marriage. The *Liberator*, June 14, 1844, reported that Ashley's marriage, "though not wholly divested from the interference of the State, was nevertheless an interesting one." Members of the community assembled under the great pine tree in the grounds, "their *summer church*." In his speech George W. Benson explained that the parties had come "for the purpose of making a public acknowledgement of their union in marriage." Marriage was "an institution of heaven," and no human action was needed to bring it about because the couple were "already married" by the will of God. Though he avowed no disrespect to the justice of the peace, Oliver Warner, human intermeddling was merely "usurping a prerogative of the Deity." Warner then "in the briefest way" obtained "the customary pledge of fidelity," and pronounced Ashley and Forward legally married.

On this and several subsequent occasions couples marrying at the NAEI accepted Warner's presence on sufferance, either to placate their own relatives or to avoid the imputation of sexual impropriety. See Christopher Clark, "'We Might Be Happyer Here'," in this volume. When Warner had married NAEI member Hall Judd to Frances Birge in 1842 at Judd's parents' house in Northampton, he had, according to Judd's father, "obtained from each a promise to perform their conjugal duties, and pronounced them husband and wife. The time occupied was not over a minute. . . . There was no eating or drinking connected with this marriage. Mr Warner refused his fee, so it cost nothing to anybody" (Sylvester Judd, "Notebook," vol. 2, Judd Manuscript, Forbes Library, Northampton, Mass., entry for June 1, 1842).

41. Lucy Richardson (1825–1905) was a daughter of James Stetson's sister Nancy Richardson and had been at the NAEI since October 1842.

42. Mary Ann Smith (b. 1825), had come to the NAEI from Bloomfield, Conn., in January 1843 and worked mainly at silk production. She had ties to various abolitionist families and groups in Connecticut.

William Haven (1800–1866) had moved to the NAEI in May 1843 with his wife Louisa Ann Haven (1802/3–1889) and their seven children, then aged from sixteen down to two years. The Havens had previously lived in Windham, Conn., where William had superintended a cotton mill controlled by Samuel L. Hill, and where in 1836 he had helped Hill and others form the Willimantic Male Anti-Slavery Society. The Havens remained at Northampton after the NAEI disbanded in 1846.

43. James D. Atkins (1817/8–1896) had come to the NAEI in September 1842 from Cambridge, Mass., where he had been a stereotyper at the university printing press. He was given training and became the NAEI's silk-dyer, remaining in the community throughout its existence.

The German dyer may have been the L. H. Plouquet or Ploucquet, referred to in letter no. 27.

44. Giles Badger Stebbins (1817–1900) lived at the NAEI from July 1843 to August 1844; he was not a member, but was studying with William Adam and David Mack. He was a nephew of Calvin Stebbins (see note 56), with whose family the Stetsons had shared a house when they first lived at the NAEI. For his recollections of the community, and of Dolly Stetson, see Giles B. Stebbins, "A Young Man in the Community," in Charles A. Sheffeld, ed., *The History of Florence, Massachusetts, Including a Complete Account of the Northampton Association of Education and Industry* (Florence, Mass., 1895), 128; and Giles B. Stebbins, *Upward Steps of Seventy Years* (New York, 1890), 62.

45. George Sharpe; see note 39.

46. On the convention of Massachusetts communities for which guests were arriving, see below, note 54.

47. On the marriage of Lorenzo Nickerson and Roxcy Brown, see note 33.

48. Hiram Wells (see note 32) had been widowed in April 1843 and was marrying for the second time. The loss of his wife and a serious injury in an accident at work had produced much sympathy for him.

49. On George Sullivan's fall, see note 38. (Sam Patch [1799–1829] had been known

as a youth in Pawtucket, R.I., for his jumps into the Blackstone River from a four-story mill building; between 1827 and 1829 he had attained national fame for his daredevil feats. Patch drowned in November 1829 after making a 125-foot jump into the Genesee River at Rochester, N.Y.).

Sojourner Truth (c.1797–1883), born into slavery in New York State, had moved to New York City after gaining freedom in 1827 and joined evangelical churches and an earlier communal movement. Having spent much of 1843 as an itinerant preacher, she came to the NAEI late that year and remained with the community for the rest of its existence. See *Narrative of Sojourner Truth* (1850), ed. Margaret Washington (New York, 1993), 69–76; Carleton Mabee, *Sojourner Truth: Slave, Prophet, Legend* (New York, 1993), chap. 3; Paul E. Johnson and Sean Wilentz, *The Kingdom of Matthias* (New York, 1994), and especially Nell Irvin Painter, *Sojourner Truth: A Life, A Symbol* (New York, 1996), chaps. 7–10. Her pithy remarks and paradoxes were among the things that Sojourner Truth would be remembered for; from this and other examples it appears that the Stetson children were collectors of her sayings. Fifty years later George R. Stetson would retell this and another of Sojourner's remarks in his memoir of life at the NAEI, "When I Was a Boy," in Sheffeld, ed., *The History of Florence*, 121.

50. This letter remains to be positively dated, but its placement is based on its reference to the marriage of Nickerson and Brown, which occurred on or about June 8th and was reported in the *Liberator* on June 14, 1844. Nickerson and Brown left the community almost immediately on being married, and this letter was written for them to carry to James Stetson in Boston on their way to Harwich, Mass.

51. Rev. Samuel J. May had conducted James and Dolly Stetson's own marriage in 1827.

52. This suggestion was probably inspired by Lydia Maria Child, *Letters from New-York* (New York and Boston, 1843).

53. William Lloyd Garrison (1809–1878) was editor of the *Liberator* and recognized leader of the radical abolitionists. He had married George W. Benson's sister Helen in 1834 and made at least two visits to the NAEI, including an extended stay in the summer and fall of 1843. The Garrisons' eldest son, George Thomson Garrison (1836–1904), was a student at the NAEI's school.

54. A convention of the three Massachusetts communities, Brook Farm, Hopedale, and Northampton, was called to be held at the NAEI on August 31, 1844; see *Liberator*, July 26, 1844.

"Association" or "Associationism" was the label adopted by American followers of the community theories of the French visionary Charles Fourier (1772–1837), which had been promoted by Albert Brisbane in a book, *The Social Destiny of Man* (New York, 1840), and in a series of articles in the *New York Tribune*, collected in a pamphlet entitled *Association: Or, A Concise Exposition of the Practical Part of Fourier's Social Science* (New York, 1843). Influenced by Brisbane and other exponents, the Brook Farm community in West Roxbury, Mass., had adopted Fourierist principles early in 1844. From her report here and from remarks in a later letter, Dolly Stetson appears to have been sympathetic to the idea. On American Fourierism, see Carl J. Guarneri, *The Utopian*

Alternative: Fourierism in Nineteenth-Century America (Ithaca, N.Y., 1991); on Fourierism at Northampton, see Clark, *The Communitarian Moment*, 173–176; and idem, " 'We
Might Be Happyer Here'," in this volume.

Nathaniel P. Rogers (1794–1846) was a noted radical abolitionist and moral reformer, and editor of the Concord, N.H., *Herald of Freedom*.

55. William Adams (not to be confused with William Adam: see note 6) migrated
from Scotland to the United States around 1820. He settled in Pawtucket, R.I., ran a
grocery, professed Quakerism, and was an ardent abolitionist, nonresistant, and advocate of women's rights. His son Robert Adams was a member of the NAEI, and associated with it for almost two years before withdrawing in April 1845.

56. Calvin Stebbins (1778 or 1780–1859) and Sarah E. Stebbins (1806 or 1807–1899)
had been members of the NAEI for one year, from May 1843 to May 1844, and had
become firm friends with the Stetsons, with whom they shared a community house in
1843. Other members of the Stebbins family had interests in community reform, and
Calvin was a financial backer of the NAEI, though see the evidence later in this letter
that he and Sarah had withheld $2,000 that they had subscribed for. A $1,000 legacy
to the NAEI from the late Ruth Stebbins was also to become the subject of a dispute
with other heirs lasting from 1844 at least until April 1846—see NAEI Records, vol. 4,
pp. 78, 108, 128–129].

57. James Stetson's mother, Mary Alexander Stetson, periodically visited the NAEI.

58. See above, note 23.

59. An "Associational Conference" had been held at Hopedale, May 24, 1844, attended by two delegates from each of the Massachusetts communities. James Boyle and
Josiah Hayward had represented the NAEI; see *Phalanx* 1, no. 12 (June 15, 1844): 175.
Correspondence with Christopher Robinson (1799–1876) is copied in NAEI Records,
vol. 4, pp. [53, 55]. Robinson was a prominent Lynn shoe manufacturer who also owned
two newspapers read by reformers, the *Essex County Washingtonian* and the Lynn *Pioneer*.

60. Abner Sanger, a merchant and abolitionist of Danvers, Mass., was, after 1843,
the NAEI's principal financial supporter.

61. Sydney [sometimes spelled "Sidney"] Southworth (b. 1817) had lived in
Brooklyn, Conn., and been an abolitionist there before moving to Boston, probably
in the late 1830s. A member of the New England Non-Resistant Society, he had
been a secretary of the 1840 Chardon Street Ministry and Sabbath Convention. He
had joined the NAEI in November 1843. The debate over marriage was closely
linked to nonresistants' and moral suasionists' arguments concerning individuals' relations with the state, and with the relative roles of conscience and legal authority in
governing social relationships; see Clark, " 'We Might Be Happyer Here'," in this
volume.

62. See above, note 42.

63. Parker Pillsbury (1809–1898) was heading for the Congregational ministry
when the opposition he encountered to his preaching against slavery led him to devote
his energies to abolitionism. He was a lecture agent at different times for the New

Hampshire, Massachusetts, and American Anti-Slavery Societies; see Stacey M. Robertson, *Parker Pillsbury: Radical Abolitionist, Male Feminist* (Ithaca, N.Y., 2000).

64. On Ruggles, see note 4. On his treatment and activities in "water-cure" (hydropathy) see Clark, *The Communitarian Moment*, 197–202 and Painter, *Sojourner Truth*, 98–100.

65. Dolly Witter had been working in the household of Rev. Dan Huntington or his son Theophilus, in Hadley a few miles east of Northampton. Like the Witters and the Stetsons, Dan Huntington and his wife were Unitarians.

66. George Sharpe.

67. Dolly Stetson's father Ebenezer Witter had died in 1841.

68. On the Hammonds, see note 30; no evidence has come to light as to the age of this child, or that the Hammonds had any other children. Nothing is as yet known about Mary W. Bryant, although two brief letters from her to James A. Stetson appear later in this series.

69. Sojourner Truth.

70. Sojourner Truth's daughters Elizabeth (1825–1893) and Sophia (c.1826–1901) are discussed in Painter, *Sojourner Truth*, 19, 23, 25, 100–102. Noting that the daughters are not mentioned in the *Narrative of Sojourner Truth*, written by Olive Gilbert and first published in 1850, Painter explains this as "a commonplace erasure of . . . women who had not been shielded from predatory men or who were possibly unchaste" (102). Dolly Stetson's account appears to confirm the existence of a predatory man, and strongly hints at sexual impropriety. Though it is possible that she was merely retelling gossip that was passing round the community after Elizabeth and Sophia arrived, the fact that she and Sojourner lived in the same building and the implication that Dolly had witnessed the reunion between mother and daughters suggest that Sojourner probably told her the story herself.

71. Louisa C. Rosbrooks (1823–1901) had joined the NAEI from Cicero, N.Y., in January 1844 with her parents and siblings.

72. Stephen Christopher Rush was a fugitive slave who had arrived at the NAEI in May 1843, had been made a member in November, and remained until April 1846. For Elizabeth Bradbury, see note 28.

73. Harriet Hayden and Sydney Southworth had become partners and, following nonresistant logic, proposed to consummate their relationship without taking formal marriage vows (see note 40). According to a sentimentalized account published under the pseudonym "Richard" in the *Northampton Free Press*, May 16, 1862, they declared themselves married after a night-time meeting under an oak tree without witnesses. In this letter Dolly reports substantial opposition in the NAEI to their action, from Lucy Hayden's determination to regard her sister as engaged, not married, to the substantial number of members said by David Ruggles to be opposed to Hayden and Southworth's formal admission to membership. "Richard's" much later story claimed that Harriet Hayden had for several months resisted Southworth's refusal to have a formal ceremony. Dolly Stetson's remarks on the subject provide no evidence to support this, and it is possible that "Richard" conflated Lucy Hayden's reaction with that of her sister.

74. The debt she is referring to in the first part of this paragraph is the Association's.

75. Oliver D. Paine.

76. This sentence refers to the Stetsons' own debts and to the possible sale of their property in Brooklyn.

77. The name written here has been deliberately cut out of the letter. From the context, it is clear that this was of one of the NAEI's leaders. Although there are other possibilities, the name most likely to have caused upset or embarrassment from being left in the letter was that of George W. Benson, who was often recognized in this period as the NAEI's principal leader, and was also James Stetson's brother-in-law and close neighbor.

78. Ruth 1:16–17.

79. On the call for the convention, see below, note 87.

80. Octavia M. Damon (1823–1903) had been an employee of the Northampton Silk Company, whose factory the NAEI had purchased, and may have been among the local women the Association hired to work at silk manufacture. In September 1844 she would marry James D. Atkins, whose brother is being referred to here, and then join the NAEI as a member.

81. She is referring to members of the Scarborough family from Brooklyn.

82. Caroline M. Gove (b. 1817) had been married to a Lynn shoe manufacturer who had died in 1842; she had come to the NAEI in late June 1844 and evidently joined the Bassett family, whom she probably knew from Lynn.

83. "Paradise" was the name given to a piece of open ground on the NAEI's property, near the Mill River.

84. Almira is referring to the community convention, discussed subsequently by Dolly Stetson.

85. Daniel 5:27: "Thou art weighed in the balances, and art found wanting."

86. Thomas Hill.

87. The *Liberator* of July 26, 1844, carried a notice signed by David Mack for the NAEI executive, addressed "To the Friends of a Re-Organization of Society," announcing a convention to be held at the NAEI on August 31. Proclaiming the ideal of substituting "fraternal co-operation for antagonistic selfishness . . . in harmony with the laws of God and of life . . . ," the notice announced that after many struggles, and although it was still "embarrassed" by debt, the NAEI "feel themselves now on the threshold of earnest progress." A new system of labor "which has given a great deal of efficiency to their industrial operations," together with new subscriptions of capital, the notice claimed, placed the community "in a situation more favorable than ever before for pecuniary success." The convention would gather those who could assist in the community's plan to expand, beginning with "the erection of a commodious edifice, which they hope to see completed and occupied by 100 families before two years more shall have passed away."

88. Nancy Richardson, James Stetson's sister.

89. William F. Parker (1811–c. 1869/70), a carpenter, and Rebecca M. Parker

(b. 1817) joined the NAEI from Nantucket in October 1842 with William's mother and their three sons, one of whom was named Lloyd Garrison Parker to betoken the family's abolitionist sympathies.

90. Though his letter to James Stetson contains news and comment on a variety of matters, it is likely that Giles Stebbins's main purpose in writing was to enlist Stetson's support for his opinion that any expansion of the NAEI should be small, and governed by moral rather than material considerations. In other places David Mack had started to call the projected new community building a "phalanstery," and it is likely that Stebbins was marshaling arguments against any proposal that the NAEI should expand and adopt Fourierism. See the discussion in Clark, "'We Might Be Happyer Here'," in this volume.

91. Sydney Southworth, Harriet Hayden, and Lucy Hayden were planning to depart for the Prairie Home Community that had recently been founded in Champaign County, Ohio; on this community, see Thomas D. Hamm, *God's Government Begun: The Society for Universal Inquiry and Reform, 1842–1846* (Bloomington, Ind., 1995), 108–122.

92. In his diary for September 10, 1844, the Connecticut radical abolitionist Cyrus M. Burleigh wrote of his criticisms of the U.S. Post Office monopoly and of the power it gave the government to obstruct righteous causes. For Hale and Co., the carrier that would convey Giles Stebbins's letter and some others now in the Stetson collection, Burleigh had praise as "a grand establishment and I am right glad that it is put in operation; . . . success I say to the independent mail" (Cyrus M. Burleigh, Journal, August 1, 1844–, Burleigh Collection, Am 8192, Historical Society of Pennsylvania, Philadelphia).

Harriet Martineau's *The Martyr Age of the United States* (New York, 1839) was a pamphlet version of an article published the previous year in the *Westminster Review* (London). Martineau's article had spread word of the American abolitionist movement in Britain and was among the first writings to compare the position of women with that of slaves.

Right and Wrong in Boston was the title of the Boston Female Anti-Slavery Society's annual report, edited by Maria Weston Chapman.

Among signatories to a petition submitted to the Massachusetts legislature for the abolition of the death penalty in the winter of 1843–44 had been Erasmus D. Hudson and George W. Benson of the NAEI, and Abner Sanger of Danvers, one of its financial backers (*Liberator*, February 9, 1844).

93. This may have been Henry Chamberlain, of Concord, N.H., whose request to join the NAEI in April, 1843 had been refused; see William Adam to Henry Chamberlain, April 17, 1843, NAEI, Records, vol. 4, p. 25.

94. Isaac Swasey (1820–1874) would marry Lucy Richardson (see note 41) later in the year (see letter no. 33). Swasey had been born in Waltham, Mass., where the Richardsons lived before they moved to the NAEI. After their marriage the couple sustained their abolitionist connections, giving the name "Garrison" to their first son, and staying in contact with the Garrisons and others.

95. George Ripley (1802–1880) had founded the Brook Farm community at West Roxbury, Mass., in 1841; Adin Ballou (1803–1890) founded the Hopedale Community at Milford, Mass., the same year. There were hopes at the NAEI that Samuel J. May (see note 37) could be persuaded to join the community and take charge of its schools.

96. Castile soap.

97. Charles Richardson (b. 1827) was a son of Nancy Richardson and so Almira Stetson's cousin. In 1855 he would marry another cousin, Mary B. Winch of New Hampshire, whom he probably visited on the tour he was now proposing to take.

98. This may have been James Palmer, an officer of the Brooklyn Bank in Brooklyn.

99. "Aunt Tyler" was Dolly Witter Stetson's aunt, her mother's sister Sophia Sharpe. Her husband, "Uncle Tyler," was Daniel P. Tyler, Secretary of the State of Connecticut in 1844 and 1845 (see *Roll of State Officers and Members of the General Assembly of Connecticut, from 1776–1881* [Hartford, 1881], 308, 311).

100. An account of the Northampton Convention on the Reorganization of Society, held at the NAEI on August 31 and September 1, 1844, was published in the *Liberator* on September 6, 1844.

"Draper" was either Ebenezer or George Draper, brothers who were prominent members and financial supporters of the Hopedale community.

Lewis Ryckman was a New York cordwainer (shoemaker) who was already interested in Fourierism when he joined the Brook Farm community in 1843, and assisted in its conversion to Fourierism the following year. Ryckman subsequently became the founding president of the New England Working Men's Association and remained at Brook Farm until 1846.

101. Charles Anderson Dana (1819–1897) had joined Brook Farm in 1841 and soon became one of its leading advocates of Fourierism.

102. Fourierite.

103. Dolly wrote "15,000," but Ryckman almost certainly meant 1,500, which was much closer to the number prescribed in Fourier's own writings and those of his American followers.

104. Henry Clapp (1814–1875) was a temperance and abolitionist lecturer, and for a time editor of the Lynn *Pioneer*.

According to the report in the *Liberator* of September 6, 1844, debate had focused on the question "ought Associations to have any moral or religious test of membership, and if so, what?" As Stetson's account suggests, there was "considerable diversity of opinion" though, thought the *Liberator*, "apparently one spirit."

105. Ezra Rosbrooks (b. 1794) had come to the NAEI from Cicero, N.Y., in January 1844, with his wife Polly Rosbrooks (b. 1794) and children.

106. This is probably the Dr. H. Jocelyn discussed in note 29.

107. William H. Channing (1810–1884) was a Unitarian minister and prominent advocate of Fourierism; on July 23, David Mack had written to invite Channing to the convention, offering to pay his expenses (NAEI Records, vol. 4, p. [67]), but Channing did not come. Horace Greeley (1811–1872) was publisher of the *New York Tribune*, whose columns promoted reform causes, including Fourierism and abolitionism.

108. The name was omitted from the text here, but this was most likely George W. Benson.

109. Ruth Stebbins's heirs prompted a bitter correspondence from NAEI leaders over their refusal to pay her $1,000 legacy to the Association; see NAEI, Records, vol. 4, pp. [78, 108, 128–129].

110. Francis Jackson (1789–1861) was a wealthy Boston merchant and abolitionist, a close friend and supporter of William Lloyd Garrison.

111. Sojourner Truth and James Boyle.

112. On B. F. Fuller, see note 27; NAEI Records, vol. 2, pp. 96–97, show that a vote on Fuller's admission for one year, taken on September 7, 1844, was tied, and that his application thus failed. William Larned, a Boston merchant, had been resident at the NAEI in 1842 and 1843, but was rejected when nominated for full membership in July 1843: see NAEI Records, vol. 2, p. 71. Larned had acted as an accountant in the community, but was also remembered in the Stetson family as a teacher of history: see Wilson, *Dolly Witter Stetson*, 30. It is possible that Larned's proposed admission fell foul of divisions in the community over the conduct of the education department and the control of productive activity (see Clark, *The Communitarian Moment*, 172), and that Fuller's case was similar.

113. Mary Cone, who apparently came from Longmeadow, Mass., studied at the community's school on terms that also required her to work a full ten-hour day in the silk room or another department. Her absence created anxiety, because Almira Stetson was away seeing relatives, and Lucy Richardson was too sick to work. On October 12, 1844, David Mack wrote to Mary Cone's father, "We are all anxious to have Mary return and her services are much needed as Lucy Richardson is unable to aid at all." Mack assured Ashbel Cone of the community's "deep interest" in Mary and her two younger sisters, who had also been working and studying at the NAEI, "and especially we are attached to Mary." Mary would soon reach eighteen, and Mack proposed that she should then join the NAEI as a full member (NAEI, Records, vol. 4, p. [72]).

114. Susanna S. Bassett (b. 1826), a daughter of William Bassett, had lived at the Brook Farm community before coming to the NAEI with her family in 1844.

Sarah Bottum (1815–1850) had, with her husband Samuel A. Bottum (1817–1901), joined the NAEI in 1842, but they had withdrawn in October 1843 and continued to live nearby. They had previously lived in Mansfield, Conn., a center of household-based and small-factory silk production, and Sarah Bottum probably worked for other silk manufacturers in Northampton as well.

115. Thomas Davis Benson (b. 1842), youngest son of George W. Benson, was about two years old.

116. Almira was writing from the home of her aunt and uncle, who ran the Central House, a temperance hotel in the Nashville section of Nashua, N.H.

117. Thomas Hill; Charles Richardson.

118. "Aunt Betsey" has not yet been identified.

119. Aunt Almira was James Stetson's sister, Almira Winch.

120. Association (NAEI).

121. In September 1844 George W. Benson had sought a meeting with Samuel J. May, to propose that May should come to the NAEI and run the community's education department. From this letter, it appears that May considered the suggestion seriously, but by December word had arrived that he was inclining toward a move to Syracuse, N.Y., and Benson wrote again to persuade him to opt for the NAEI instead (George W. Benson to Samuel J. May, September 26, 1844, Boston Public Library, MS. A.1.2.14.59, and December 23, 1844, MS. A.1.2.14.82). In the event May became the Unitarian minister in Syracuse, where he would remain until his death in 1871.

122. Brook Farm.

123. Anna Jackson.

124. James D. Atkins and Octavia Damon were married on September 30, 1844, and boarded at George W. Benson's until a room was found for them.

125. "Ploughcut" was a silk dyer named L. H. Plouquet or Ploucquet, who seems to have been hired to work during the winter of 1844–1845. Letters from S. L. Hill to R. M. Niles, January 27 and February 13, 1845, refer to batches of silk sent by Niles from Hartford to be dyed at the NAEI (NAEI Records, vol. 4, pp. [83, 92–93]). Ploucquet apparently developed a dye using bark to add weight to the silk, but when this proved to add insufficient weight to a batch, he proposed "a new and superior dye," which "will use . . . sumac which he considers more sure in adding weight." See also note 43, above.

126. Sophia Foord, the Parkers, and others were followers of Sylvester Graham (1794–1851), noted writer and lecturer on health and dietary reform, who lived in Northampton and who occasionally lectured at the NAEI. Graham advocated temperance, sexual restraint (including in marriage), avoidance of meat and refined flour, a diet based on vegetables, fruit, and coarse bread flour ("Graham flour"), regular exercise, frequent bathing, well-ventilated rooms, and sleeping on hard wooden beds to avoid the dangers of sensuality posed by feather mattresses. See Stephen Nissenbaum, *Sex, Diet, and Debility in Jacksonian America: Sylvester Graham and Health Reform* (Westport, Conn., 1980).

127. The Welsh-born social and educational reformer Robert Owen (1771–1858) founded or inspired a number of cooperative communities in the British Isles and the United States between the 1820s and the 1840s, of which that at New Harmony, Ind., from 1825 to 1827 was the best known. Owen's condemnation of the conventional connections between property, marriage, and religion had outraged members of orthodox American churches in the 1820s and gained him, at their hands, a lasting reputation as an infidel. When he revisited the United States in the mid-1840s, Owen took steps to explain his opinions; his article, "Address of Robert Owen to the People of the United States," originally published in the New York *Daily Tribune* on September 24, 1844, restated his views on marriage, which Dolly Stetson evidently found quite reasonable. See Robert Owen, "Address of Robert Owen to the People of the United States," in John R. Commons et al., eds., *Documentary History of American Industrial Society*, 11 vols. (Cleveland, 1910–1911): 7:155–60.

128. Boston.

129. Nancy Richardson's husband Luther Richardson had died in 1837; Dolly and James Stetson had lost one small child in the 1830s and another in the early 1840s, as well as their ten-year old son Ebenezer in 1843.

130. Sophia, Sojourner Truth's daughter, was said to be pregnant.

131. Francis Winch was the husband of James Stetson's sister Almira.

132. Robert Wesselhoeft (1797–1852), a Prussian-born lawyer, fled the German state of Weimar in 1840 on account of his suspected revolutionary politics, sailed to the United States, and settled in Cambridge, Mass. Turning to medicine, he became the pioneer American practitioner of hydropathy, and would set up a water-cure establishment at Brattleboro, Vt., in 1845. His patients in Cambridge or Brattleboro would include several members of the Benson family, William Lloyd Garrison, and Maria and David Mack.

133. Apparently, he did so: James O. Adams, *Directory for the City of Manchester, September 1846* (Manchester, N.H., 1846), 89, lists Charles Richardson as a clerk at the Amoskeag manufacturing corporation.

134. Swasey.

135. L. Maria K. Mack (1809–1882) had married fellow teacher David Mack in 1835; together they had run a school in Cambridge, Mass., before moving to the NAEI in 1842.

136. Anna Jackson.

137. Nashua, N.H.

138. The Hutchinson family singers had a farm in Milford, N.H., which, inspired by their visits to Brook Farm and the NAEI, they were running collectively with a "community treasury"; see Cockrell, *Excelsior*, 102, 104, 264–270, 274.

139. She had suggested this before; see note 52.

140. Isaac Swasey. Two weeks earlier Dolly Stetson had reported his comments on the NAEI and the unlikelihood that his parents would, as contemplated, move there; presumably Swasey was by now felt by some members to have outstayed his welcome.

141. Hamm, *God's Government Begun*, 119–120, discusses the collapse of the Prairie Home community in Ohio. Of NAEI residents who had gone to join that community, Sydney Southworth and Harriet Hayden subsequently returned to the NAEI; Elizabeth and Cyrus Bradbury, who had been at the NAEI during the summer of 1844 before moving to Ohio, eventually joined the Hopedale community in Milford, Mass.

142. Dolly Stetson is saying that going through the "usual forms" of marriage would be a sacrifice for Isaac. This is the context for Mary Stetson's suggestion in the next letter that the formalities were in fact kept to the absolute minimum.

143. Hall Judd (1817–1850) was a nonresistant who was among the early members of the NAEI, remained connected with it throughout its existence, and in its latter period became its Secretary; see Clark, *The Communitarian Moment*, 15, 17, 23–24, 179–180. On Sophia Foord, see note 3.

144. Edwin Richardson (b. 1829) was Lucy Richardson's younger brother. Mary was noting that the justice of the peace's role was kept to the minimum necessary to fulfill the legal requirement for marriage.

145. Caroline Gove and Charles May both left the NAEI a few weeks later, and married in February 1845 before moving to live at the Hopedale community.

146. Profile.

147. George W. Benson.

148. In the 1830s Bassett had been censured and then excluded from the Society of Friends because his membership in antislavery and nonresistance groups was held to violate Quaker constraints on associating outside the Society. William's father, Isaac Bassett, had been prominent in the attempt to discipline his son. Bassett's case was regarded by radical abolitionists and nonresistants as emblematic of the churches' corrupt involvement with slavery. For Benson, who had Quaker sympathies and some of whose family were Quakers, the issue had been a personal one, and on this occasion he evidently revealed his animosity towards Isaac Bassett's stance.

149. For Rosbrooks see note 105; for Hammond see note 30.

Joseph C. Martin (1808–1865), from the small farming town of Chaplin, Conn., had joined the NAEI with his family in April 1844 and would stay for the rest of its existence. He was elected its President in 1845, in succession to George W. Benson. One of a group of devoted abolitionists in Chaplin, Martin had described their disputes with and subsequent expulsion from the town's church in a letter to William Lloyd Garrison, published in the *Liberator* on January 5, 1844. Chaplin was near Brooklyn, and Martin's relatives were among the Stetsons' neighbors and acquaintances in that part of Connecticut.

150. Romulus Fowler Hudson (b. 1828), a son of Erasmus D. and Martha T. Hudson, had remained in the NAEI after his parents withdrew in 1843.

Sarah Brigham (1825–1886) and Martha Brigham (b. 1827) had joined the community in November 1843 with their recently widowed father; like Lydia B. Pierce, who had been there since February 1843, they may have worked in the silk department. "Morgan" may have been Littleton T. Morgan (b. 1820), from Cambridge, Mass. Their move to the Dedham silk factory probably proved a mistake, because that mill was soon destroyed by fire.

Francis Rosbrooks (b. 1825) was a son of Ezra and Polly Rosbrooks (see note 105); George Hill (b. about 1822) had lived at the NAEI for almost a year after its founding, but had subsequently moved, probably to a nearby farm.

151. H. W. Macomber (b. about 1808), though not a member of the NAEI, was hired to peddle its silk products in 1844 and 1845. After the breakup of the community, Macomber and a local merchant employed Samuel L. Hill to continue running its silk operations in conjunction with them.

152. The sisters Angelina and Sarah Grimké, from South Carolina, had toured New England in 1837, lecturing against slavery under the auspices of the American Anti-Slavery Society and provoking indignant orthodox Congregational clergy to reiterate biblical strictures against women's speaking in public. Abby Kelley was the first New England woman to gain prominence as an abolitionist lecturer; her appointment to an otherwise-male committee of the American Anti-Slavery Society prompted the departure of evangelicals from the society and the division of the abolitionist movement in

1840. Almira Stetson's admiration for these women as speakers and "illustrious person-ages" denoted both her allegiance to radical abolitionism's promotion of women's rights and her own ambitions to further that cause.

153. Elizabeth and Sarepta Martin are mentioned in note 2.

154. Abner S. Mead (b. 1822), from Danvers, Mass., had joined the NAEI in 1843. He later returned to Danvers and worked as a shoemaker.

155. Ezra Rosbrooks, see note 105, and his son John Milton Rosbrooks (b. 1830); on the Loomises, see note 29.

156. Valentine.

157. Mary's.

158. Anne Paul lived at the NAEI for a year from June 1844, sponsored by aboli-tionist friends in Boston. Originally from England, Paul had married an African Amer-ican minister who had subsequently died, and she faced both poverty and ostracism from conventional social circles for having made a "mixed" marriage.

Pamelia or Pamela Small (b. 1795) had come to the community from Norwich, Conn., when it was founded in April 1842 and was a member until May or June 1845.

159. The reference is probably to [Katherine Parker Gordon] *Fresh Flowers for My Children* (Boston, 1842); "George Thompson" was George Thompson Garrison (1836–1904), eldest son of William Lloyd Garrison and Helen Benson Garrison, who lived at the NAEI while he attended the community's school.

160. This was Charles May, who had left the NAEI a few weeks before.

161. "Wendy" was William and Helen Garrison's third son, Wendell Phillips Gar-rison (1840–1907). The Garrisons' daughter, Helen Frances Garrison, had been born in December 1844.

162. James Willson or Wilson was evidently a former slave, probably a fugitive. Mailing the letter in Boston may have been intended to conceal his whereabouts.

163. Margaret Fuller's *Woman in the Nineteenth Century* (New York, 1845) had just been published.

164. Brooklyn.

165. The Unitarian church, formally the First Society in Brooklyn, may have held a mortgage on Dolly Stetson's portion of her late father's property.

166. See note 163, above.

167. Samuel L. Hill.

168. Elijah Powers was a Northampton storekeeper from whom the NAEI ob-tained some supplies and who took some of its products in exchange.

169. George W. Benson.

170. Merchants "put out" palm leaf to households in various parts of rural New England for braiding by women and children preparatory to manufacture into hats. On this industry see Christopher Clark, *The Roots of Rural Capitalism: Western Massa-chusetts, 1780–1860* (Ithaca, N.Y., 1990), chap. 5, and Thomas Dublin, *Transforming Women's Work: New England Lives in the Industrial Revolution* (Ithaca, N.Y., 1994), chap. 2.

171. David Mack, Jr. (1836–1894), son of David and Maria Mack.

172. James Atkins.

173. George W. Benson.

174. Catharine Benson.

175. Stephen C. Rush.

176. Fitch's name does not appear in other sources relating to the NAEI; but see note 203, below.

177. Joseph Stetson (b. 1798), James A. Stetson's elder brother, had been running the Central House, the only temperance hotel in Nashua, N.H.; he subsequently moved to Manchester, N.H.

178. James Kerr. Jason H. Sulloway (b. 1815) had been a member of the NAEI since April 1842. In June that year he had married Mary Eliza Pierce (b. 1822), who had then joined the community; they had a daughter in 1844. Sulloway was probably a mechanic. Later in the 1840s he was in a manufacturing partnership with George W. Benson, and after that failed he and his family moved to Boston, where the 1850 census listed him as a machinist, living in a boarding house.

179. Joseph Conant and Samuel A. Bottum were both former members of the NAEI who had remained in the locality. Conant, a silk manufacturer, had various business interests. Bottum was less prosperous; his wife was probably hiring Mary E. Sulloway to do domestic tasks so that she could herself devote time to skeining silk for Edward Valentine, another local silk manufacturer.

Neither in this nor in the next paragraph was Dolly Stetson merely passing news idly to James. This information, both about the community and about changes in the silk industry, might affect James's business and the Stetsons' plans for their own future.

180. Joseph Conant (1792–1870), from Mansfield, Conn., had been manager of the Northampton Silk Company mill before the NAEI purchased the property. A relative by marriage of Samuel L. Hill, Conant was among the founders of the community and was a member for the first six months of its existence. He subsequently ran a local silk business with two sons-in-law who had also belonged to the NAEI for a short while, and had other interests in Northampton and Mansfield. His marriage, mentioned here, to Caroline Williams of Mansfield, was his third. He later moved back to Mansfield and ran a farm and silk factory in what became the Conantville section of the town.

181. George Prindle (1818–1895) had come to the NAEI from New Haven, Conn., in May 1843. He and Louisa Rosbrooks married on April 23, 1845, and moved the next month back to New Haven, where George worked as a tailor for a period. They later migrated to Wisconsin and subsequently Iowa.

182. Sarah Thurber Benson (1799–1850), an elder sister of George W. Benson, and Olive Gilbert (1801–1884), both of Brooklyn, Conn., had been active with Dolly W. Stetson in the Brooklyn Female Anti-Slavery Society in the 1830s. Gilbert moved to Northampton in the mid-1840s and was the ghostwriter of the *Narrative of Sojourner Truth*, published in 1850.

183. Sojourner Truth.

184. Mary Ann Smith; see note 42.

185. This passage condenses Matthew 23:23–24.

186. Susan Byrne (b. 1816) had been at the NAEI since 1843, and was previously

active in the Female (Working) Anti-Slavery Society of Willimantic, Conn., of which she was Treasurer in 1842.

"George" was George W. Benson and "Anna" Anna Jackson.

187. George R. Stetson.

188. David Reed was long-time editor of the *Christian Register*, the leading Boston Unitarian newspaper, which he had founded in 1821.

Theodore Parker (1810–1860) was a Unitarian minister with close links to Transcendentalist and antislavery circles. Noted for his theological liberalism, he was by the mid-1840s disowned by many conservative Unitarians.

189. Joseph C. Martin; see note 149. George and Eliza (Forward) Ashley; see note 33. Their daughter, Lydia L. Ashley, was born on March 12, 1845. George Ashley was probably Joseph Martin's brother-in-law.

190. The letter is undated, but refers to the celebration the following Monday, April 7, 1845, of the third anniversary of the founding of the NAEI on April 8, 1842.

191. Dolly is referring to Frederick Douglass, who was speaking at an antislavery meeting in Northampton Center. See below, note 194.

192. That is, to visit Brooklyn.

193. At the Hampshire, Franklin, and Hampden Agricultural Society's annual cattle show in October 1845, Dr. J. W. Smith exhibited "A full set of Artificial Teeth, showing great mechanical skill," beating his rival to a $2 "premium" or prize (*Hampshire Gazette*, October 21, 1845).

194. Frederick Douglass (1818–1895) escaped from slavery in 1838 and in the early 1840s became a lecturing agent of the Massachusetts Anti-Slavery Society. By the middle of the decade he was criticizing northern racial prejudice as well as slavery.

195. "On the tapis," i.e., under consideration. Trusdell has not been identified.

196. Hall Judd.

197. During Frederick Douglass's visit to the NAEI, Elisha Hammond painted his portrait for a patron in Philadelphia. In a report on his visit to the community, published in the *Liberator* on June 20, 1845, Pennsylvania abolitionist Benjamin S. Jones noted the "capital likeness of Douglass" that "almost speaks." The portrait, Hammond's only known completed painting, later passed to the Rhode Island Historical Society and was purchased in 1974 by the National Portrait Gallery, Smithsonian Institution, Washington, D.C. (accession number NPG.74.45).

198. Mrs. Loomis was the wife of G. Gorton Loomis; see note 29.

199. C. M. Hartwell was hired as a silk peddler in upstate New York; see Hall Judd to Hartwell, August 1, September 25, October 6, 1845, NAEI Records, vol. 4, p. [101, 106, 108].

200. William Robert Small (b. 1824) was the son of Pamelia Small (see note 158). He was at the NAEI from April 1842 to June 1845 and was, with his mother, a resident of the factory boarding house. His account of an antislavery meeting in Northampton in April 1844, which included a speech by Frederick Douglass and songs by the Hutchinson family, was published in the *Liberator* on May 10, 1844.

201. Theodore Parker; see note 188.

202. The two Ross families were: Austin Ross (1812–1901) and his wife Fidelia Ringe Ross (1813–1902), who arrived from Chaplin, Conn., in late March 1845 and remained at the NAEI for the rest of its existence; and probably the family of Abel Ross (c.1774?–1860).

203. A J. D. Fitch had been active with Samuel L. Hill and George W. Benson in organizing an Eastern Connecticut Anti-Slavery Convention at Willimantic in March 1841 (reported in the *National Anti-Slavery Standard*, March 18, 1841), and it is possible that it was he or his brother who had lived for a time at the NAEI.

204. Johnson's identity is not known. The 1850 Census listed a black woman named Lucinda Johnson, aged 20, in the household of the machinist Hiram Wells; possibly she was this man's daughter.

On Willson, see notes 34 and 162; on Luther Brigham, see note 28.

205. Association.

206. Dating this letter is a puzzle. Almira did not date it, simply noting that she was writing on "Sunday night 11 o'clock," but someone else, probably James Stetson, wrote "A. B. Stetson May 11th" on the outside of the folded letter. May 11, 1845, was a Sunday, but Almira also wrote to her father on Monday morning, May 12, 1845, without referring to having written the night before, and saying explicitly that she only had time to write a short letter. The May 11 date may therefore be misleading. The year and month are fairly clear: the letter is addressed to James at the Boston address he had between December 1844 and July 1845, and Almira refers to a decision not to go to Boston for the Massachusetts Antislavery Society "anniversary" in May, as she had expressed a wish to do in her letter of April 25. May 4 was also a Sunday. However the opening lines of the letter imply that James had recently visited Northampton, and no evidence that he made such a visit in late April or early May has come to light.

207. Brooklyn.

208. Hall Judd; Eliza Boyce Wall (b. 1816) was an abolitionist and nonresistant, and sister of a Lynn, Mass., shoe manufacturer. In 1841, she had married Joseph S. Wall, editor of a nonresistant newspaper, the *Reformer* (Worcester, Mass.) that was largely a vehicle for the writings of their Lynn fellow campaigner William Bassett. The Walls had joined the NAEI soon after its founding in April 1842; after Joseph had died of consumption in Worcester that October, Eliza returned to live at the community until the summer of 1845. It is not certain what traits or behavior merited her fierce denunciation by Hall Judd, but her links to the Bassetts suggest that she may have shared their liberal views about "amusements."

209. William J. Bumstead (b. 1810) and Lucia B. Bumstead (b. 1807) had moved to the NAEI from Bloomfield, Conn., in November 1842 with their three small sons. Bumstead was probably a tanner by trade. The family were among a group of radical abolitionists or nonresistants who had fallen out with their church in Bloomfield, several of whom came to the NAEI; Hall Judd had been part of this group when he had worked in Bloomfield in the early 1840s.

210. Eliza Hammond.

211. Though this letter is undated, Almira says she is writing on her seventeenth birthday.

212. 1 Peter 4:3: "For the time past of our life may suffice us to have wrought the will of the Gentiles, when we walked in lasciviousness, lusts, excess of wine, revellings, banquetings, and abominable idolatries."

213. John Prouty was a member of the NAEI from June 1844 to August 1845; he had been in Wisconsin before moving to the Association, but nothing else is presently known about him.

214. Sydney Southworth and Harriet Hayden; see notes 36, 61, 73, 91.

215. Lydia Maria Child, *Letters from New-York* (New York and Boston, 1843) or idem, *Letters from New York* (New York and Boston, 1845).

216. On the Parkers, see note 89. The next letter makes it clear that they were not withdrawing from the Association, but going on a short trip that would take them to Boston.

217. Mary Ann Smith.

218. Robert Wesselhoeft; see note 132. When David and Maria Mack withdrew from the NAEI as of July 1, 1845, they moved to Wesselhoeft's new water-cure at Brattleboro, Vt. On David Mack's subsequent engagement with water-cure therapy and on the practice of soliciting treatment or advice by letter, as Theodore Scarborough was attempting here, see Clark, *The Communitarian Moment*, 196–202.

219. An account of Hayden's death and funeral appeared in the *Northampton Free Press*, May 16, 1862.

220. Frederick Douglass's *Narrative of the Life of Frederick Douglass, an American Slave, Written by Himself* (Boston, 1845) had recently appeared and was much in demand among reformers; it would sell 30,000 copies in the United States and Britain within five years.

221. Edwin Richardson; see note 144.

222. This letter is undated and its placement at present conjectural.

223. On Sylvester Graham, see note 126. Many abolitionists shared Graham's opposition to the growth of Odd-Fellowship: see the editorial in the *Liberator*, July 12, 1844, and the notice of this speech, reprinted from a Northampton paper, in the *Liberator*, July 18, 1845.

The church of the Boston Society of the New Jerusalem, or Swedenborgians, had recently been completed on Bowdoin Street.

224. These lectures have not so far been identified.

225. Frederick Emerson, *The North American Arithmetic: Part Third, for Advanced Scholars* (1834); idem, *Key to the North American Arithmetic; Second and Third Parts, for Teachers* [1845?].

226. Mt. Sugarloaf, at the southern end of the Pocumtuck range in Deerfield, Mass., commands a view of the Connecticut Valley southward to the Holyoke range and Mt. Tom. Mary's comments on the relative merits of Mts. Sugarloaf and Holyoke were shaped by the fact that the latter was already popular with tourists.

227. Mary Ann Smith.

228. Danielson Village, in Killingly, Conn., the railroad depot for Brooklyn.

229. I.e., well.

230. George Sharp or Sharpe (see note 39) and his brother Davis, of Abington, Conn., were Dolly W. Stetson's uncles; their wives were, respectively, Lucretia and Syrena.

231. For Rogers, see note 54; Dolly Witter may have met him at the NAEI, where he visited from time to time.

232. Sarepta Martin; see note 2.

233. Northampton.

234. Martin, Judd, and Hill were writing formally as the Executive of the NAEI.

235. The Stetsons moved from the NAEI on or about March 16, 1846, to rented accommodation in the town of Northampton. S. L. Hill to Abner Sanger, April 2, 1846 (NAEI Records, vol. 4, p. [129]), noted James A. Stetson's withdrawal from the NAEI. In a place where Sunday was usually observed strictly, Dolly Stetson had to restrain her children, who were used to the NAEI's refusal to recognize the Sabbath as a special day.

236. Frances Birge Judd (1820–1894) had married Hall Judd in 1842 and joined the NAEI immediately afterward. She wrote two short memoirs of her life in the community, one dated 1853 in the A. J. Macdonald Collection, pp. 67–70, Beinecke Rare Book and Manuscript Library, Yale University, and the other, Frances P. Judd, "Reminiscences," in Sheffeld, ed., *History of Florence*, 115–118.

237. Bailey Birge (1793–1868?), father of Frances Judd, had moved with his wife and other children to the NAEI in November 1845 and remained to become a clerk in the silk business that succeeded the community.

238. Community Boarding House.

239. Thomas Hill and Mary Ann Smith.

240. Accounts of Barron's attempted murder of his wife, his subsequent suicide by hanging in Northampton jail, and Mrs. Barron's slow recovery with "homeopathic remedies" appeared in the *Liberator*, May 15, 1846, and the *Hampshire Gazette*, June 2, 1846, the latter correcting inaccuracies in earlier reports. On Martha Brigham, see note 150; she apparently returned to work or board at the NAEI after the destruction of the Dedham silk factory.

241. This was Samuel May, Jr. (1810–1899), a cousin of Samuel Joseph May. A Unitarian clergyman who became disillusioned with organized churches, in 1847 he became General Agent of the Massachusetts Anti-Slavery Society.

242. Samuel L. Hill.

243. Abolitionists were prominent among protesters against the Mexican War.

244. In 1846 Parker's followers had organized the 28th Congregational Society in Boston and installed him as their minister.

245. John Clapp, from Pomfret, Conn., had been hired to work the farm in James Stetson's continued absence.

246. Anna Jackson.

"We Might Be Happyer Here"

Marriage, Education, and Conduct at the Northampton Community

Christopher Clark

SCHOLARS OF intentional communities like the Northampton Association have in recent years focused on the wider contexts that gave rise to these collective efforts to build an ideal way of life, and on the legacies such efforts had in the lives of the people who took part in them. Donald E. Pitzer, one of the leading historians of utopian communities, pioneered this approach with the concept of "developmental communalism," which recognized communities not merely as institutions in themselves, but as phases in the history of the reform movements they were part of, and in the lives of the people who joined them. Some years ago, I discussed the Northampton community from a similar viewpoint in my book *The Communitarian Moment*.[1] The discovery of the Stetson letters, and the opportunity they afford for a close look at the experience of a single family before, during, and after their membership in a utopian community greatly enrich our means of grasping the significance of this experience for those who took part in it. Allowing us to link together previously fragmented evidence, the correspondence of Dolly Stetson, her husband, and their children enables us to trace the evolution of the abolitionist movement, and the intermixture of religion, ideology, education, reform, and practical necessity in the lives of ordinary abolitionists.

Discussions of people who joined utopian communities have often tried to distinguish those whose reasons for doing so were idealistic from those whose motives were more pragmatic. Shakers referred to "Winter Shakers," the men and women who entered their communities for the support they could provide during the cold season or "hard times," and who left again when times or the season improved. Historians have noted the farmers and poor frontier folk who flocked to Robert Owen's New Harmony community in Indiana in the mid-1820s, supposedly not from dedication to the community's ideals, but because they were eager for the chance of free support. Brian J. L. Berry has argued that the impulse to set up such communities was correlated with downward phases of "long-swing" economic cycles. Either directly, as people sought economic shelter in communities, or indirectly as economic hardship fostered millenarian movements that in turn led to the formation of communities, communalism was, according to Berry, associated with economic depression.[2]

On the face of it, the American utopian upsurge of the 1840s conformed to this pattern. Communities were formed in unprecedented numbers in the early part of the decade, when economic depression was at its toughest; and many failed or dwindled in size after 1844, when conditions began to ease. Yet separating "idealistic" reasons for participating from supposedly more "pragmatic" motivations can obscure some of the subtle and powerful ways in which these different elements combined to make communal life attractive to the families and individuals who ventured into it. The example of the Stetsons at the Northampton Association demonstrates how different concerns and motivations arose and were worked out in a particular family. What we might in the abstract distinguish as "ideals" and "practical motives" frequently overlapped and acted together to influence the decisions that were made about joining, remaining at, and eventually leaving a community. As their letters can show, especially when interpreted in the light of other supporting evidence, the Stetsons' motivations for participating in an intentional community were linked to an array of personal, familial, and social concerns.

WHEN JAMES A. STETSON and Dolly Witter Stetson moved to the Northampton Association from Brooklyn, Connecticut, in April 1843, they were not venturing among strangers. Kinship, neighborhood, and their connections in the abolitionist movement were overlapping themes among the factors that drew them to join. As Garrisonian abolitionists, they were sympathetic to the radical ideals of Northampton's founders. They had built close ties to fellow abolitionists among their Connecticut neighbors, a significant number of whom also joined the community at Northampton. Kinship reinforced these ties. George W. Benson, one of the Association's founders and most active leaders, was James Stetson's brother-in-law. By the time

The Stetson family homestead in Brooklyn, Connecticut. (Courtesy, Anne Beaman)

the Stetsons reached Northampton, the community included various abolitionist acquaintances from Connecticut and Massachusetts, and yet more
relatives. At different times there were as many as twenty-seven other
people at the community to whom James Stetson was related by kinship or
marriage.[3]

The Stetsons had also faced a long period of financial difficulty, as James
had struggled to make a go of his chaise-making business in Brooklyn. After
the panic of 1837 aggravated his problems and the removal of Brooklyn
neighbors to Northampton impaired his network of local support, the offer
of the Northampton Association's agency for selling silk may have been
James Stetson's best chance to rebuild his financial affairs and business connections.[4] As he started to peddle silk around New England, the combination
of ideals, kinship, and economic concerns influenced James and Dolly to
make common cause with their friends at the community. When he proposed
to Dolly in February 1843 that they should join the Association, James
made these issues explicit. New egalitarian arrangements for its members'

subsistence that the community had just adopted would provide the family with $338.60 per year for board and clothing. At the same time, the community would offer Dolly sociability and companionship with people of compatible beliefs and commitment to reform. A learned and forthright woman, to be remembered in her family as "a great reader, a clear thinker and a fluent talker," she would, James assured her, find at Northampton "congenial spiritts here with whome you will be happy." Above all, the Association's plans to combine education and work promised schooling for their children superior to that in Brooklyn, offered throughout the year and available to girls and boys equally.[5] In particular, the community might provide their eldest child, their daughter Almira, an opportunity to equip herself for a start in life that James and Dolly, in their reduced circumstances, could not ensure in Connecticut. For men and women with the Stetsons' reform interests, educational aspirations, local connections, and financial means, joining the Northampton Association and participating in its cooperative patterns of work and mutual support offered better prospects of realizing their ideals than remaining in their own household.

The Stetsons and many of their neighbors were quite typical of the types of people who, across New England, New York, and the Old Northwest in the 1830s and 1840s, became adherents of radical abolitionism. Scholars such as Nancy R. Hewitt, Judith A. Wellman, and John L. Brooke have identified strong pockets of abolitionist support in regions and neighborhoods of farmer-mechanics. These were rural areas that during the first decades of the nineteenth century underwent considerable change, through population growth and migration, and through the adoption of new economic activities, especially craft-based rural industries. Such regions were among those susceptible to the evangelical revivals of the Second Great Awakening and to the notions of human perfectibility that promoted "immediatist" campaigns to sweep away evils such as slavery and intemperance. Such areas, in which farming continued to thrive, but in which many families also branched out into other activities, including small-scale manufacturing, embodied the particular mixture of ideals that could sometimes end up in the founding of communities like that at Northampton.[6]

Over half the men and women who came to the Northampton Association had previously lived in rural settlements which combined the farming and manufacturing activities that made for a "rural-mechanical milieu" consistent with communitarian values. Though farmers and craftsmen saw themselves as "independent" and often believed in the self-help and self-discipline that lay at the heart of the moral reform impulse, their neighborhoods also relied considerably on patterns of local cooperation and mutual assistance. The cooperative ideals of "community reform" or "Association" were not far removed from the normal assumptions of local obligation and moral economy. Indeed, some of their contemporary critics claimed that utopian communities were merely emulating the relationships that had long been common in New England towns; Samuel Griswold Goodrich, who had grown up in late eighteenth-century Ridgefield, Connecticut, recalled "a sort of communism or socialism which prevailed in our rural districts long before Owen or Fourier was born." In most parts of the North and Northeast, such local circumstances gave rise to voluntary associations and reform movements, such as temperance and antislavery societies, which remained "single-issue" organizations. But in some instances, of which Brooklyn, Connecticut, was an example, circumstances could generate the effort and aspirations that gave rise to an attempt at a broader "community reform" aimed at more radical social change.[7]

Two things worked together to shatter the local patterns of cooperation and mutual obligation that had operated in Brooklyn for much of the 1820s and 1830s. Financial embarrassments like those suffered by James Stetson cut across local ties of financial support. As economic hardship deepened, particularly after 1837, strands of credit and trust became strained, and some relationships will have broken. On top of this, the disputes arising from abolitionism put further stress on relationships in the town. Samuel J. May's resignation from the Brooklyn church, the closure of churches to abolitionist meetings, and the split within the national abolitionist movement at the end of the 1830s made cooperation on reform efforts increasingly difficult. The Windham County Anti-Slavery Society faced both internal divisions and a rift among abolitionists statewide. The Brooklyn Female Anti-Slavery Society was virtually moribund by the time its members formally abandoned it in 1840.

First the Bensons, then local families such as the Scarboroughs, the Prestons, and later the Stetsons themselves moved to Northampton and joined with others to form the Northampton Association. In part, they were recreating the fractured world of their old town. Brooklyn was the largest single source of Association members. But it was only the clearest instance of a general tendency. Other Northampton members were drawn from

Connecticut towns, such as Chaplin and Bloomfield, which had also suffered economic reverses and religious dissension. And from across New England, New York, and the upper Midwest came enquiries from men and women who contemplated Northampton as a shelter from similar circumstances in their own localities.

The Stetsons entertained many doubts about the Northampton Association, and their letters help explain the background to their decision to withdraw from it in 1846. But the letters also suggest many reasons why women like Dolly Stetson could find benefits from living in a community. Though communal domestic arrangements could severely burden the people, usually women, who had to run them, they also provided some notable advantages over life in individual, isolated households. When he had persuaded her to join the community, James held out to Dolly the prospect of "more rest," and "advantajes for mental & moral improvement which I Know you so much long for." Dolly Stetson's move, soon after James's departure for Boston, into the Association's factory boardinghouse, seems to have enabled her and the elder daughters to enjoy the community's sociability and to use cooperative working arrangements to lighten some burdens of household work. Other commentators of the 1840s, including various Fourierist authors and the Maine writer Jane Sophia Appleton, regarded individual households as excessively burdensome and isolating for women, and advocated cooperative arrangements to alleviate these problems. In their letters Dolly Stetson and her elder daughters testified to the realism of these arguments.[8]

For the radical abolitionists and nonresistants at Northampton a cooperative community served the ideal of accomplishing a wholehearted reform of society. Community was, for one thing, an outgrowth of the kind of associative activity that had been the reform movement's institutional expression. Local reform societies to promote temperance, antislavery, or other causes were models of "association" that admitted individuals of varied religious and political persuasions. A nonsectarian residential community like that at Northampton was in many ways merely a logical extension of an already established set of practices. Furthermore, for nonresistants, who rejected the authority or legitimacy of any institution based on the use of force or violence, a community represented the means and opportunity for self-government by those who had freed themselves of obligation or loyalty to established, corrupt institutions.

Nonresistance, too, was an extension of the radicals' doctrine of moral suasion: the insistence that moral pressure and witness for truth, rather than the use or threat of physical force, was the power that could bring about social change. By accomplishing the reform and purification of individuals, moral suasion would expunge the sins in society. Though by no means all nonresistants subscribed to community principles, to some of them cooperative communal action seemed the ideal means of putting moral suasion into practice. In the absence of a strong State based on the capacity to exert physical power or violence, community reform, as an embodiment of collective action, might be an effective force for change, and communities would become visible embodiments of a reformed citizenry. The Stetsons did not fully endorse the ideas of their most radical nonresistant colleagues at Northampton, but their Unitarianism, their belief in human perfectibility, and their commitment to educational equality put them in sympathy with the broad aims of their fellow members.[9]

Early in the community's existence, one of its women members, Frances Judd, led its Sunday afternoon meeting in a discussion of a text that was particularly important to nonresistants, the third chapter of Paul's epistle to the Galatians. This passage put forward two important propositions. It suggested, first, that "reformed" people could abandon the law, under which they had been schooled, and bring themselves into self-government, under God rather than under civil or state institutions. Second was the faith that a reformed society would become egalitarian, without distinctions of religion, race, gender, or status: "there is neither Jew nor Greek; there is neither male nor female; there is neither bond nor free; for we are all one in Christ Jesus."[10] The "community of interests" developed in a cooperative association such as that at Northampton could be the medium in which these ideals of social reform and equality could be realized in practice. The passage from Galatians, however, also posed a problem: were people in the community already reformed, and therefore not subject to "law," or were they only approaching perfection and hence still requiring institutional tutelage? That issue would underlie some of the Northampton community's difficulties.

As they stepped into community, the Stetsons and other members were fully conscious that they were only among the first to accomplish equality in a still-sinful, still-inequitable world. As realists they had to reconcile their own actions in joining a community with their recognition that others had not followed them, and that even many radical reformers were not taking the community path that they had chosen to follow. Members had to face the charge of their opponents that their actions had done nothing to further the cause of abolition or other reforms. From the community in 1844, the former slave Stephen C. Rush answered this charge in an impassioned letter to William Lloyd Garrison's *Liberator*: "We are here to honor liberty and to denounce slavery . . . to proclaim the dictates of eternal justice and to rebuke the wrongs done by man to man."[11]

Rush was not just expressing an abstract ideal. For those who, like the Stetsons and their Brooklyn neighbors, had come from fractured churches and reform organizations, joining the Northampton community was a practical means of reestablishing connections in the reform movement, and of repairing the damage caused by the economic upheavals and doctrinal splits of the late 1830s. They realized, too, that the need for such reconnection was related to their social position and personal circumstances. Though Dolly Stetson's father had been a prosperous farmer, she was not a member of the New England elite. Marrying James, a craftsman, had been likely to draw her away from such circles, although involvement in the antislavery movement kept her closer to them than she might otherwise have managed. Underlying Dolly's wishes and ambitions, as she expressed them in her letters to James, was a desire to keep in contact with people who shared her religious, intellectual, and reform interests. As another Northampton member, Martha Turner Hudson, asked her husband, "can we not be so situated as to do good & be with our children & benefit the world too?" For the Hudsons the answer, as it turned out, would lie outside the community, but Dolly Stetson saw staying at Northampton as essential to pursuing such ideals. "Can we do as much good to our race," she asked James rhetorically, "to return to our isolated condition where whatever of moral power we may possess will be rendered powerless because we have not the wealth and station to render us worthy of notice[?]" Membership in a community enabled ordinary men and women such as the Stetsons to make their calls for radical reform carry weight that they would otherwise have lacked.[12]

A PERSISTENT THREAD in James and Dolly Stetsons' letters to each other was the standing of their marriage and the relationships within their family. In a recent study of abolitionists' marriages, Chris Dixon has emphasized couples' efforts to achieve spiritual equality and, beyond that, even to establish more substantive equality between partners. For Dolly and James Stetson, their membership of the Northampton community and, not least, their

These portraits of James Alexander Stetson and Dolly Witter Stetson were taken in the 1860s, more than fifteen years since the Stetson family had left the Northampton Association. (Courtesy, Constance Renner)

reactions to James's doubts about staying there were for several years inter-twined with the fabric of their marriage. Equality between them was deli-cately negotiated.[13]

At first sight, their relationship may appear not to have been equal at all. Several times Dolly Stetson expressed to James her deference, her duty, or her sense of inadequacy. In May 1844, for instance, in a letter marking the seventeenth anniversary of their marriage, she acknowledged "many omis-sions of duty if not comm[i]ssions of crime on my part," though having just delivered her ninth child she could observe wryly that "there is one point where my conscience does not accuse me of neglect of duty and that is in 'multiplying and replenishing [the Earth]'." She sought advice from James, sometimes invoked his authority, and expressed a willingness to defer to his wishes about the family's future.[14] Such deference would not have conflicted with the Northampton Association's ideals. Its constitution specifically up-held "the family relation, the relation between husband and wife and be-tween parents and children," as "the root and foundation of all human excel-lence and happiness."[15] As we shall see later, the question of who had authority over children did become an issue at the community, but there seems to have been no wish to interfere in married partners' relations with each other.

To be sure, membership in the community could to an extent provide women with a basis on which to exercise power and relieve themselves of some of the burdens of marriage and household work. Women members had equal rights with men to participate and vote on community business, and some achieved a degree of prominence in its affairs. A woman could, as we noted, lead the reading at a community meeting for discussion of religious subjects. On several occasions Sojourner Truth led singing or prayers at meetings or funerals. Maria Mack, already an accomplished teacher well before she joined the community, seems to have occupied a significant role: she was appointed to committees and regarded by at least one observer as the leader of the domestic side of the Association's activities.[16] An Associa-tion officer, answering a claim in the *Liberator* in 1843 that women had been prevented from voting at a public antislavery meeting organized by the com-munity, not only rebutted the charge, but noted that the community had women members, who voted at meetings, "and a woman among its Direc-tors, who has perhaps more onerous duties than any other officer." On some occasions when community matters were debated, husbands and wives took different sides of a question. Maria and David Mack, for example, spoke opposite each other in a discussion on Fourierism in 1844, while Hall and Frances Judd sometimes voted differently from each other.[17]

Yet though the community could provide a forum for women and a chance for them to practice its proclaimed ideals of equality, its own attachment to the sacredness of marriage and the family prevented it from interfering in husbands' and wives' own relationships. There is no sign, for instance, that anyone sought to prevent wives from deferring to their husbands against their own better judgment. Once, the day after an important decision, a woman member requested the Association's secretary to alter the record of her vote so as to make it conform with her husband's. She claimed to have misunderstood the question put, but in a memoir Frances Judd wrote scathingly of women who had insufficient courage to counter their husbands' opinions.[18] The community would not contest a husband's claim to authority over his wife if he asserted it.

Dolly Stetson, though, did not need the community's help to demonstrate that she was far from being her husband's cipher. Although she affirmed her duty and submission to James's authority, the reality was more complex. On some issues, such as her decision to move to the factory boarding house in April 1844, she tried to consult James (or said she did) but then took action herself and presented him with a fait accompli. Indeed, Dolly seems to have made her firmest professions of deference to James in connection with the question on which she actually resisted him most successfully: namely, whether the family should stay at the Northampton Association at all. While avowing her duty to make his opinion hers, and to follow his guidance, in fact, with her elder daughters' help, she waged a long campaign to dissuade James from making them leave the community.

Dolly acknowledged James's discontent with the Association, but underlined the advantages of remaining there. Would the alternatives available to them be any better? Was anywhere perfect? Would it really be best "to put to sea alone"? Against James Stetson's persistent reluctance to stay at Northampton, Dolly and her daughters coaxed him to do so. When the community faced reorganization in the spring and summer of 1845, James told the leadership that the Stetson family would be leaving. Dolly successfully countered even this effort to go behind her back. "Certainly," she affirmed, "[I] do not wish to stay if you cannot see things here in a more favourable light," but stay they did—in this instance for another nine months.[19]

169

An early twentieth-century snapshot of the former silk factory and community
boarding house of the Northampton Association. The building no longer stands.
(Courtesy, Historic Northampton)

The letters that Dolly Stetson and her daughters wrote to James Stetson
during his absence in Boston formed part of a conscious effort to persuade
him to let the family remain at Northampton despite his own doubts and
anxieties about the community. Dolly and her elder daughters each evinced
an attachment to life at the community that survived a number of attempts
by James to persuade them to leave. This attachment was revealed at times
of crisis, when it appeared possible that the community would decide to
disband.[20] James Stetson was by no means the only male member of the
Association to have severe doubts about its viability, and women like the
Stetsons were among those who helped ensure that the community would
continue despite such doubts and difficulties. Along with others they worked
to sustain community even when many leading men wanted to abandon it;
and they abandoned it themselves only when the advantages it gave them
had been effectively eroded or compromised.

Though Dolly Stetson's influence was partly attributable to smart maneu-
vering, it is apparent that she and James in fact shared a considerable measure
of equality in their marriage. James's few surviving letters to her suggest that
he could defer to Dolly as much as she did to him. As he was arguing in early
1843 in favor of joining the Northampton community in the first place, and

wrestling with the practical issues such a move would pose, he confessed to her: "Ever I am confounded myself & it will take your own Clear mind to lead me out of the Laberyanth." If rather self-consciously, he laid the decision at Dolly's feet: "I am almost ready to give up my manhood & say wherever you direct but keep me with you and I will submit."[21] The letters Dolly Stetson wrote to James were facets of his absence, and time and again they expressed frustration or disappointment at the length of his time away, or his failure to return home when hope or expectation had suggested that he would. But James's absences were not new in their marriage. He had traveled considerably in the 1830s in connection with his chaise business; Dolly had even accompanied him once, on a trip to Philadelphia. Alongside the frustration and the campaigning for influence were strong expressions of affection.[22]

The Stetsons' correspondence was relatively open. They consulted each other or—when James failed to consult—faced firm, if gentle reproof for not doing so. Having read the British reformer Robert Owen's views on property, religion, and marriage, Dolly commented that the ideas were less objectionable than she had been led to imagine from the reputation that Owen had gained in conventional American opinion. Holding that social institutions should comply with the "divine or natural" principle of ensuring the happiness of each individual consistent with the greatest happiness of the whole society, Owen had argued that no marriage should outlast the partners' consent to it, and "no parties . . . should be compelled to associate as husband and wife after the natural affections . . . have been so far separated that no probability remains of effecting a reunion of them."[23] Dolly's tacit approval of this principle may suggest that she was confident in the essential security of her own marriage and content to contemplate it as the continuing fruit of mutual consent, rather than of custom or force. In letters about the ideas of the liberal Unitarian pastor Theodore Parker, whose preaching James had attended in Boston, Dolly signaled her ability to disagree with her husband, and to make clear her own religious opinions in spite of possible differences between them.

Affection is also apparent between father and children, whose letters to him were often lighthearted, even playfully critical. The children were respectful to James, but not in the manner that they might have been to a more authoritarian parent. Almira Stetson made use of her membership in the community to negotiate her relations with her parents, particularly with her father, and to work out the balance between her duties within the family and the fulfillment of her own ambitions. Almira's letters avowed her affection for and obedience to her father, though she dreamed that he could be made proud of her through a public role. While acknowledging that the family's circumstances had obliged her to curb her ambitions and to be satisfied with "small acts of virtue" and the duties of everyday life, she implicitly challenged her father to support her hopes of independence. She contrasted her own position with that of her Brooklyn friends, the Martin sisters, who had, she said, been made prisoners of their father's "inhuman" will. Almira enlisted her father in her campaign to "free" the sisters by urging him to take them newspapers, in defiance of their father's prohibition. Almira's letters to James bespoke a frank and even relatively equal relationship.[24]

In that, they emulated her mother's. Though seventeen years of marriage, childbearing, and anxiety had knocked much of the playfulness out of Dolly's expressions of affection for James, the essential elements of independence, self-confidence, and assertiveness were present still. Here was a marriage that to a considerable degree met the test of equality that abolitionists idealized. Dolly Stetson emerges as a comparatively stronger figure, more forceful in her family's affairs than, for example, her friend and former neighbor Helen Benson Garrison, or probably (as far as we can presently tell, in the absence of many letters) her sister-in-law Catharine Benson.[25] When Samuel J. May observed that Dolly Stetson "moves like a power," he could have been referring to her marriage.

Community membership was an important element in the balance of influence between James and Dolly Stetson. Belonging to a community figured as a factor in Dolly's conception of her marriage and family life. One reason that she was attached to the Northampton community was that it seemed to fulfill purposes that would be harder to satisfy elsewhere. The Stetsons' past had been difficult. They had had to face James's financial troubles. Three times they had suffered the death of a child, most recently that of their ten-year-old son Ebenezer in 1843 after they had been at the community for several months. Disconcerted by James's absence, Dolly saw the community as a place where the family might heal its wounds. For a considerable time, she resisted returning to Brooklyn, where taking up her mother's farm was now the only prospect open to them. In October 1844, James Stetson relinquished the Boston store and went on the road instead, peddling silk in eastern Massachusetts. Dolly expressed disappointment, revealing a hope that perhaps the store might have offered an opportunity for the family's future: "I hoped that if you continued in the store . . . it might lead to a business that would help us to live. . . ." But she was not hoping for an escape from the community. This was a contingency plan, as she made plain: "a business that would help us to live that is if the Association were obliged to break up."[26]

THROUGHOUT THEIR connection with it, however, the Stetsons' strongest purpose for being at the Northampton Association was to obtain educational advantages for the children. James cited this reason in his early 1843 letter proposing that they should move there. More than once, when James suggested they should leave the community, Dolly reflected that the access it provided to affordable education was their most powerful motive for staying. The children, too, seemed to find pleasure in the opportunities they were getting. By the same token, if education was the strongest reason for being at the community, the decline of the Association's schooling during 1845 was one of the main factors that would finally convince the Stetsons to withdraw from membership in the early months of the following year.

Their emphasis on the Northampton Association's value as a place to educate the children grew out of tendencies in their own, particularly Dolly's, earlier lives. Dolly Stetson was her parents' only child. Her mother (Dolly Sharpe Witter, whom we meet in the letters) had ensured that she received a sound basic education at home and in the short summertime schools for girls that were held in early nineteenth-century Brooklyn. Later her parents sent young Dolly for a year to a private school for young ladies in nearby Thompson, Connecticut, though the Stetson family memory of this was as a "finishing school," rather than as a seat of learning. Yet Dolly Sharpe Witter, who was known in the family as "the philosopher," had managed to combine reading with the demands of running a busy farm household. She imparted to her daughter a habit of reading fast and working hard that would shape Dolly Stetson's own life.

Friends were astonished at the way Dolly Stetson managed to read widely while meeting the demands of unrelenting domestic work. One remarked that to watch her work would be to imagine she never read, and to note her learning would be to assume that she could not have time for work. Her letters, with their references to abolitionist writers and the Unitarian and reform press, suggest participation in a world of news and debate that complemented the regular weekly discussions and the periodic conventions that took place at the community. During their first year there, before James Stetson went to Boston, he and Dolly shared a house with the family of Calvin Stebbins, a prosperous farmer of Wilbraham, Massachusetts, with whom Dolly was friendly and with whom she probably had much in common. Stebbins was remembered as a freethinker and a reader; it was said that he owned more books in Wilbraham than anyone except the minister, and it is likely that Stebbins and Dolly Stetson shared their interests while the former was at Northampton.[27] It was easy to be deceived into underestimating her learning. When Calvin's nephew, the student Giles B. Stebbins, did so he received a lesson he never forgot. Long afterward Stebbins recalled a conversation on slavery in which, with the "complacent self-satisfaction" of a "Massachusetts youth, who was a Whig, a Unitarian, and a prospective clergyman," he contested Dolly Stetson's use of some biblical texts as arguments for freedom. As Stebbins talked, he recalled, a look of "amused pity" appeared on Stetson's face, and when he had finished "she took up the matter and expounded the Scriptures in the light of liberty." As she demolished Stebbins's argument he became "confounded . . . that I, one of the lords of creation, . . . should be so utterly humiliated by a person unlearned, as I supposed, in clerical lore, and that person a woman!" After a night of "mental and moral confusion" Stebbins realized that Stetson was correct and went to thank her. "We became cordial friends," he wrote, "and, having come into a teachable mood, I learned much from her." The incident was still sharp in his memory forty-five years later.[28]

Just as her old friend Abby May Alcott managed to juxtapose childcare with reading and writing during the 1830s, so Dolly Stetson may have achieved something similar. She bore ten children during the first twenty years of her marriage, and later said that she spent these years "with one foot in the cradle," but her son George claimed that she read while nursing her babies. If so, perhaps the advantage of delaying the weaning of young James E. Stetson in the spring of 1845 was the opportunity to sustain this habit of informing herself that she might have lost had she been obliged to switch to other tasks.[29] One of the attractions of community life may have been that it helped Dolly Stetson reconcile the demands of work and her intellectual interests. The burdens of work were still considerable, but her letters suggest that they were less onerous in community than they had been when she was running her own household.

Unitarianism and the influence of Samuel J. May were further important factors in the Stetsons' emphasis on education. May had been among the leaders of an educational reform movement in Connecticut in the 1820s, and his church helped convey the general emphasis on the importance of education for women that retained a strong role in the Stetsons' lives. As the

James Ebenezer Stetson was born at the Northampton Association in April 1844. This portrait dates from the early 1860s. (Courtesy, Constance Renner)

historian Dorothy May Emerson has noted, Unitarianism's encouragement of education for religious women had a direct influence on their participation in reform movements and their belief in the possibility of social change through antislavery, temperance, and peace campaigns. The Stetsons in many ways exemplified this influence. Their early adoption of temperance, Brooklyn's connections with the peace movement, and their commitment to antislavery in the 1830s were directly linked to their participation in education for their son and daughters.[30]

The Unitarian focus on girls' and women's education had been rooted partly in the assumption of all individuals' spiritual equality, but also in the presumption that educated women would provide appropriate practical and emotional support for their husbands. Good reformers, the assumption went, would have well-informed, cultivated women standing behind them. Dolly Stetson's education in childhood and young adulthood fit this pattern. She had married at age twenty, and it was as the energetic keeper of her household and mother of young children that she was first given praise and recognition by neighbors impressed with her talents. But the publication in 1833 of Lydia Maria Child's *An Appeal in Favor of that Class of Americans Called Africans* spread the view that women should move beyond merely supporting male reformers and become active reformers themselves. Dolly Stetson and the women among her Brooklyn neighbors quickly put Child's precept into practice, forming the Brooklyn Female Anti-Slavery Society and becoming activists in their own right.[31] Though women who already had obligations to children and family were less able than single women, such as Abby Kelley, to take on public antislavery roles, they nevertheless combined family and reform obligations. Abby May Alcott did it by writing, Dolly Stetson by participation in her local organizations. Once those had declined, by the 1840s the Northampton community provided the best opportunity for her family of limited means to further its educational and reform ideals.

The ability to do this lay in the combination of teaching and manual work that the community offered its children and boarding pupils. Its formal title, the "Northampton Association of Education and Industry," embodied its commitment to joining learning and work in the lives of its members. Teaching methods and syllabus followed some of the patterns of progressive education of the period. There was a strong emphasis on learning by doing and the teaching of "object lessons" to children whose moral sense, as well as their knowledge, was to be fostered. The rejection of conventional methods of rote learning and of discipline by corporal punishment invited skepticism from some observers, and probably from some members of the community too. Even so, the concepts of combining education with work and of using the observation of the natural and human world to provide moral and practical lessons could be made to fit reasonably well with the habits and practical assumptions of a rural society.

Given the value they placed on it, it is not surprising that one of the functions of Dolly Stetson's letters to James was to report on the children's educational progress. During 1844 she and the children wrote with enthusiasm of the community's schooling, and expressed the hope that James could participate in the voluntary evening classes on various subjects that were instituted that October. The community's provision of schooling for the children was one of its main attractions to Dolly Stetson, and she cited it repeatedly in her discussions with James about whether to stay or leave.[32] The community also helped foster Almira's ambitions. As she grew up in the abolitionist movement Almira had dreamed of emulating its most prominent women, becoming a public speaker and "illustrious personage" in the cause of freedom. Although because of her family's financial difficulties, "these dreams of bliss are passed and I find myself nothing but Almira still," she determined to use the opportunities that Northampton provided to embark on her own program of study and improvement. In 1845, aged seventeen, she mapped out for herself a complete syllabus of learning by private reading that would be facilitated by remaining in the community, and she announced her admiration for Margaret Fuller as a model to follow.[33]

Almira had expressed her "love for this Community" and her intention "to bring all my energies" to fulfilling its plans for improvement. For her, as for her mother, part of the attraction lay in the community's educational opportunities. Yet these opportunities would prove impossible to sustain. For reasons that Marjorie Senechal helps explain in her essay on silk production, the Northampton Association struggled financially. As an abolitionist visitor noted, the Association's members had "a heavy debt resting upon them; a phantom guest which has ever been present at the feasts of all advocates of community reform."[34] During 1845 financial difficulties had a particularly corrosive effect on the community's educational provision. Despite many efforts, the Association could not throw off the incubus of debt. First it expanded. Then, over the winter of 1844–1845, it contracted in numbers again. Finally in the summer of 1845 the community's property was divided

This photograph is believed to be of Lucy D. Stetson, taken in the late 1860s or 1870s.
She was born in 1841 and spent her early childhood at the Northampton Association.
(Courtesy, Constance Renner)

to raise some capital, and it continued on a smaller scale. Each of these changes increased demands on the women of the community, who were a minority of the members, and also required more work from children and young members, who came to form over half its total population. The demand for labor resulted in the reorganization of the community's schooling.

Early in the Northampton Association's existence, children had studied in the mornings and labored for the community in the afternoons. Subsequently this pattern was reversed and work was literally and symbolically placed before schooling. As economic pressures increased, the tendency for work to drive out attention to learning increased also.[35] The Stetsons' letters reflected the pressures. The silk-growing department employed children for from one hour and three-quarters a day upwards according to their age, and Dolly noted the effects of tiredness and overwork on the children who worked there.[36] In October 1844, thirteen-year-old Mary told her father that "I work in the Silk Room now every day"; and a few months later her seven-year-old brother George wrote that "I braid palm leaf an hour every day." Behind these matter-of-fact statements lay an increasing reliance by the community on the labor of its children and young adult members.[37] Almira also felt the pressure. Her work for the silk department had once given her pleasure, but by 1845 her letters began to reflect frustration at the long hours, incompetence, and poor organization of an operation desperately striving to earn profits.[38] Dolly Stetson questioned the burden that the workload imposed on all the community's members, and particularly on its children.[39]

The demand for children to labor rather than study caused tension during the spring of 1845 and prompted the withdrawal of some members who, led by James Kerr of Pawtucket, Rhode Island, had urged the importance of schooling. "[Y]ou say you have been unusually depressed," wrote Dolly Stetson to James that May, "—so have I—but from a different cause. . . . Mr. Kerr and family have gone."[40] Teachers departed too, disappointing Stetson children who had respected or befriended them. The community schools were closed to fee-paying outsiders, and then from June 1845 were cut almost entirely. What had started out as a forward-looking experiment in balancing novel methods of schooling with labor had evolved into a system of child labor essential to the community's survival. The change eroded the educational advantages James and Dolly Stetson had sought for their children. With those advantages went part of the family's rationale for staying on as members.

YET THE DECLINE of the schools was not alone sufficient to detach the Stetsons from the Northampton community. Their commitment had also been to cooperating with other members to further the cause of reform, and financial difficulties could not dampen that. Nevertheless the community always faced issues of moral principle that were directly related to the dilemma posed by Galatians chapter 3: were the members already "reformed" or not? To what extent were they to be subject to conventional concepts of law and authority, and to what extent were they as individuals and as a group now free to exercise their own will? Several recurrent themes in the Stetsons' correspondence touched on aspects of this question. Some proved tangential to their concerns and to their future in the community, but divisions over issues of morality at length both assisted in breaking the community up and led the Stetsons to distance themselves from it.

While the community did not interfere with the internal workings of its members' marriages, the civil and moral standing of marriage as an institution was a subject of debate during 1844. The issue was closely linked to nonresistants' and moral suasionists' arguments concerning individuals' relations with the state, and with the relative roles of conscience and legal authority in governing social relationships. James and Dolly Stetson observed the debate closely, and her reports to him regarding the conduct of a succession of community marriages seem to reflect a concern that their fellow members should not diverge too radically from acceptable social norms.

Nonresistants held that human actions and relationships should be regulated by conscience and the dictates of righteousness ("the government of God"). Habit or tradition, law or human government should not hold sway, because they might be in contradiction with truth, and because their power rested ultimately on coercion or force. Many Northampton Association leaders and members were strongly sympathetic to nonresistance, but the question of marriage put them in something of a quandary. The community's published declarations upheld the sanctity of marriage, but their nonresistance principles led many of them to question the notion that this sanctity was rooted in the legal standing of marriage. Sydney Southworth, known as a radical on the issue, appears to have stated the distinction quite clearly, that "true" marriage was a spiritual, not a conventional or legal institution. However, rejecting legal forms exposed radicals on the marriage question to the accusation that they were opponents of marriage, or advocates of "free love." When Southworth and his partner Harriet Hayden declared in 1844 that they were married without having gone through the formality of obtaining legal authorization, the community, its supporters, and its critics were much exercised about the matter. From Dolly Stetson's letters, it is evident that James was quizzing her frequently about the community's discussions on such issues. David Ruggles, she told him, had conveyed to Southworth and Hayden the members' opinion that they should depart.[41] Her reports on the marriages of several other community members in 1844 and 1845 suggested that formalities, however exiguous, were followed in other cases.

When she commented on the presence of a justice of the peace, or recounted a community leader's remarks about the irrelevance of legal formalities to marriage, she was not just relating idle gossip. She was assuring James that the social conventions that he and Dolly had themselves observed were in practice being maintained.

Dolly Stetson also provided James with a commentary on the debates over the future of the community and "community reform" in general at Northampton. James Stetson's absence coincided with a period in which there was much consideration of the ideas of the French social theorist Charles Fourier and the community plans put forward by American Fourierists. Some of its members contemplated the possibility that the Northampton Association might follow Brook Farm in adopting Fourierist principles and arrangements, such as constructing a large community building or "phalanstery," and organizing a pattern of work-groups to enable members to rotate jobs frequently. Though they never joined a Fourierist community, the Stetsons appear to have been among those who were sympathetic to the prospect. At the various conventions held in Northampton and elsewhere in 1844 to generate support for Massachusetts communities, Dolly Stetson paid particular attention to the presence of Fourierist speakers and advocates. A letter to James that summer from the student Giles B. Stebbins marshaled implicit arguments against adopting Fourierism, and may indicate Stebbins's recognition of James as an influential figure who needed to be persuaded. In October, Dolly reported that there was to be a lyceum debate on adopting Fourier's system, and that she wished James could be there "to help the cause along." Though her letters remain tacit on the precise extent of their interest, it is likely that the Stetsons were allied with David Mack, William Bassett, and other Northampton members who considered Fourierism a promising vehicle for tightening control of the community's members and securing the Association's financial future.[42]

This put them at odds, however, with members who held more closely to a moral suasionist or nonresistant distrust of organization. Most moral suasionists objected to Fourierism because they considered it to put too much faith in the power of social institutions and material arrangements to reform humanity. They believed that, as William Lloyd Garrison expressed it, social reform would come about only through the reformation of individuals. Northampton's discussions about Fourierism faded out late in 1844. Support for it had been insufficient, and in any case the community's very survival was a more pressing issue. But the debate was linked to what would prove to be the single most serious ideological difficulty for Northampton's members: a conflict of opinions about "cultural" issues that were rooted in different religious views. The Stetsons' letters throw valuable light on that question.

Religious diversity and tolerance was one of the Northampton community's hallmarks, proudly claimed by its leadership. When an inquirer asked in 1846, "Of what religious sect are your members?" the Association's acting secretary replied, "Of no particular sect. Each one is at liberty to chose his own."[43] The community's opponents, of course, criticized this freedom, and even some of its supporters were skeptical that it could survive the disagreements that would break out between proponents of different views. In a memoir half a century later Frederick Douglass implied that religious disagreement had been a source of the Northampton Association's demise. There is direct evidence too that argument took a serious toll on members. When William Bassett left in late 1844, he explained to an English friend, "Divers considerations influenced me to that course." The Association "was embarrassed with a heavy debt" and lacked "productive power," and Bassett's family felt "discontent . . . with their situation." But, in addition, "it was constantly convulsed and its peace destroyed by most violent dissensions, not only in reference to its pecuniary concerns, but on account of religious differences. I never met with more painful exhibitions of bigoted intolerance than among those who had there congregated to work out the problem of true social life!"[44]

Dolly Stetson's letters show, however, that the incidents that drove Bassett to leave were only indirectly religious in character. Their ostensible cause was a disagreement over aspects of behavior that caused rifts in the group on several occasions. Most members of the Association agreed with its published egalitarian, antislavery, nonresistant ideals. But many areas of culture and behavior were not amenable to constitutional definition and should, nonresistants held, be regulated by individuals' consciences and moral scruples. Some of these areas posed little difficulty at the community. Temperance and teetotalism were so widely accepted among reformers by the early 1840s that there was no evident dispute over the consumption of alcohol. But conflicts did arise over matters which nonresistance was ill equipped to resolve. With individual conscience as the sole arbiter of behavior, members seem to have relied on the authority of constraints they had grown up with or grown used to. Over several issues, especially dancing, playing cards, and the behavior of young people, rifts emerged between what we could call "liberal" and "puritan" factions. Though she rarely engaged directly in the debates herself, Dolly Stetson seems to have been among the "liberals." As with aspects of Fourierism and the marriage question, this put her at odds with some of the community's nonresistant majority.

At a community picnic in the summer of 1844, Sojourner Truth's daughters danced a waltz. "It was," wrote Almira Stetson, "quite a wonder to the people here."[45] Whether the "wonder" was the waltz itself, or the fact that the two young women dared to dance it, is not entirely clear; but either way it would be surprising if Sojourner had approved. As Paul Gaffney notes in his essay in this volume, Sojourner Truth often displayed the moral strictness that she drew from her evangelical experience. Not long afterward, as Dolly Stetson recorded, Sojourner and the radical perfectionist James Boyle were lambasting the community's young people for their frivolous amusements and open flirtations with one another. Such arguments could cause people to withdraw from the community. Boyle had been credited before with driving out members he regarded as morally loose; on this occasion, wrote Dolly, he "used most unjust language and produced a great deal of digust," and she reported William Bassett's remark that "if he and his children have got to hear such language here he shall go somewhere else."[46] Soon enough, Bassett himself was under attack. At a community meeting that November, Sojourner Truth criticized the teacher Charles May for letting children under his charge play cards. When Bassett spoke up to explain that May had merely been demonstrating a mathematical game, he was promptly "censured" and told by community leader Samuel L. Hill that "he had better go." Asserting the right to follow his own conscience in private, Bassett prepared to leave Northampton with his family and return to their home in Lynn. Dolly Stetson regretted the departure of a member she regarded highly, and it is likely, too, that Bassett's withdrawal denied the community the services of one of its best managers of silk production. Some weeks later, Charles May also left Northampton, depriving Dolly Stetson of a cherished family connection and her children of a much-liked teacher and friend.[47]

The curbs on what "puritans" saw as moral laxity continued. In a dramatic scene four months after the Bassetts departed, Hill prevented several women, including Dolly Stetson, from dancing at the dedication of a new community kitchen and dining room. What might have been a joyful celebration ended with "a great deal of grumbling."[48] Dancing and card games had been a part of her own upbringing, and Dolly Stetson doubted the wisdom of the restrictions that some of her fellow members wished to impose. "I cannot oppose innocent amusements for the young," she wrote; "I think I can look back to my past life and see where I may have been saved from what might have been far worse by a game of whist." In 1845, she noted, "The subject of Amusements is the great matter that seems to devide the members," and she remarked critically of the individuals who "take the same ground against games or sports of all kinds for children even playing ball &c."[49]

The Stetsons' concerns about education, work, Fourierism, and conduct were linked to the broader question of who, in a community that consisted of nuclear families and claimed to uphold the sacredness of the "family relation," should actually exercise authority. Many of the issues arising over "amusements" were concerned with the activities of children and young people. Disputes over dancing, playing cards, ball games, and flirtation touched on the competing claims of the community and of parents to regulate children's behavior. Drawing Dolly Stetson toward sympathy with what I have called the "liberal" side of the argument was her reflection that individual adults should be trusted to provide appropriate guidance to the young without community interference. With apparent approval she reported David Mack's argument, in a debate about "the relation in which children were to stand to this Association," that "Parents were instituted by God as the protectors Guardians and Governors of their children untill they were capable of reasoning judging and acting for themselves and any institution that intefered with this relation whether Associat[ion] or any think else must be contrary to the divine law and deserved only to come to naught."[50] This aligned her with Charles May, William Bassett, and others who advocated latitude on these matters of judgment, and also with James Kerr and other parents who had claimed the right to give priority to the education of their children over the community's needs for labor. It placed her at odds with the individuals I have labeled "puritans," such as James Boyle, Sojourner Truth, Samuel L. Hill, and the Judds, who were more content to support community regulation of children's and young people's behavior, not by making rules but by criticizing individuals for "immorality." Ultimately the Stetsons upheld "family" above "community" in their order of priorities.

Dolly Witter Stetson and other women in the Association were among those who determined to keep the community going when, on several occasions in 1844 and 1845, decisions could have been made to disband it. Beyond this, however, women's influence on the business and financial affairs of the Association remained relatively limited. On one hand, they had little access to or control over the material property that was essential for the community's credit and financial viability. On the other, even though they were nominally equal with the male members and had the opportunity to vote in community affairs, they were rarely able in practice to participate in decision-making as fully as their male colleagues. Evidently, too, meetings took place from which women were excluded.

At one such private meeting in early April 1844 several leading men of the community discussed a proposal to bring the Association to an end. Shortage of funds prompted the crisis but, wrote Martha Turner Hudson as she relayed reports of the meeting to her husband, the sudden promise of fresh subscriptions halted the movement to disband. "The failure that I wrote you about has all passed at present at least. Samuel [L. Hill], Theodore [Scarborough] Hiram [Wells] and Mr. [David] Mack were willing to stop and thought they must but George [W. Benson] comes home with (it is said) $12000 and would not hear to giving up at all says he shall certainly carry it through." Meeting again shortly afterward, the men "talked the matter over and concluded to go on." But a suggestion was floated at this point that would in the long run guide the final disposition of the community and its resources. Martha Hudson reported that Hall Judd "would form a neighborhood Com[munity] and so would Samuel." A year later, according to Dolly Stetson, several members again contemplated replacing the Association with an "Agricultural and mechanical community" based on individual households.[51] Between 1844 and 1846, leading members of the community helped it to evolve toward such an arrangement. Samuel L. Hill and his family were already living in a house off the Association's "domain" and, during 1845, Hill was having a new house built. Elisha L. Hammond, too, was building a house for himself and his wife; Dolly Stetson noted the date its frame was raised in 1845. At length, after the Association formally disbanded in November 1846, no fewer than sixty-seven of its members remained in the immediate vicinity. Many of them, including Hill, Hammond, and Hall Judd, participated in the formation of a local neighborhood along the lines that Judd had contemplated more than two years earlier.[52] Dolly and James Stetson were not among this group, however. For reasons to do both with their own circumstances and with the conflicts in the Northampton community, settling in the newly created neighborhood with their remaining fellow communitarians proved for them neither practicable nor appealing.

Staying might, in fact, have made a good deal of sense for the Stetsons. James continued for several years to be employed as a sales agent by the Association's successor firms. Almira and Mary wanted to stay in Northampton anyway, and remaining there would have enabled them to do so without breaking up the family. Dolly could have sustained the reform commitments and companionship that she would miss when she left. Several times in the period after the family had moved from the Association but were still living in town, her letters revealed the eagerness with which she met some of her community friends. Yet the Stetsons' main material asset was the Witter farm in Brooklyn, which had always been their most realistic alternative to being at the Association. With the needs of Dolly's mother to consider as well as their own, remaining at Northampton and buying property there was not readily within the Stetsons' means. Moreover the divisions within the Association during the latter part of their membership had driven away many of the people with whom Dolly Stetson felt most compatible.

It is likely that many of the men and women who remained to form Northampton's "neighborhood community" were not those whom she regarded as particularly sympathetic. After disputes over "amusements" or other "cultural" issues, it tended to be "liberals" like Charles May and William Bassett who had packed up and left. As the community struggled with its financial difficulties in mid-1845, the question, as Dolly Stetson saw it, was who "can agree [to] go on with the rest[?]"⁵³ For the time being, she and her family did so, but as others withdrew she found herself left among members, including Samuel Hill, Sojourner Truth, Elisha Hammond, and the Judds, with whose opinions she had differed. Having already found them unduly rigid in their views, Dolly seems to have evinced no strong wish to join them in disbanding the Association and organizing their new "neighborhood community."

EVEN SO, their three-year residence at the Northampton Association seems to have done a good deal to shape the Stetson family's future lives and memories. For Dolly Stetson in particular, departing from the community and leaving the mutual support, friendships, and companionship it had provided her remained a matter of regret. According to her granddaughter, she long missed "the close contact with the men and women who stimulated and enriched her life, and whose companionship had been so congenial to her." Despite his reluctance to remain in the community, even James fostered warm recollections of his family's time there. "I have ever been thankful that I went," he later wrote; "altho I returned as poor as I went, in money, the advantages to my family were very great in schooling, and in association with the best people I ever knew."[54] It is a reasonable guess that the fondness of their parents' recollections and their own memories of community days led the Stetson children and grandchildren to preserve the family letters written from the Northampton Association. The letters would remain as memorabilia of a distinctive phase in their family's history, and of their connection with a distinctive episode in the story of American radical reform.

Dolly Stetson and most of the children returned to Brooklyn, Connecticut, in 1847 to live along with her mother on what had been her parents' farm. That year, Dolly would give birth to her tenth and last child, their son Joseph. Within a few years James A. Stetson gave up his job selling silk for his Northampton associates. According to one version of the story he "resigned his position on account of a proposed transaction which he considered dishonest," and returned home to take charge of the farm. Initially he was the butt of neighborhood jokes. No man in his late forties, it seemed, had been known to take up farming for the first time and make a success of it, but James appears to have disproved the local wisdom and returned the farm to a measure of its former prosperity. He also found on the land a peace of mind that he had not achieved in trading: "I have been freed from buying and selling," he wrote, "a business I came to dislike more than I can tell." He regained his standing in the town and, by the Civil War, had become sufficiently reconciled to politics that he joined the Republican Party and was elected as Brooklyn's representative to the Connecticut General Assembly for the 1864 session.[55] James and Dolly would remain settled in Brooklyn for the rest of their long lives; each of them lived to the age of ninety-two, and their marriage lasted for over sixty-five years, until James's death in 1893. In some respects they remembered their sojourn at Northampton as the last episode of an eventful early marriage, and their move back to the farm as the initiation of a long, peaceful retirement from the concerns of the world.

If anything, the Northampton Association and the wider family connections it represented played a greater role in the children's futures than in Dolly's and James's own. The experiences of Almira and her siblings

James Alexander Stetson at age seventy-five. This portrait was taken in May 1877 for the Stetsons' fiftieth wedding anniversary. (Courtesy, Anne Beaman)

Dolly Witter Stetson sits for her fiftieth wedding anniversary portrait, May 1877. She is sixty-nine years old. (Courtesy, Constance Renner)

measured some of the changes that were taking place in mid-nineteenth-century New England society and in the reform movements in which they had been involved. They participated, in different ways, in the formation of new middle-class occupations during this period, and in the retreat from radicalism that the collapse of the Northampton community and many similar efforts at realizing a utopian vision represented. Like Louisa May Alcott and the other children of Dolly's old acquaintance Abby May Alcott, the younger Stetsons found expectations and opportunities structured differently in the middle decades of the nineteenth century than their parents had in the 1820s.[56]

The Stetsons' educational ambitions for their children shaped the desire that both Almira and Mary evinced to become teachers. Almira remained in Northampton when her mother and siblings moved back to Brooklyn in 1847, and obtained a post teaching school that summer. Perhaps with money she saved herself, or with help from family or friends, she then managed to fulfill her hope of extending her full-time education by enrolling at Mary Lyon's Mount Holyoke Female Seminary in South Hadley for the 1847–1848 school year. Yet, although this gave her the opportunity to study, the school can hardly have suited her well. She could surely have coped with the strict regimen, and with being placed in the Junior Class with much younger students, but Mount Holyoke was a bastion of theological orthodoxy, where students were strenuously encouraged to seek a conversion experience and Unitarians like Almira were viewed as infidels. The contrast with the Northampton community's free discussion would have been profound. The future poet Emily Dickinson, who spent that same year in the seminary's Middle Class, was miserable. Almira apparently did not complete the year, but went back to Brooklyn and taught school for a period, before returning to Northampton to live and teach again in the familiar and more congenial surroundings of Broughton's Meadow.[57]

Mary had from the start wanted to join her there. In the summer of 1847, Dolly Stetson wrote that Mary would rather be assisting her elder sister in Northampton than staying at the farm in Brooklyn "knitting socks or picking whortleberries." At length she was able to do so. By the summer of 1850 Almira and Mary were both living in the household of Habor Haborson, a Norwegian-born machinist who lived close by their aunt and uncle Catharine and George W. Benson. They would remain teaching in Northampton until 1853, when Almira returned once more to Brooklyn to marry the town's new Unitarian minister.[58] Mary, alone among the Stetson children, did not marry. The legacy of her time at Northampton continued to influence her life, as she pursued a teaching career in various parts of New England. In 1857 she was in Brooklyn, where she signed an American Anti-Slavery Society petition calling for the disunion of the United States, perpetuating the campaign for dissociation from slavery that had begun in 1844. Since their time together at the Northampton community, Mary's closest friend had been her cousin Mary Richardson, who also became a teacher. The bond lasted throughout the two women's lives. Mary's youngest sister Lucy, the baby whom Dolly Stetson was carrying on the wagon ride to the community in April 1843, would get married in 1868 to a Northampton man, and the couple settled in the town. It may have been at their house there that Mary Stetson eventually died in her old age, sometime after 1915.[59]

The career of George R. Stetson, the eldest son to survive childhood, measured both the influence of the family's Northampton period and the rapidity with which circumstances changed in the decade and a half after the Northampton Association disbanded. Later in his life Stetson wrote a reminiscence of his childhood in the community, one of a relatively few memoirs that marked the communities of the 1840s with fondness, rather than with criticism. In the meantime, however, he had taken new directions. With the help of his sister Almira, the young Stetson secured in 1855 an apprenticeship with the firm of a former Northampton community member, and he returned to Broughton's Meadow, which by now had been renamed Florence. His employer, Hiram Wells, a machinist, had been a founder of the Northampton Association, had remained there throughout its existence, and was among the group who had stayed to settle in the neighborhood after it disbanded. Wells was no soft touch. The year before Stetson joined him, he had faced down a brief strike for higher wages with a stubborn refusal to give in to his workers; even Wells's own wife had apparently described him as "obstinate as an ass."[60] Stetson recalled that he worked for Wells for one dollar a week plus room and board while he received a basic training as a machinist. In 1857, however, he moved to take a job in Springfield at a works where the pay was better and there was much more for him to learn.

Quitting Hiram Wells's shop quite possibly saved George Stetson's life, because in 1859 the hard-driving Wells blew himself and two workmen up by ordering the safety valve on a stationary steam engine held down to raise pressure. At the beginning of the Civil War, though, Stetson returned once more to Florence to work for the firm that had succeeded Wells in the shop, a company now controlled by the former Northampton Association leader Samuel L. Hill. The works was being used to make weapons, but Hill's pacifist principles led him to switch it into the production of Florence sewing machines. George Stetson's training, however, was in arms production, and he soon moved to another factory nearby, making rifle barrels and bayonets on contract for the federal armory in Springfield.

This move broke George's last link with his former community past. While Hill, exemplar of the generation that had founded the Northampton Association, adhered to its nonresistant ideals, George R. Stetson, like many others of his younger generation, accepted the logic of war as the instrument for ridding the United States of slavery. Over the next two decades he would become an expert toolmaker and machinist in the small-arms industry, and establish patents in barrel making and cartridge manufacture. Though his later career was in gas and electricity supply, it was the skills of war, not the principles of peace that he deployed to this end. The Northampton community would remain an active memory, and a spur to efforts by him and other members of his family to memorialize their connection with it, but it ceased to be an active presence in George Stetson's life.

LATER IN THE CENTURY, along with other former abolitionists the Stetsons celebrated the eventual triumph of the effort to destroy slavery that they had once taken great risks to support. Dolly Stetson would remember that the young lawyer she had once been dissuaded from courting had eventually become a congressman, and then disgraced himself in her eyes by voting for the Compromise of 1850 and the notorious Fugitive Slave Act. James Stetson would take pride in the Connecticut legislature's vote to ratify the Thirteenth Amendment in 1865. Yet for the Stetsons, abolitionism had always been a personal matter as well as a public campaign, a movement closely linked to their family, kin, and neighborhood. When in May 1877, Dolly and James celebrated the fiftieth anniversary of their marriage, they were proud to receive from William Lloyd Garrison a congratulatory message that praised their long devotion to ending slavery.[61] A brother-in-law of James Stetson's sister, Garrison was part of their kinship network as well as a public leader. Activism and family were intertwined.

Late in the nineteenth century and early in the twentieth, George Stetson and his own kin took several steps to memorialize his parents and their involvement in reform. He wrote an essay recalling his experiences as a small boy at the Northampton community; arranged the printing of a memoir of his mother, compiled by Almira's daughter—his niece; and wrote or dictated his own autobiography for his children, who in turn printed it after his death in 1915.[62] In all these efforts, the Northampton Association and the family's membership in it occupied a distinctive place in their memories. But the family was also preserving the letters that their mother and siblings wrote while they were living at the community, and these letters, now that we have

George R. Stetson, born in 1837, was a young boy when the family joined the Northampton Association. (Courtesy, Constance Renner)

James Stetson died March 5, 1893, and Dolly Stetson died on June 5, 1899. They are buried in Brooklyn, Connecticut. James's epitaph reads: *The honest man's the noblest work of God;* Dolly's is inscribed: *For who is like a Mother among all them that are in the earth.* (Courtesy, Anne Beaman)

been able to read them, have taken us back into that world with an intimacy and immediacy that memoirs alone could not recreate.

Notes

Parts of this essay previously appeared in Christopher Clark, "A Mother and Her Daughters at the Northampton Community: New Evidence on Women in Utopia," *New England Quarterly* 75, no. 4 (December 2002): 592–621, and are used with permission.

1. Donald E. Pitzer, ed., *America's Communal Utopias* (Chapel Hill, N.C., 1997); Christopher Clark, *The Communitarian Moment: The Radical Challenge of the Northampton Association* (Ithaca, N.Y., 1995; Amherst, Mass., 2003).

2. Priscilla J. Brewer, *Shaker Communities, Shaker Lives* (Hanover, N.H., 1986); Ann Taylor, *Visions of Harmony: A Study in Nineteenth-Century Millenarianism* (Oxford, Eng., 1987); Brian J. L. Berry, *America's Utopian Experiments: Communal Havens from Long-Wave Crises* (Berkeley, Calif., 1992).

3. On abolitionism, kinship, and neighborhood as themes at the Northampton community, see Clark, *The Communitarian Moment*, 34–46, 78–85.

4. Kate deNormandie Wilson, *Dolly Witter Stetson: A Sketch of Her Life* (Brooklyn, Conn., 1907), 77–79, outlines James Stetson's financial difficulties. For the loss of his workshop, compare "Abstract of the Assessment Lists of the Town of Brooklyn," Town Clerk's Office, Brooklyn, Conn., for 1838, with that for 1837. See also the memoir by George R. Stetson, "When I Was a Boy," in Charles A. Sheffeld, ed., *The History of Florence, Massachusetts, Including a Complete Account of the Northampton Association of Education and Industry* (Florence, Mass., 1895), 118–123; Northampton Association of Education and Industry, Records, 1836–1853, American Antiquarian Society, Worcester, Mass. (hereafter cited as NAEI, Records), vol. 2, p. 21, notes an instruction to Benson to write to James to arrange for him to visit with a view to his "joining the Association and acting as permanent agent for the sale of silk."

5. James A. Stetson to Dolly W. Stetson (hereafter JAS and DWS), [February 20, 1843] (letter no. 2). Stetson Family Correspondence, Manuscript Collection, Historic Northampton, Northampton, Mass. References are to letters in this collection unless otherwise indicated, and include the letter number assigned in this volume. On Dolly Stetson's character and interests, see Wilson, *Dolly Witter Stetson*, 39; other descriptions of her appear in Giles B. Stebbins, "A Young Man in the Community," in Sheffeld, ed., *The History of Florence*, 128; and idem, *Upward Steps of Seventy Years* (New York, 1890), 62.

6. Judith Wellman, "Women and Radical Reform in Antebellum Upstate New York: A Profile of Grassroots Female Abolitionists," in Mabel E. Deutrich and Virginia C. Purdy, eds., *Clio Was a Woman: Studies in the History of American Women* (Washington, D.C., 1980); Judith Wellman, *Grass Roots Reform in the Burned-Over District of*

Upstate New York: Religion, Abolitionism, and Democracy (New York, 2000); John L. Brooke, *The Heart of the Commonwealth: Society and Political Culture in Worcester County, Massachusetts, 1713–1861* (Cambridge, Eng., 1989), 363–66.

7. On neighborhood exchange, work-swapping, and mutual interdependence, see Christopher Clark, *The Roots of Rural Capitalism: Western Massachusetts, 1780–1860* (Ithaca, N.Y., 1990), 23–38, 64–71; S. G. Goodrich, *Recollections of a Lifetime, Or Men and Things I Have Seen*, 2 vols. (New York, 1857), 1:75.

8. [Jane Sophia Appleton] "Sequel to the Vision of Bangor in the Twentieth Century," *Letters from the Kenduskeag* (Bangor, Me., 1848). In an article on the "isolated household," the Fourierist journal *The Harbinger* [1, no. 22 (June 21, 1845)] had argued that women not living under the benefits of cooperation were "slaves" of the "social mechanism"; see also Kathryn Tomasek, "Children and Family in Fourierist Communities," *Connecticut History* 37 (1996–1997): 159–173.

9. These principles were evident, for example, in the letter James Stetson wrote to Dolly Stetson during a sales trip to Vermont in October 1842, excerpted above in "Stetson Family Correspondence," note 1: "I hope our dear children will never think meanly of . . . [the] powers . . . God has given them, and seek to exalt them by adding virtue and increase in knowledge and excellence until they arrive at the perfect stature of men and women in Christ which lies in perfecting our mental, moral and religious abilities." See Edward J. Lee, Jr., "The Old Letter," *Vermont History News* 33, no. 6 (November–December 1982): 88–90.

10. Galatians 3:20–28.

11. Stephen C. Rush to William Lloyd Garrison, July 21, 1844, Boston Public Library MS. A.1.2.14.43.

12. Martha Turner Hudson to Erasmus D. Hudson, October 1, 1843, Hudson Family Papers, Box 1, folder 20, Special Collections and Archives, W.E.B. Du Bois Library, University of Massachusetts, Amherst; DWS to JAS, April 13, 1845 (letter no. 47).

13. Chris Dixon, *Perfecting the Family: Antislavery Marriages in Nineteenth-Century America* (Amherst, Mass., 1997).

14. Quotations are from DWS to JAS [early May 1844] (letter no. 5); other examples are in DWS to JAS, July 26, [1844] (letter no. 13); August 25, 1844 (letter no. 21).

15. NAEI, Constitution, 1842, article VI, A. J. Macdonald Collection, p. 71, Beinecke Rare Book and Manuscript Library, Yale University.

16. Dolly Stetson shared this high regard for her, writing to James on April 13, 1845, "I think Mrs Mack one of the most accomplished women I ever met and one whose influence over girls as far as education and manners is concerned is most salutary" (letter no. 47).

17. William Adam to *Liberator* (Boston), November 1843; DWS to JAS, October 26, [1844] (letter no. 31).

18. Frances P. Judd, "Reminiscences," in Sheffeld, ed., *History of Florence*, 117.

19. DWS to JAS, July 26, [1844] (letter no. 13); April 13, 1845 (letter no. 47); June 19, [1845] (letter no. 61).

20. See Christopher Clark, "A Mother and Her Daughters at the Northampton Community: New Evidence on Women in Utopia," *New England Quarterly* 75, no. 4 (December 2002): especially 606–608.

21. JAS to DWS, [February 20, 1843] (letter no. 2). A later reference suggests that it was indeed her word that decided the family's move: see DWS to JAS, August 4, 1844 (letter no. 17).

22. DWS to JAS, June 3, [1844] (letter no. 7).

23. DWS to JAS, October 6, 1844 (letter no. 27), referring to Robert Owen, "Address of Robert Owen to the People of the United States," New York *Daily Tribune*, September 24, 1844, reprinted in John R. Commons et al., eds., *Documentary History of American Industrial Society*, 11 vols. (Cleveland, 1910–1911), 7:155–160, quotation from 157.

24. Almira B. Stetson to JAS, December 10, 1844 (letter no. 35).

25. A fresh perspective on Helen Benson Garrison is, however, provided in Harriet Hyman Alonso, *Growing Up Abolitionist: The Story of the Garrison Children* (Amherst, Mass., 2002).

26. DWS to JAS, April 21, [1844] (letter no. 3); October 12, 1844 (letter no. 28).

27. Wilson, *Dolly Witter Stetson*, 39; Ralph Stebbins Greenlee and Robert Lemuel Greenlee, *The Stebbins Genealogy*, 2 vols. (Chicago, 1904): 1:348–349.

28. Stebbins, "A Young Man in the Community," 128; idem. *Upward Steps of Seventy Years*, 62, gives another version of the same story.

29. Wilson, *Dolly Witter Stetson*, 39; George Ripley Stetson, *The Story of My Life, and Incidents Connected Therewith* (n.p., n.d.), 19; DWS to JAS, July 26, [1844] (letter no. 13).

30. Dorothy May Emerson, ed., *Standing before Us: Unitarian Universalist Women and Social Reform, 1776–1936* (Boston, 2000), 4. Samuel J. May had organized an education convention at Brooklyn in 1827 that led to the founding of a Society of the Friends of Education for Windham County, whose first president was Dolly W. Stetson's uncle George Sharpe; see Ellen D. Larned, *History of Windham County*, 2 vols. (1880; rpt. ed., Chester, Conn., 1976), 2:477.

31. [Lydia Maria Child] *An Appeal in Favor of that Class of Americans called Africans* (Boston, 1833); Brooklyn Female Anti-Slavery Society, Records, 1834–1840, Connecticut State Library, Hartford.

32. DWS to JAS, July 26, [1844] (letter no. 13); Almira B. Stetson to JAS, [July 27, 1844] (letter no. 14); DWS to JAS, August 4, 1844 (letter no. 17), October 6, 1844 (letter no. 27); Mary S. Stetson to JAS, October 13, 1844 (letter no. 29).

33. Almira B. Stetson to JAS, December 10, 1844 (letter no. 35); March 4, 1845 (letter no. 42).

34. Benjamin S. Jones, quoted in *Liberator*, June 20, 1845.

35. DWS to JAS, October 6, 1844 (letter no. 27).

36. DWS to JAS, August 4, 1844 (letter no. 17). The Fourierist journal *The Phalanx*, September 7, 1844, reported that the Northampton Association's silk-growing depart-

ment included twenty or so small girls and boys "who, in the ordinary state of society would be of no service whatever to their parents or themselves."

37. Mary S. Stetson to JAS, October 13, 1844 (letter no. 29); George R. Stetson to JAS, March 2, 1845 (letter no. 41). For a discussion of child labor in the community, see Clark, *The Communitarian Moment*, 168–172.

38. Almira B. Stetson to JAS, February 19/23, 1845 (letter no. 40), March 4, 1845 (letter no. 42), May 12, [1845] (letter no. 55).

39. DWS to JAS, March 18, 1845 (letter no. 45).

40. DWS to JAS, May 4, 1845 (letter no. 52); on the dispute, see Clark, *The Communitarian Moment*, 171.

41. DWS to JAS, July 26, [1844] (letter no. 13).

42. DWS to JAS, October 26, [1844] (letter no. 31); Giles B. Stebbins to JAS, August 7, 1844 (letter no. 18); on Fourierist ideas at Northampton, see Clark, *The Communitarian Moment*, 173–176.

43. Bailey Birge to Ephraim Otis, June 29, 1846, NAEI, Records, vol. 4, pp. [135–136].

44. William Bassett to Elizabeth Pease, August 14, 1845, Boston Public Library MS. A.1.2.15.49.

45. Almira B. Stetson to JAS, August 4, 1844 (letter no. 17).

46. DWS to JAS, September 1, 1844 (letter no. 22).

47. DWS to JAS, November 19, [1844] (letter no. 32). Charles May was elder brother to Rev. Samuel J. May and to Abby May Alcott, both of whom (as we have noted) had played important roles earlier in Dolly's life.

48. DWS to JAS, March 18, 1845 (letter no. 45).

49. DWS to JAS, October 6, 1844 (letter no. 27), May 11, 1845 (letter no. 54); on amusements in Dolly's early life, see Wilson, *Dolly Witter Stetson*, 5, 17.

50. DWS to JAS, October 6, 1844 (letter no. 27).

51. Martha Turner Hudson to Erasmus D. Hudson, April 7, 1844, typescript Hudson Family Papers, folder 23, Sophia Smith Collection, Smith College, Northampton, Mass.; DWS to JAS, April 15, [1845] (letter no. 48).

52. Clark, *The Communitarian Moment*, 180, 186–187.

53. DWS to JAS, May 11, 1845 (letter no. 54).

54. Wilson, *Dolly Witter Stetson*, 39.

55. The quotation is from a undated letter of James Stetson's printed in Wilson, *Dolly Witter Stetson*, 79. Other details of Stetson's later life are drawn from *Roll of State Officers and Members of the General Assembly of Connecticut, from 1776–1881* (Hartford, 1881), 388, and *Commemorative Biographical Record of Tolland and Windham Counties, Connecticut* (Chicago, 1903), 961–962; Stetson was also a Mason and temperance advocate, and remained a Unitarian.

56. On the "retreat from radicalism," see Clark, *The Communitarian Moment*, 189–196. On the occupations available to women, see Louisa May Alcott, *Work: A Story of Experience* (1873; rpt. ed., New York, 1977).

57. *Annual Catalogues of the Teachers and Pupils of the Mt. Holyoke Female Seminary from 1847–57* (Northampton, Mass., n.d.), 4, lists Almira B. Stetson of Brooklyn, Conn., as a member of the Junior Class, and Emily Dickinson, of Amherst, Mass., as a member of the Middle Class for 1847–1848. A vivid description of the Mt. Holyoke seminary that year appears in Alfred Habegger, *My Wars Are Laid Away in Books: The Life of Emily Dickinson* (New York, 2001), 191–212.

58. DWS to JAS, May 12, 1847 (letter no. 75); United States Seventh Census, 1850, Population Schedules, Hampshire County, Mass., National Archives (microfilm).

59. On Mary Stetson, see Wilson, *Dolly Witter Stetson*, 59, and disunion petitions in Slavery in the United States Collection, American Antiquarian Society, Box 1.

60. Clark, *The Communitarian Moment*, 210–211, discusses Wells and his eventual fate, referred to in the paragraph below.

61. Wilson, *Dolly Witter Stetson*, 61.

62. George R. Stetson, "When I Was a Boy,"; Wilson, *Dolly Witter Stetson*; George Ripley Stetson, *The Story of My Life*.

The Camel and the Needle

Silk and the Stetson Letters

Marjorie Senechal

In the attic with the family letters, Dolly and James Stetson's great-great-grandchildren found a large latched box of dark and gleaming wood (figure 1). It bore no nameplate, no label, no clue to who made it or why or when, but whoever put the box in the attic with the letters knew it belonged with them. Inside, glass plates framed dot-sized eggs, crumbling silkworms, ancient cocoons, skeins of raw silk, and tiny brown paper packages tied with white silk thread.[1]

Had the box been James Stetson's? A skilled craftsman, he might have built cases to display the silk he peddled on the road or sold in the Boston store, but this is not silk he would have sold: there is no colored thread, no knitted purse, no finished product of any kind. The rough, gray silk marked "Florence" looks crude beside the more lustrous "Italian" skein. What salesman would advertise a competitor's superior product?

The mystery recedes when we look at the box in the light of the letters. Silk was the chief business of the Northampton Association of Education and Industry, and the Stetsons were occupied, and preoccupied, with it. Almira raised silkworms, reeled their cocoons, and wrapped finished thread in packets for her father to sell, Mary twisted silk into thread, and George picked mulberry leaves and fed them to the worms. When James was away from Northampton, Dolly kept him apprised of silk department affairs. *My Dear Husband — I have a few moments of leisure and commence a letter hoping to get a sheet full before Mr Bassett sends a box to you—*[2] Dolly and Almira and occasionally the younger children tucked letters in with the thread that the stage brought to James. And they threaded comments on silk through their letters.

As Christopher Clark points out in his introduction to this volume, the letters were not written to us. James understood their casual allusions to people and problems, but sometimes we do not. The references to silk are especially mystifying. Why was the NAEI making silk, of all things? What is a cocoonery, why worry about the weather, and what does it mean to weight silk? Why was it so difficult to sell?

FIGURE 1. The Stetson family's silk box. Photograph by Stan Sherer.

This chapter reconstructs the missing context. First I review silk making in Connecticut and in Massachusetts in the decade before the founding of the NAEI. Then I juxtapose excerpts from the letters with the silk department activities to which they refer. In the concluding paragraphs, I consider some of the reasons why silk production at the NAEI was problematical and ultimately failed.

UNTIL THE MASS production of synthetics in the 1880s, all textiles—sheets and blankets, towels and tablecloths, clothing and rugs—were made of natural fibers, principally wool, cotton, linen, and silk. In today's acrylic, kevlar, and polyester world, we forget how central the manufacture of thread and yarn once was, and how time-consuming. No fiber comes from nature ready to use; all are wrested from their sources—sheep, cotton plants, flax plants, cocoons—with difficulty. Wool, cotton, and linen are short fibers that must be twisted together to make a continuous yarn or thread. This process, called spinning, is only the last step in a long sequence of preparations. Before you can spin, you must raise the sheep, or plant and cultivate the cotton or flax, and then shear the sheep, pick the cotton, ret and hackle the flax, and finally comb, card, and clean them. At first glance, making silk looks easier: the silkworm does it for you. Its cocoon is a single filament, half a mile long. But the silkworm is fragile, and completely dependent on humans for food and for shelter. And humans must unwind the thin, uneven filaments from the cocoons and twist them into smooth, sturdy thread.

The NAEI's founders did not choose silk for "the business of utopia" after weighing its many pros and cons:[3] the "business" came first. "400 acres, more or less, together with all buildings, mill and water privileges, machinery, fixtures, water wheels and gearing thereon or thereto appertaining," states the deed in a sloping 1841 hand. A tourist attraction in the four years it operated, the Northampton Silk Company was now in receivership, but its mulberry trees, mature at last, could be stripped of their leaves to feed the silk worms, and the four-story brick factory still housed state-of-the-art silk manufacturing machinery and a steam engine. One of the new purchasers was Joseph Conant, an experienced silk manufacturer from Mansfield, Connecticut, who had managed the property for the previous two years. Another was Samuel Lapham Hill, a Connecticut cotton manufacturer. "Over the course of the year, as prospective partners were assembling," notes Clark, "the manufacturing project turned into a wider effort to promote social change by creating a community of reformers."[4] Their "utopia" would be built on a solid economic base for, as a convention of New England silk growers pointed out, "inasmuch as in America and China the mulberry tree is found in the native forests, it is a manifest indication of Divine Providence, that this country, as well as China, was designed to be a great silk growing country."[5]

The Chinese domesticated the silkworm, *Bombyx mori*, over five thousand years ago, and China is the origin of most of the world's silk today, but over the millennia silk has also been raised and manufactured throughout the world's temperate zone, from Sweden and Russia to Italy and France to Madagascar and Brazil.[6] When the NAEI embarked on it, silk in America was not a new idea: its time had come and gone—over and over again.

From 1619, when King James I sent silkworms to Jamestown, until the Revolution, when more pressing concerns pushed silk growing aside, interest in and production of silk in the southern colonies waxed and waned in inverse proportion to the price of tobacco.[7] James had hoped that sericulture—the cultivation of the silkworm and the mulberry tree—would supplant tobacco and wipe out smoking, "A custom lothsome to the eye, hatefull to the Nose, harmefull to the braine, dangerous to the Lungs, and in the blacke stinking fume thereof, neerest resembling the horrible Stigian smoke of the pit that is bottomelesse."[8] In the end, tobacco wiped out the silkworm.[9]

Most of the silk raised in the southern colonies was destined for English mills, which may account for the colonists' lack of interest in it. Benjamin Franklin and others encouraged domestic manufacture, but their efforts foundered. Silk growing survived the Revolution only in Connecticut, where it had just begun. Encouraged by such practitioner-advocates as Ezra Stiles, the president of Yale University, raising silkworms and reeling silk from their cocoons became routine household chores, especially in Mansfield and other towns in the northeastern part of the state. "Not only the care of the silkworms, but the manufacture of silk, and in most cases its sale, were part of the business of the matron of the house," recalled Alfred Lilly, a Mansfield resident who later moved to Northampton to work for the NAEI's successor company. "Trade of that period took largely the form of barter. Having dyed her silk with her own hands, the matron repaired to the country merchant to exchange it for dry goods or groceries."[10]

Although the work was seasonal—silkworms were raised only in the spring—it was extensive and intensive. A few families raised as much as 130 pounds of silk in a year. That is, they raised 390,000 silkworms (each bushel of cocoons yields a pound of silk, and 3,000 cocoons fill a bushel.) And 5,000 mulberry trees: one pound of leaves feeds forty worms, and a mature mulberry tree produces two pounds in a season. But if the quantity of this household production was impressive, its quality was not. Lilly explains, "Compared with the Italian sewing silk, the American was inferior. . . . Consumers found the thread too fine and of an uneven size, that gave it a rough appearance. Frequently the great objection was urged that there was too much floss upon it. The color was often defective, both as to shade and permanence."[11] Nevertheless, as a sideline the work was profitable.

The industrial revolution was, at its start, a revolution in textile production, and if cotton could be manufactured successfully with power machinery, why not silk? America's first silk mill was built in Mansfield in 1810 by the brothers Rodney and Horatio Hanks; it soon closed, but a full-scale replica of this tiny factory still runs in Henry Ford's Greenfield Village near Detroit. The Hankses' second mill failed too, but a third Mansfield effort, the Mansfield Silk Company, formed in 1827 or 1828 for the "manufacture of silk by machinery," lasted a decade and had a greater impact. "This vigorous undertaking aroused, far and near, an interest in the industry, both as to culture and manufacture," the silk historian Linus Pierpont Brockett opined in 1876. "It stimulated the efforts of the other pioneers in the business, and made a permanent impression as to the solid reality of the silk manufacture in this country."[12] The partners in this undertaking included Lilly's father and NAEI cofounder Joseph Conant.

The problems the Mansfield Silk Company encountered were also instructive, or should have been. "The machinery was very crude," Lilly explained, and ". . . proved inadequate for the manufacture of American silk as that was then reeled." The company imported raw silk for a time until an English visitor explained "the true process of reeling" to the manufacturers. Now the company could use cocoons raised in Mansfield, but the improved quality of its products also increased the demand for them. To keep up, the factory had to operate year round, and this required a much larger supply of raw silk than Mansfield's seasonal sericulture could supply. They decided to raise silkworms all summer.

The Mansfield Silk Company was unaware, perhaps, that raising successive crops of worms required great skill and more luck. For best results, the eggs of the *Bombyx mori* silk moth must be kept in a cool place for months after they are laid.[13] Traditional silk growers stored the eggs over the winter and brought them to hatching temperature in the spring when the mulberry trees set out their first tiny leaves. To raise successive crops of worms in a single season, they had to keep eggs laid the previous season in cold storage much longer, a difficult feat in the days before refrigeration. The problems were not confined to storage: silkworms are sensitive to temperature, and worms that thrive in the spring may perish in the summer heat. "You have with great propriety discarded [the foreign writers'] artificial heat, thermometers, barometers, hygrometers, and all their variety of troublesome methods, minute regulations and useless implements, which make the culture of silk a difficult and intricate science," Peter Du Ponceau wrote to the Massachusetts sericulturist Jonathan Cobb in 1831, who proudly reprinted the letter in his manual.[14] But in fact the culture of silk was just that.

Compounding the problems of raising its own silk, the Mansfield Silk Company attempted to weave it, but silk was too delicate for the power looms of that day. Distracted by difficulties with moth and cloth, the harried owners neglected the intermediate step, the manufacture of thread. Their competitors filled the gap, with the help of improved thread-making machinery devised by Nathan Rixford, a Mansfield mechanic.[15] At the end of the decade, the company closed.

Meanwhile, in Northampton, the Northampton Silk Company was attracting visitors too. Before its founder, Samuel Whitmarsh, moved to town in 1830, sericulture had been a minor cottage industry throughout the Connecticut Valley, though not on the Mansfield scale. Dr. Daniel Stebbins was one of several citizens who raised silkworms and mulberry trees on his own property.[16] Stebbins was a friend of Samuel Whitmarsh and his brother Thomas, which may explain why they left the successful tailoring business they had established in New York and settled in Northampton. Whatever their inspiration, Northampton would never be the same. With Samuel Whitmarsh, Charles Sheffeld remarked in *A History of Florence*, "to reach a conclusion was to act upon it."[17] Within a few years he had built a cocoonery, or silkworm nursery, for two million silkworms, and two long greenhouses for mulberry shoots on his large estate near the center of town.

If Whitmarsh was aware of the Mansfield Silk Company's misadventures, he was unfazed. In 1835, with the support of New York and Connecticut backers, he bought property along the Mill River, including an old linseed oil mill (figure 2), and commissioned Rixford to fit it out with silk machinery.

FIGURE 2. Samuel Whitmarsh's first silk mill, 1834. From L. P. Brockett, *The Silk Industry in America*, 1876.

FIGURE 3. Whitmarsh's brick factory, later the boarding house and silk factory of the Northampton Association. From Charles A. Sheffeld, ed., *A History of Florence, Massachusetts*.

That autumn he toured Europe to visit silk farms and factories in France, Italy, and Switzerland, and brought mulberry seedlings and packets of seeds back with him.[18] Soon he moved his machinery out of the oil mill and into a new four-story brick factory (figure 3) that later became the residence, as well as the manufactory, of the NAEI. In the factory, steam powered the looms (probably built by Gamaliel Gay, who patented a power silk loom in 1835). Of the nine steam engines in western Massachusetts in 1838, Whitmarsh owned two:[19] a five-horsepower engine in the factory, and a single-horsepower engine in his cocoonery.

My Dear Father, I am writing you this letter in the belfry of the factory there is a beautiful view of the river and meadows . . . , wrote Mary Stetson.[20] The scale of Whitmarsh's ambition is evident when we consider the varied activities the NAEI later carried on there. "In the basement was the laundry; on the floor above or second story, besides two rooms given to silk manufacturing, was a room fitted up with 'bunks' in which several men slept," noted Sheffeld. "On the third floor at one end was the kitchen and long dining room, and at the other end were several sleeping rooms. The 'finishing room,' where the silk was skeined and packed, and the 'Community Store' were on this floor also. The fourth story was divided into sitting and sleeping rooms for families and single persons."[21] The Stetson family was one of several that would live on the fourth floor.

Whitmarsh encountered predictable difficulties and created others of his own. Only a few workers stayed for more than two seasons.[22] His newly planted mulberry trees could not yet be stripped of their leaves, so he imported large quantities of raw silk and bought leaves and cocoons, reeled or unreeled, from local farmers. Imported silk was expensive and the quality of the domestic silk uneven, making manufacture even more problematic. Nevertheless, Whitmarsh filled a little manual (figure 4) on what he called the "American System" of sericulture with exhortations to farmers to raise more trees: "Be not alarmed by the frequent croakings about the high price of labor in this country and the impossibility of raising silk, in competition with other countries; it is too late in the day for any such arguments. . . . I urge you all to plant mulberries in the full assurance that they will be wanted."[23]

SUCH STATEMENTS lend credence to charges that selling mulberry trees interested Whitmarsh more than manufacturing silk. "The actual fact was

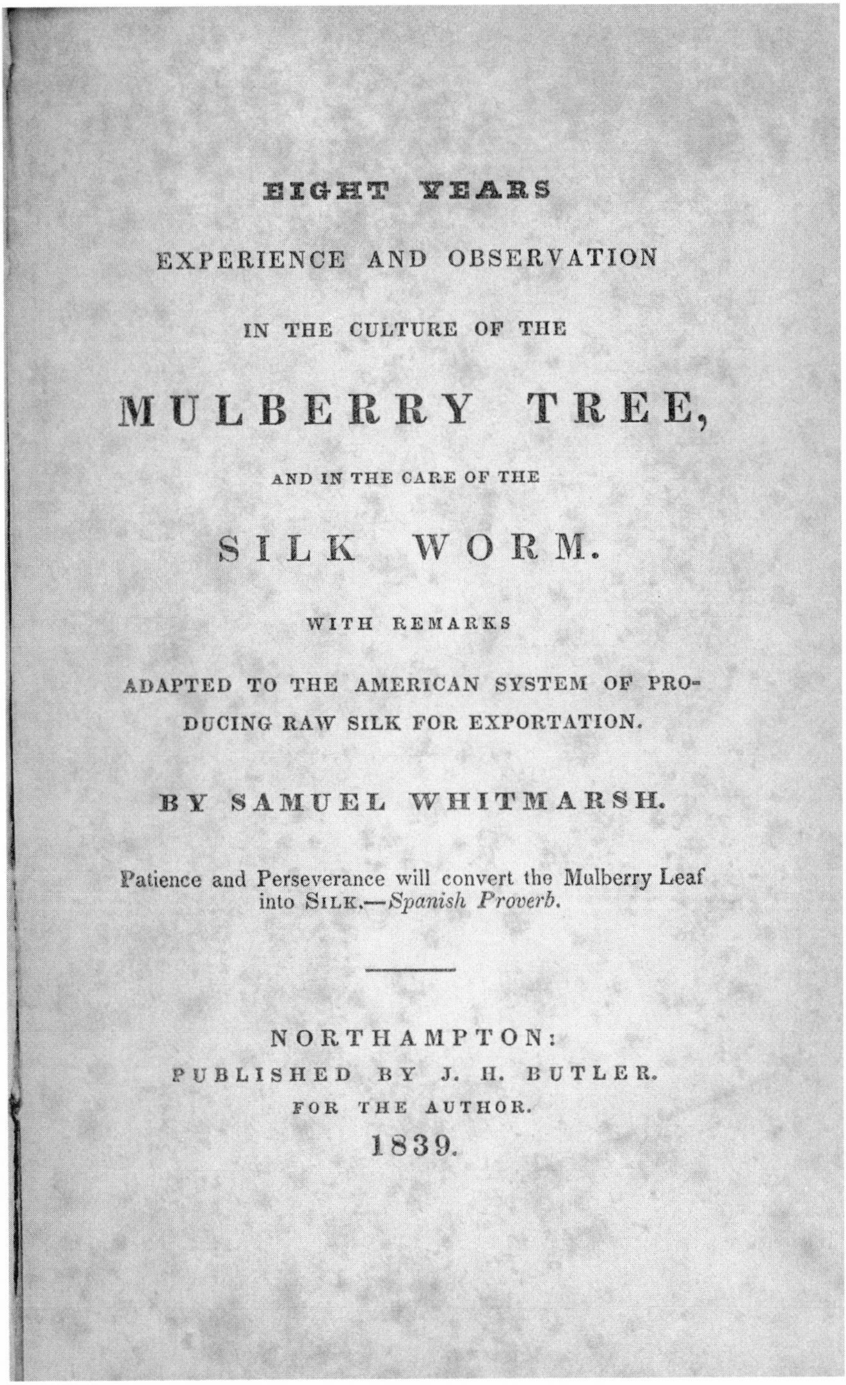

EIGHT YEARS

EXPERIENCE AND OBSERVATION

IN THE CULTURE OF THE

MULBERRY TREE,

AND IN THE CARE OF THE

SILK WORM.

WITH REMARKS

ADAPTED TO THE AMERICAN SYSTEM OF PRODUCING RAW SILK FOR EXPORTATION.

BY SAMUEL WHITMARSH.

Patience and Perseverance will convert the Mulberry Leaf into SILK.—*Spanish Proverb.*

NORTHAMPTON:
PUBLISHED BY J. H. BUTLER.
FOR THE AUTHOR.
1839.

FIGURE 4. *Eight Years Experience and Observation in the Culture of the Mulberry Tree, and in the Care of the Silk Worm, with remarks adapted to the American system of producing raw silk for exportation,* by Samuel Whitmarsh, Northampton, 1839.

that the manufacturing there, at that period, was carried on for a mere show," a weaver in Whitmarsh's factory later told Brockett. "The works were overrun with visitors, and the appearance of an active business in manufacturing silk filled their minds with notions of the wealth to be derived from silk culture. In short, the mills were kept running in order to increase the sale of mulberry trees."[24] Whether or not the accusation was justified, speculation in mulberry seedlings, especially the *Morus multicaulis* variety that Whitmarsh avidly promoted, drove up prices throughout New England until the plants sold for their weight in gold.[25] When the bubble burst, Whitmarsh and hundreds of others lost the fortunes they had lashed to these slender stalks. In 1840, only a year after the publication of his book, the adventure was over. Whitmarsh withdrew from the Northampton Silk Company and went on to fail at other enterprises.

The year before, when his superintendent resigned, Whitmarsh recruited Joseph Conant to run the factory. Conant brought his sons-in-law Orwell Chaffee and Earle Dwight Swift, both experienced silk manufacturers, from Mansfield with him. Edward Vallentine, a young English dyer who emigrated to Mansfield in 1838, moved to Northampton at the same time. On Whitmarsh's departure, the company's trustees leased the property to Conant, who continued the operations on a reduced scale. Until it was sold, he contracted with Vallentine for dyeing and with Stebbins for mulberry leaves.

The failures of the Mansfield and Northampton companies did not augur well for the founders of the Northampton Association as they took over the orchards and factory and resumed raising and manufacturing silk. But many NAEI members came from silk-raising areas of Connecticut. Joseph Conant grew up in a silk-raising milieu; Dolly Witter Stetson's mother raised silkworms when Dolly was a child. They knew, and thought they knew how to avoid, the mistakes of the past.[26] A residential community, with a stable labor supply, would minimize turnover. With proper care, Whitmarsh's neglected orchards could be revived to feed the worms.[27] A spate of patents in silk machinery—reelers, winders, twisters, and looms—promised a new level of technical perfection in manufacture.[28]

"THE SILK INSECT affords a display of the wisdom of Divine Providence in the adaptation of means to ends, calculated to excite high interest and admiration," gushed Cobb. "The extraordinary effect produced by this little animal in the short space of six weeks is no less than the conversion of the vegetable substance of the mulberry leaf into threads of rich and durable silk."[29] Ralph Waldo Emerson likened this miracle to the mind's conversion of experience into thought.[30] For the Northampton Association, however, the hoped-for miracle was the conversion of leaves into food for the table.

"We number thirty men above the age of 18; 26 women, with 6 more, hired to work in our silk room; 46 children under the age of 18," wrote David Mack in April, 1843.[31] In 1844 a visitor noted about twenty small girls and boys working in the silk-growing department "who, in the ordinary state of society, would be of no service whatever to their parents or themselves."[32] The NAEI accorded rights to the children along with their responsibilities. Children over the age of five, including Almira, Mary, Sarah, and George Stetson, were paid for their labor, could hold stock in their own names, and were permitted to speak at community meetings (whether they did is not recorded).

At first, the silk department appointed two directors, one for silk growing and one for manufacture, but within a few months of the Stetsons' arrival in Northampton, there were four sub-departments: for silk growing, manufacture, dyeing, and finishing and sales. The Stetson letters speak to the work of each of them.

Silk Growing: Hatching, Feeding, Worrying, Cocooning, Reeling

I am in the cocoonery to work I like it very well . . . wrote Almira to her father.[33] "The children did the work, under the supervision of a couple of men to keep us in order, and see that it was not all play and no work," Almira's cousin Anna Benson recalled many years later. "The long, rather low cocoonery had shelves on each side of a passageway, running lengthwise with it, upon which the eggs were hatched, and the boys brought the leaves in baskets, while the girls distributed them over the shelves, and worms soon devoured them. The work was clean and wholesome, done at regular times, between school hours, and really enjoyable."[34]

The NAEI's cocoonery, built in 1843, was 100 feet long, 25 feet wide, and high enough for two tiers of shelves to hold the growing worms. It probably looked much like Whitmarsh's (figure 5), but Almira's fall from the upper level in 1844 suggests that the upper tiers of shelving were mounted on parallel platforms instead of on a second floor. The legend in Whitmarsh's drawing refers to vents in the roof, walls, and flooring. Like Cobb and other American silk growers, Whitmarsh scoffed at most details, but he understood the importance of circulating air.

To persuade the silkworm to spin a cocoon of good quality, the caretaker must anticipate its needs at each stage of the life cycle (figure 6), from egg to larva to pupa to moth. The work in the cocoonery included hatching the silkworm eggs, chopping mulberry leaves and feeding the worms, keeping

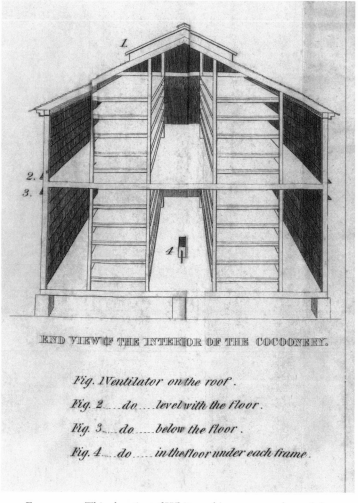

FIGURE 5. This elevation of Whitmarsh's cocoonery formed the frontispiece of his *Eight Years Experience*. . . .

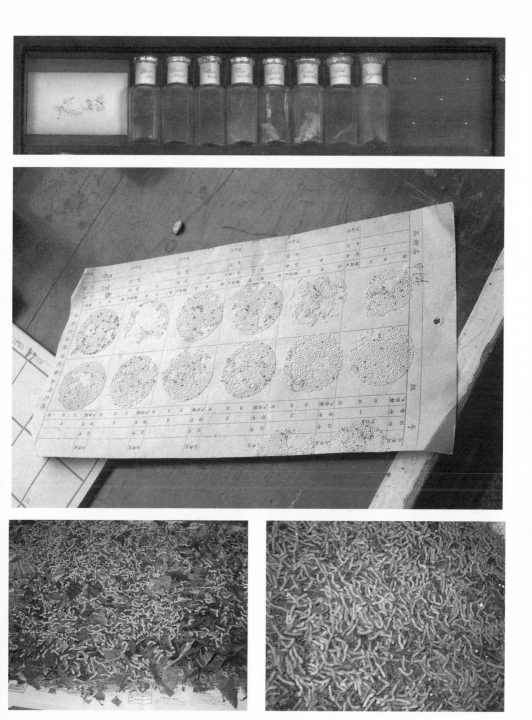

FIGURE 6. (*Top*) The Stetson silk box: jars that once displayed the silkworm's life cycle, labeled One Day, Three Days, One Week, Two Weeks, Three Weeks, Four Weeks, Silk in Worm, and Chrysalis. Photograph by Stan Sherer. Silkworms in Zhenjiang, China, 2002: (*center*) hatching; (*bottom left*) about two weeks old; (*bottom right*) about four weeks old. Photographs by Marjorie Senechal.

the cocoonery aired and cleaning the trays on which the silkworms munched leaves and excreted waste, preparing the shelves for cocooning, and unwinding the silk from the cocoons.

In charge of all this was Oliver Paine, appointed director of the silk-growing department in 1842 at the age of twenty-two. He had joined the NAEI two days after its founding because, he explained in a personal statement, the Association promised a "better way of lieving [sic]."[35] Paine had been "brought up in the woods" in Chesterfield, Massachusetts, a village in the hills northwest of Northampton, and started school at the age of twelve, after the death of his father. He left school to go to work after only a few years and "learnt the Silk bisiness" from Whitmarsh on the job. We may assume he followed Whitmarsh's practices unless experience dictated otherwise—which, the Stetson letters show, it sometimes did.

From one ounce of eggs, black or gray dots about the size of sesame seeds, hatch 40,000 hungry worms. Their appetites increase dramatically as they pass through the larval stage, which makes caring for large numbers of worms impossible unless they are hatched at the same time. Around the world, in traditional sericulture societies, women brought the eggs from cold storage to hatching temperature by placing them in sachets tucked into their bosoms. In nineteenth-century America, setting the eggs in a warm room, out of direct sunlight, was the preferred technique.

Had they brought magnifying glasses to the cocoonery, the community children would have noted that the newly hatched worms looked like spiky black dragons, but within a few days turned gray and then white. The larval period comprises five stages, called *instars*: black dragon, tiny gray worm, large white worm, larger white worm, and much larger white worm. The stages are demarcated by a twelve-to-twenty-four-hour pause while the silkworm stops eating to shed its skin; only then can the caretakers rest. In the fifth instar, the noise in the cocoonery is deafening, as the worms chomp noisily around the clock. *Mary says that they are so much engaged feeding the worms that they have no time to knit purses but in school and they are tierd then and dont wish too knit. . . .*[36]

"Work was interspersed with our lessons," George Stetson reminisced. "We gathered the mulberry leaves for the silkworms, being watched over and directed by a member appointed for that purpose."[37] Whitmarsh to the contrary, details mattered. "Strip the leaves upwards, not downwards, as this injures the buds," instructed William Kenrick, a horticulturist in eastern

Massachusetts.[38] "When you begin a tree strip it complete; leave not a leaf, take all, as it injures the tree less unequally." And after stripping, the leaves must be properly cared for. "Wet leaves are injurious, they cause disease," Kenrick warned. "When gathered they should be preserved from wilting . . . being often turned, and aired, and shifted alternately to new and dry parts of the floor." "We are directed to '*chop* the leaves small for the worms,'" snorted Whitmarsh (see figure 7). "For this I can see no good reason, but rather many against it. I do not practice it myself, nor do I recommend it." Paine knew better. Dolly told James, . . . *one day last week they cut 200 bushells of foilage before tea and all hands turned out after tea they were in such a drive.*[39]

The NAEI raised several crops of worms in the summer of 1844. *We had 25 bushels of cocoons of the first best quality they came off very well indeed much better than we feared having so much unfavorable weather and new hands put on to feed, and all other things considered we went beyond of best expectations,* Almira wrote. *We have a larger crop on now and very ~~unfa~~ bad weather indeed I do not know what will be the effect but we are rather fearful that they will not do as well as the first crop.*[40] Bad weather and hot weather were only two of many things to worry about. An ancient Chinese manual warned of sixteen "injurious things to silkworms." The Chinese strictures echo in the first English-language sericulture manual, a book-length poem written in 1599,

Colde sometimes kills them, sometimes ouer-heate,
Raine, oyle, salt, old and wet, and musty foode,
The smel of onyons, leekes, garlick, and new wheat,
Shrill sound of trumpets, drums, or cleauing woode:

Yea some of them are of such weaknesse great,
That whisperings soft of men or falling floud,
Doth so their harts and senses ouer-wheele,
That often headlong from the boord they reele.[41]

"The Rush Letter"—a report by the secretary of the Treasury, in 1828, on the growth and manufacture of silk in the United States—restated the injurious things as early nineteenth-century silk growers understood them: "errors in hatching the eggs, and treatment of very young worms; bad air of the district in which they were bred; impurity in the air in which they are kept, arising from deficient ventilation, from exhalations of the litter of the

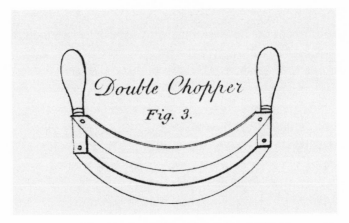

FIGURE 7. A tool for chopping mulberry leaves. From U.S. Treasury Dept.,
Growth and Manufacture of Silk, 1828.

worms, and of their manure, which has been permitted to accumulate; too
close crowding, owing to which cause their spiracles, or breathing holes,
were stopped, and the expiration and inspiration of air prevented; the quality
and quantity of food; improper change of food; peculiar constitution of the
air in certain seasons, against which no precautions can avail; frequent
changes of temperature in the room in which they are kept."[42] There is no
mention of bacteria, viruses, parasites, or other live modes of transmission:
their role in disease was not yet understood.

Whitmarsh had nothing to say about silkworm diseases, though others
struggled to cope with them.[43] But he gave some thought to the weather.
"Do thunder storms affect the worms?" he asked rhetorically in his little
book. No, he concluded, the problem was not thunderstorms, but inadequate
ventilation. He had "carefully observed them during repeated severe thunder
storms, and have tried experiments which prove to my mind, that the ill
effects which have been supposed to be caused by thunder, have arisen from
suffocation" because "it is natural for anyone in the approach of a thunder
cloud to fly to the windows—like sailors in a squall—to make all snug before
the thunder comes."[44] Hence the vents in his cocoonery. But on tobacco he
was emphatic: "You must not mention *Tobacco* in the presence of silk worms.
In regard to this drug they show good taste: *they had rather die than smell it.*"[45]

Silkworms that manage to survive heat, cold, thunder, trumpets, onyons,
bad air, and tobacco have but one goal: the nirvana of the cocoon (figure 8).

FIGURE 8. Detail of the Stetson silk box: broken cocoons and raw silk skein.
Photograph by Stan Sherer.

Throughout its instars, the silkworm converts mulberry leaves into a liquid protein, which it stores in a special pair of glands. When it is time for its metamorphosis, it looks for a bundle of straw or twigs on which to spin. Having climbed onto this—the first and only physical exercise of its short life—the worm nods and bobs while ejecting two fine streams of liquid silk from spinnerets on either side of its head. A gummy substance, called sericin, ejected with the silk, binds the streams together into a single filament and the filament into a nearly watertight cocoon. The silkworm's human care-taker provides the bundles for the worms to climb on and ensures that they are not too close together: overlapping cocoons cannot be unwound.

Inside the cocoon, the silkworm rearranges itself into a moth which, left to nature, will emerge after a few weeks through a hole it creates with a special enzyme. The moth's only adult task is to initiate a new life cycle. Unlike the Monarch butterfly, which sips nectar and vacations in Mexico, the silkmoth can neither fly nor eat nor drink. After mating, the female lays about 300 eggs; within a week or so, both males and females die. The Chi-nese discovered, those millennia ago, that by *not* leaving this to nature—by intervening before the moth emerges—they could unwind the entire cocoon into a filament up to half a mile long and, after processing, use it as thread. Sericin, solid at room temperature, softens in simmering water. (According to one legend, a Chinese empress discovered this when a cocoon fell from a mulberry tree into her cup of steaming tea.) The softened cocoon can be unwound, or reeled, with the living pupa inside; alternatively, the pupa can be smothered, by steaming, baking, or prolonged exposure to intense hot sunshine, and the cocoon stored and reeled later. A few moths may be allowed to emerge, to provide eggs for the next silk-growing season, but the NAEI seems to have bought its eggs from dealers each year.

I believe the silk growing business is quite lively they have a large crop just ready to wind . . . , wrote Dolly.[46] Unwinding the silk of a single cocoon is straightforward, but the manufacture of thread is not. The filament ejected by one silkworm is too thin and too uneven to be used for sewing or weaving. Both defects are repaired simultaneously by the process of reeling, in which several cocoons are unwound together (enough sericin remains to bind them) and new filaments added as old ones thin out or break. The reeling may be done with a simple wheel or with a more sophisticated machine powered by hand, water, steam, or—today—electricity. But whatever the machine, whatever the power source, the key mechanism was the human hand. It took years to learn to reel properly (estimates range from five years to twenty). Paine won prizes for his raw silk and reeling machines in local fairs,[47] but "it is, and ever will be, in vain to talk of 'the inventive genius of Americans, doing away with the difficulty of reeling'," Whitmarsh observed with uncharacteristic appreciation of the need for skill. "*Practice* makes perfect, and when the first principles are understood, time and practice only, will perfect it."[48]

In the summer of 1843, her first at the NAEI, Oliver Paine taught Almira and three other girls how to reel.[49] In 1844, when her letters begin, she was one of the community's most experienced reelers.

Let's imagine Almira reeling for a minute or two using the machine shown in figure 9. Sitting on a low stool (not shown) in front of the basin, she tosses two dozen or so cocoons into the simmering water. As they float about, she stirs the pot with a stalk of broom straw until the fuzzy silk surrounding them—the silk that the silkworm ejects first, as it begins to spin—unravels and clings to it. (This "waste silk" is not reeled, but it can be spun like flax, wool, or cotton.) She is hot and miserable: the water in the basin is nearly boiling, and she must plunge her hands into it again and again. In the summer of 1843, the water was heated by a fire under the basin; 1844 was better in that respect. *I think it will be a very pleasant part to reel, (compared to what it was last summer) as the warter to be heated by steam so no heat will be in the room.*[50] "A steam pipe passes through the vessels containing the water in which the

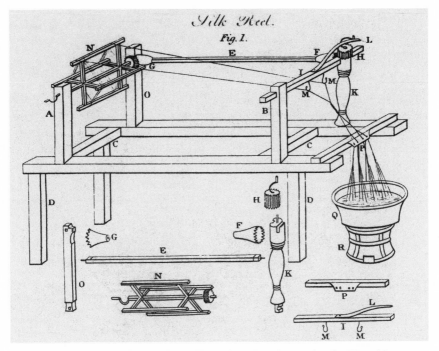

FIGURE 9. Schematic drawing of the Piedmont Reeler, used in the United States at the time of the Northampton Association. From U.S. Treasury Dept., *Growth and Manufacture of Silk*, 1828.

cocoons are immersed, preserving it at an equal warmth," Kenrick reported after visiting Whitmarsh's cocoonery. "These vessels are emptied at once by a cock at the bottom; when the water becomes discolored, it is drawn off. Other cocks placed above supply them with both hot and cold water when needed."[51]

When Almira has gathered the ends of sixteen unraveling cocoons and removed the waste silk, she divides the filaments into groups of four and passes them through the holes in the metal plate on the machine, above the basin. Then she joins the four groups into two, eight strands in each; thanks to the sericin, they bond quickly. After winding these two strands around each another several times, she passes them through the eyelets below the bar and ties them onto the reel at the back. The holes, the winding, and the eyelets clean the silk and squeeze out some of the water it absorbed in the basin. (The silk will be cleaned again before it is dyed.) The most ingenious feature of the reeling machine is the traverse bar in front, to which the eyelets are attached. Moving back and forth horizontally, it spreads the silk out on the reeler to dry so that the next layer doesn't stick to it.

In the summer of 1843, the reeler Almira used was like the one shown, its handle turned by one of the community children. The child had to pay attention to her work: the cocoons would leap out of the water and hit the metal plate if she turned the crank too quickly, while if she turned it too slowly, the filaments would tangle. In 1844, steam may or may not have turned the reel; steam both turned the reels and heated the water in Whitmarsh's cocoonery, but other cocooneries of that time used it just to heat the water, if they used it at all.

Whatever the power source, Almira can't look up to watch the reel or admire her work: she must keep her eyes on the cocoons. When the skeins (figure 10) have reached the desired size, she removes them, tosses more cocoons into the basin, and starts the process all over again.

Manufacture: Doubling and Twisting

After reeling, the first step of manufacture is to wind the skeins of raw silk onto bobbins. *Mary Ann Smith says tell Uncle James that three of us can wind five ounces per Day day with Mr Havens help; . . . The silk manufactory I think is looking up — two new winders are comeing tomorrow.*[52]

The skeins of raw silk were slipped onto the rails of the winding machine (figure 11), an end of each skein drawn over the porcelain guides on the traverse bar and attached to the bobbins above. After the silk was wound onto bobbins, the bobbins were placed on the spindles of a "doubling" machine that twisted the threads of two (or more) bobbins together and wound the doubled thread onto a single bobbin or reel. To make the thread stronger, two or more doubled threads were again wound together and twisted, either in the same or in the opposite direction (handspinners know this step as plying). There were as many variations on doubling and twisting as there were types of thread: the variations defined the types. *They have got a beautiful lot of sewing and saddlers silk ready for you but they would like to keep it to show to the people that may be here . . . ,* Dolly reported.[53] "Sewings" was used for hand sewing (the first sewing machine patent would be granted to Elias Howe in 1846); "saddlers" was used for heavy duty stitching, such as saddles. Sewings was twisted in the same direction twice; saddlers was reverse twisted.

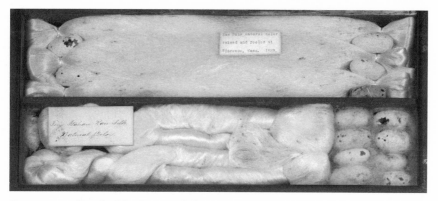

FIGURE 10. Detail of the Stetson silk box: skeins of Florence (Mass.) and Italian raw silk. Photograph by Stan Sherer.

The doubling and twisting machine the NAEI used was based on a design less than fifty years old. From medieval times through the seventeenth century, Italian silk manufacturers fiercely guarded the secret of doubling and twisting on an industrial scale. Their machine consisted of two room-sized concentric circular cages. The stationary outer cage held both the bobbins of threads to be doubled and twisted and the bobbins or reels onto which they were wound. The inner cage, attached to a center pole turned by a water wheel or donkey below the mill floor, held paddle wheels that turned the bobbins and reels as it whirled around. The Italian monopoly on mechanical "throwing," as doubling and twisting were called, was broken early in the eighteenth century by John Lombe, who copied the design and smuggled it home to England. But the simpler, belt-driven rectangular machine devised by the French inventor Jacques Vaucanson replaced the cages everywhere by the century's end. Subsequent improvements in the mechanism have not altered Vaucanson's basic design.

I work in the Silk Room now every day, Mary wrote.[54] The NAEI's version of Vaucanson's machine was patented by Harrison Holland in 1838.[55] Holland, a partner in the Hanks brothers' short-lived second mill, had migrated with his wife and younger children from Mansfield to Northampton. Desperately poor, he and several of the children, including Josiah Gilbert Holland, the future poet and essayist, did odd jobs for Whitmarsh. After Whitmarsh departed, Harrison Holland continued to work, off and on, for the NAEI. The patent model for his "Silk Spinner" (figure 12) belongs to the permanent collection of the National Museum of American History in Washington, D.C.[56] The full-sized machine had, of course, many more spindles and was turned by a water wheel, not by a crank. Sarah Stetson alluded to the trials and tribulations of water power when she remarked, . . . *the cakes of ice came so abundantly that it filled the river and this morning Mr Atkins and Mr Haven and some boys went on the cakes in the river and pushed them down so that the wheel could run. . . .*[57]

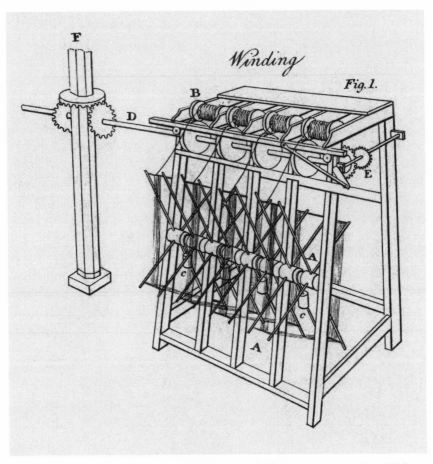

FIGURE 11. A machine for winding skeins onto bobbins, or vice versa. From U.S. Treasury Dept., *Growth and Manufacture of Silk*, 1828.

In his patent application, Holland stated that he had "invented, made and applied to use a certain machine or improvement in the spinning, doubling, and twisting of silk to be performed by one operation . . . ," the improvements being two: a device that would automatically stop the machine when a thread broke, and a simple method for changing the twist. When a thread broke, as often happened when the quality of the silk was poor, the girls tending the machine had to tie it and restart the twisting. Work in the silk room continued into the night. As Dolly noted, *Our new kitchen and dining*

Figure 12. Patent model for Harrison Holland's Silk Spinner, 1838.
Photograph by Stan Sherer.

*room are completed the latter of which was formily dedicated last Tuesday Evening
. . . brilliantly illuminated with hanging lamps borrowed for the occasion from the
silk room.*[58]

The Smithsonian patent model collection also includes a machine designed by Adam Brooks of Scituate, Massachusetts, intended for home use,
that reeled the cocoons and doubled and twisted the filaments into thread,
and Kenrick mentioned another by Gamaliel Gay.[59] Oliver Paine seems to
have tried something similar. Dolly told James, *Pain has got his reeling opperations started reeling onto bobbins or little reels about the size of bobbins whether it
answers his expectations or not I do not know.*[60] The patent record of the era is
like the Burgess Shale, replete with fossils of primitive life forms that failed
to evolve. None of the all-in-one machines stood the test of time.

Dyeing

After doubling and twisting, the thread was wound from the bobbins back
into skeins and sent to the Dye House. In June 1843, when the NAEI made
dyeing a separate sub-department, its director, James Atkins, was still a nov-
ice. The community had contracted with the expert dyer Edward Vallentine
the year before, but then decided, for financial or ideological reasons or both,
that their dyer should be one of themselves. Atkins, a new member and a
printer by trade, agreed to take the job, but dyeing, like reeling, required
years of apprenticeship. The ensuing drama is not recorded in the NAEI's
business letters and minutes, but other observers were less discreet.[61] When
Vallentine refused to train Atkins, the NAEI threatened to bring a competitor over from England. In October 1842, for the sum of one hundred dollars,
Vallentine gave in and signed a painfully detailed agreement in which he
promised to teach Atkins everything he knew within four months. But even
if Vallentine faithfully carried out his part of the bargain,[62] Atkins could not
have learned the subtleties of dyeing in that brief time any more than Almira
Stetson learned the art of reeling in one short summer. In 1843 David Mack
explained to a customer that the order he had placed for thread could not be
filled "because we intend to confine ourselves to staple colors."[63]

The work of the Dye House included cleaning and degumming the raw
silk, bleaching it, adding mordants, dyeing, and weighting. Degumming—
removing the remaining sericin—is essential if the silk is to be dyed, as
sericin imparts its own color to the silk.[64] The cocoons of some varieties of

Bombyx mori are "white" (of many shades, including pale pink and pale green), while others are "yellow" (ranging from the palest of ales to deep amber). In addition to stiffening and coloring the silk, sericin prevents the dye from being absorbed. To clean raw silk, the dyer hangs the skeins on a long pole and immerses them in a large vat of boiling soapy water. *James Atkins thinks that the castele soap is a great improvement in point of softness and lustre,* noted Dolly.[65] When the sericin has dissolved, he rinses the silk clean in the running river. (To prepare silk further for certain dyes, the dyer may also bleach it.) After cleaning, the skeins, still on the pole, are steeped in a water bath in which a mordant, usually alum, has been dissolved: mordants help the silk absorb the dye and make it colorfast. After soaking the silk in that solution for the requisite time, the dyer plunges it into a broth of water, dyes, metals, and other ingredients. When the desired hue has been achieved, he carries the pole to the river again, rinses the silk, and hangs it up to dry.

Before the discovery of synthetic dyes, all dyes were made from plants, animals, or minerals. From the dyer's point of view there were five primary colors, explained Elijah Bemiss in *The Dyers Companion* (1815), "blue, red, yellow, brown, and black. Each of these can furnish a great number of shades, from the lightest to the darkest; and from the combination of two or more of these different shades, arise all the colours in nature."[66] If the community's children visited the Dye House, they would have learned how brown dyes were made from tree bark (butternut, walnut, hickory, oak, chestnut, maple, and others), black dyes from logwood and additives such as "blue vitriol" and barks, yellow from fustic and other plants, blue from indigo, red from madder and from the insect cochineal.[67] Magically, it seemed—modern chemistry was in its infancy—these colors could be modified by the addition of certain colorless ingredients (figure 13). The children would also have learned how the dyer increased his palette by dyeing the silk first one color and then another.

Recipes for dyes resembled the food recipes in cookbooks, and were often included in them. Both are mystifyingly vague to modern eyes. To dye cloth green, said Bemiss,

> Take two pounds of fustick, boil well, till the strength is well out, then take out the chips, and add a quarter of a pound of allum, and six ounces of blueing, prepared as in receipt No. 6; stir it with the dye till it is well mixed, then handle your silk fifteen or twenty minutes: stir it lively, and keep it

open and loose in the dye; (silk should never be wenched as woollen goods) air, and if not deep enough, add a little more blueing; and if not yellow enough, then a little allum, run again fifteen minutes; then air, and if the colour suits, rince immediately.[68]

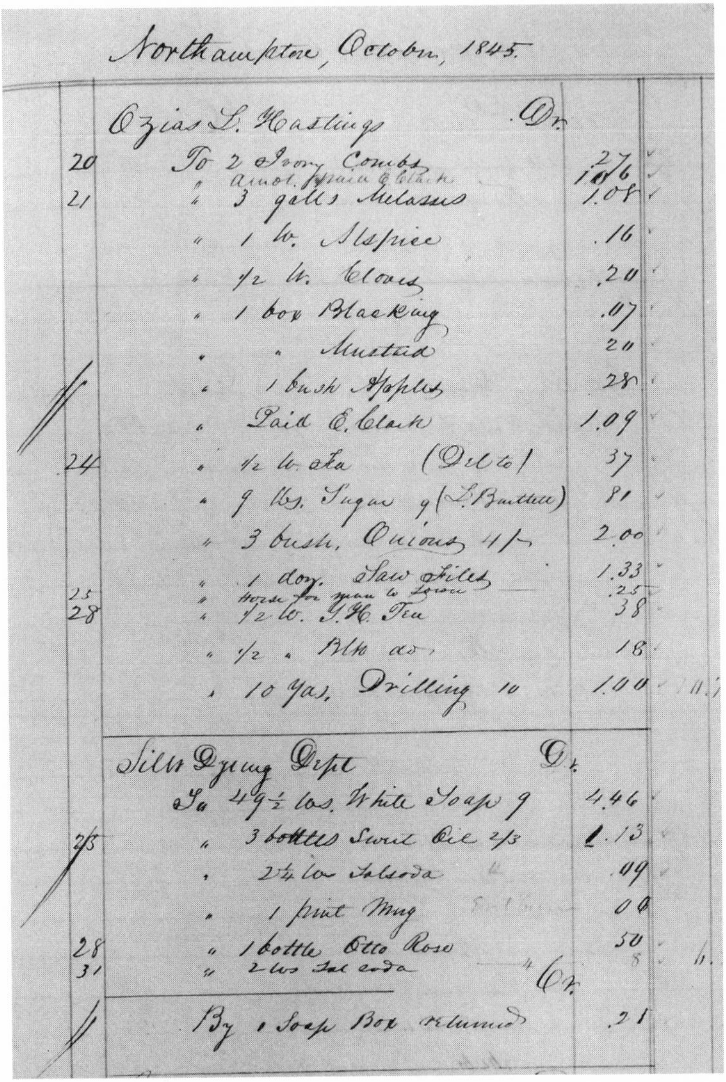
Northampton, October, 1845.

Ozias L. Hastings Dr.

20 To 2 Ivory Combs .27
" Amt. paid E. Clark 1.06
21 " 3 galls Melasses 1.08
" 1 lb. Allspice .16
" 1/2 lb. Cloves .20
" 1 box Blacking .07
" " Mustard 20
" 1 bush Apples 28
" Paid E. Clark 1.09
24 " 1/2 lb. Tea (Ditto) 37
" 9 lbs. Sugar 9 (L. Bartlett) 81
" 3 bush. Onions 4/- 2.00
" 1 doz. Saw Files 1.33
25 " Horse for man to town .25
28 " 1/2 lb. Y.H. Tea 38
" 1/2 " Blk do 18
" 10 yds. Drilling 10 1.00

Silk Dyeing Dept Dr.

To 49½ lbs. White Soap 9 4.46
25 " 3 bottles Sweet Oil 2/3 1.13
" 2¼ lbs Salsoda .09
" 1 pint Mug 06
28 " 1 bottle Otto Rose 50
31 " 2 lbs Sal soda 8

Cr.

By 1 Soap Box returned .21

Figure 13. A page from the record books of the Northampton Association's silk-dyeing department. American Antiquarian Society, Worcester, Mass.

Then there are 2 lbs 5½ oz of Green, wrote Almira. *I guess I wont say much about this, it will speak for itself.*[69]

Minus its sericin, silk weighed less when it left the Dye House than when it arrived. In 1843, NAEI leaders judged the losses unacceptably high;[70] some lots of silk may have been so badly dyed that they had to be thrown out, but Atkins was also unskilled at weighting, the technique of "restoring" the lost weight by adding extra ingredients. Dyers weighted silk to fool customers and to make silk, especially black silk, stronger and more colorfast.

There has been a German here that professes to/// [. . .] the art of Dying silk in the Italian manner/// [. . .] weighting it more than James has done with/// [. . .] less expense, Dolly informed James.[71] The Italians were masters of the ancient art: "in Milan in 1606 the entrepreneurs picked a furious fight with the dyers, even accusing them of adulterating black silks by adding nothing less than bacon fat, wine, olive oil, or honey to the regular dyes to give the silks greater weight and to save on raw materials, thus causing countless specks to appear on the cloths as soon as they were exposed to dust."[72] Brockett, writing in 1876, remarked that "the salts used to effect this increase, are compounds with iron, tin, and the alkalies as bases—mostly astringent salts, but among them are the cyanides, all of which are prompt and deadly poisons. The weight and apparent lustre of the fabric are preserved, and there is a semblance of silk with a good 'body' that attracts purchasers. Very brief wear reveals the deception."[73]

The "German dyer," L. H. Ploucquet, was well known in Connecticut, where he lived, and may have been recommended by customers there. He stayed at the NAEI for several months in the winter of 1844–1845: besides teaching Atkins to weight silk in the Italian manner, he dyed wool, cotton, and linen for local residents.[74] Despite Ploucquet's tutelage, Almira remained unimpressed with Atkins's colors. *. . . I think you will find the silk superior to any thing yet from Northampton especially the hundred skeins of <u>blue black</u>. we compared it with the Italian and could scarcely tell the difference (Oh what a lie).* But Ploucquet's weighting was effective: *We are getting off 50 pounds, like what you told James you wanted so that you could take it and throw it across the room and have it ~~lay~~ lye as ~~y~~ it fell. We might throw it to Boston and ha[ve?] it land safely at 228 Wash[ington] St. and not a skein would be tangled. It is exactly like the Italian in this respect. . . .*[75]

Finishing and Sales

Although its main product was and would be sewing thread, the Association briefly considered manufacturing other silk goods too. "Bolting cloth," a sturdy silk gauze, was quickly supplanting wire mesh in wheat milling machines. The NAEI signed a contract with Rollin White of Vermont to use the bolting cloth loom he had patented in 1842, but then withdrew from it. A plan to manufacture warp and weft thread for weavers also failed to materialize.[76] The Stetson letters refer only to sewings and saddlers.

Mary Cone has gone to Springfield and I do not know when she is to return Mary Ann Smith is in very miserable health and is going to Hartford tomorrow So you see that skeining is left to Susanna Bassett I believe however that they have hired Mrs Bottom to help . . . Dolly wrote.[77] In the days before sewing machines, silk thread was sold in skeins, as embroidery thread is today. In the finishing room, the newly dyed—and very long—skeins were rewound into shorter ones and then packed (figure 14) and sent to James Stetson in Boston by stage. Almira wrapped the skeins in ¼ lb papers "which is our common way of putting up our silk when we do not tie it up in hundred bunches."[78] *Dont laugh at the way they are done up for I did them and there is no one else that knows any thing about it to teach me. If we are to do up our silk so, I think I shall have to go to Boston to learn or else have very explicit instruction by letter.*[79]

JUDGING FROM the dates on the letters, boxes of silk were sent to James at least every other week. In addition, the NAEI bartered silk for goods from local merchants, and community members traveling as abolitionist lecturers carried silk goods to sell to sympathizers. The NAEI placed advertisements—announcements, in those days—in newspapers and abolitionist newsletters. An ad in the *Liberator* stated, "Sewings, Saddlers, silk and Twist for sale wholesale and retail. 2½ Hanover St. by J. A. Stetson ONE OF ITS MEMBERS We strongly recommend the examination and purchase of this silk to all who are in want of any."[80]

The Hampshire, Hampden, and Franklin Agricultural Society's annual fair, held in Northampton each October, was also an advertising venue, and the prizes and premiums were announced in the *Hampshire Gazette.* In October 1842, NAEI silk thread won prizes in this fair and in the exhibition of the American Institute of New York; a Hartford, Connecticut, newspaper remarked that a sample of sewing silk from the community was "the most

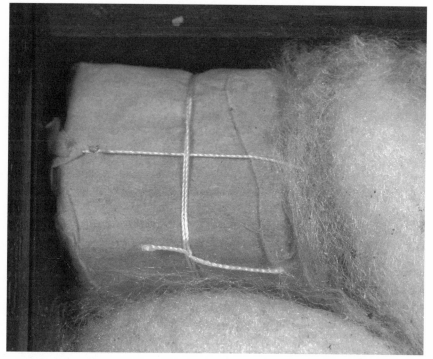

FIGURE 14. Detail of the Stetson silk box: a package illustrating finished silk.
Photograph by Stan Sherer.

splendid specimen of American excellence in reeling, spinning and dyeing silk that we have ever seen."[81] Oliver Paine's reels and raw silk continued to win prizes for the next few years, but after a modest showing in 1843 the NAEI did not enter, or was not awarded prizes for, its sewings.[82]

"When the cold weather drove us indoors . . . we were taught sewing, braiding straw, knitting silk and beaded purses, and other useful things," Anna Benson recalled.[83] The children's first purses were not, in any case, effective advertisements for NAEI silk: *I have made up the purses that were knit last winter they are mostly poor silk and many of them poorly knit.* But their knitting had improved, as Dolly added, *I thought it better to make tassils than to sew on the drops that would do for the better ones that the girls are now making.* . . . [84] The purses would be sold. *Mr Mack says that a new kind of purse was introduced at a fair in Boston made small and attached to a clasp and selling for 2 or 3 dollars apiece — he thinks that you had better look about and obtain one as a sample if there can be so much profit on them.*[85] Mary wrote later, *I have knit a purse for Aunt Tyler and had it carried into the fair in town but I did n[ot] get it in early eneough to get the prize.*[86] The NAEI's knit purses were never cited in the prize lists.

CLARK HAS described the community's financial difficulties in detail, showing how the business of utopia became, by 1845, "locked in a descending spiral from which it could not escape."[87] The NAEI's struggles with silk production were the single most important cause of the nightmare. At an unpleasant community meeting in May 1845, James Stetson blamed poor sales on "an insufficient supply of silk and sometimes unsuitable silk," James Atkins complained of delays in obtaining suitable dyes, and "Mr. Stetson and others expressed disappointment that this department [silk growing] had fallen so far short of the estimated earnings at the commencement of this year without explanation." In the finishing room, the tension rose. Almira snapped: *[with] every one handling the silk and misplaceing it. I think I ought to have some praise for ever getting it in to the box in any shape whatever. You wanted to know about the weight I will send it as I have it—but I cannot ~~vough~~ vouch for its correctness. I packed the box Thursday afternoon and Friday morning when I got there I found James A—had been to it, and how or what he did with it I do not know. I had a really crying spell about the silk and the box after it ~~wh~~ went away but it did no good.*[88] Under pressure, the utopians panicked and, like countless silk manufacturers before and since, stooped to decidedly nonutopian practices: *"I am authorised to write to you by "the directors" of the finishing room—the trinity which co[n]sist of James 1st 2nd Octavia and 3rd Mrs Hammond "to get some Otto of Rose and put into the silk that smells so bad and make it smell better no matter if it is [dearly?] sold for it is too bad to lose such a good lot of silk"!!!*[89]

Financial pressures, overwork, confusion, mistakes: the price was steep. *I wonder if it is like rational beings to be up poreing over account books till 1 or 2 oclock at night?* wrote Dolly, *or to be so driven for money as to have girls set up till that time skeining silk and have to suffer months and perhaps loose her sight like Marion Smith. Oh! ye Scribes and Pharisees hypocrites who strain at a gnat and swallow a Camel.*[90] The name of the Camel was Silk.

The decade 1838–1848 was, Brockett reminded his readers, a time that "tried the souls of the silk producers and manufacturers."[91] Finicky silk-worms, winter-killed mulberry trees, storage problems, poor reeling, and uncertain markets: the silk producers' trials were daunting, and many gave up in the wake of the mulberry craze.[92] The silk manufacturers agonized over the vagaries of the raw silk supply and the primitive state of their machinery. The Northampton Association shouldered both sets of problems and, in the end, was crushed by their weight. Yet the effort made sense at the time.

"No enterprise, large in its inception, comprehensive in its designs, widespread, far reaching, and beneficent in its results, can claim an exemption from difficulties, in the infancy of its movements," the New-England Silk Convention declared. With the dabblers and charlatans out of the picture, the serious business of silk could begin. The Mansfield Silk Company and the Northampton Silk Company had tried, and failed, to raise their own silk, but they had lacked the resources a residential community could afford.

The Shaker communities in Kentucky and the Harmonists in Economy, Pennsylvania, had raised and manufactured silk successfully since the 1820s. But there were important differences between their silk industries and that of the NAEI that may not have been obvious then. The most important difference was scale. Only 11,000 silkworms were raised in the Shaker village at North Union in 1840; in the late 1830s the Harmonists produced at most 151 pounds of silk in a season.[93] These modest quantities reflected modest goals. The Shakers wove silk kerchiefs and neckties for their members and for gifts; they sold small quantities too, but sales were never the rationale. The Harmonists' silk was widely acclaimed, and their factory, with steam reelers and a Jacquard loom, widely admired. But silk was just one of many successful manufacturing activities of these communities. Losses could be absorbed.

The Northampton Association raised silk successfully too. Neither the Stetson letters nor the NAEI records hint that a single silkworm fell ill, despite worry about the weather. The 1844 mulberry blight that put an end to silk growing in Mansfield did not, it seems, make its way to Northampton. But the Association staked its existence on selling silk thread in a crowded, competitive market. Almira's twenty-five bushels of cocoons would not suffice for a week.

Some shortfall had been anticipated: Oliver Paine was instructed to buy cocoons and raw silk in 1842.[94] But, it was assumed, the gap would narrow, not widen. A few days after the difficult meeting in May 1845 described above, Paine withdrew from the NAEI. The supply problem grew worse with the cessation of sericulture: the cocoons on the market were often poor quality and the reeled silk they bought proved inferior to the samples, or even rotten. *The silk that Georg///[e] got in Boston they cannot work at any rate,* Dolly reported.[95] By 1845 the NAEI gave up on American raw silk. "We have had so little confidence in being able to supply ourselves with raw material in that way that we depend mostly upon purchasing foreign stock," Samuel Hill wrote in response to an inquiry. "We should be glad however to get in the way of being supplied with stock of our own country's growth whenever we can safely depend upon it."[96] Like their competitors, none of which raised silk, the NAEI bought Chinese raw silk from merchants in New York, Boston, and Hartford. But even this was sometimes unworkable because Chinese reeling machines lacked the traverse bar. Throughout the 1840s, American manufacturers sent reelers to China, urging their suppliers to copy and use them; they eventually did so, in the 1850s, too late to help the NAEI.[97]

Consumers scorned American-manufactured silk products no matter where the silk was grown. The Italians set the standard for manufacturers and customers alike. But, owing to the vagaries of transport, Italian silk was often in short supply. The NAEI's competitors won customers for their products by adopting Italian-sounding brand names.[98] James Stetson deplored this ruse and the NAEI did not practice it.[99]

But principle was not the only source of the NAEI's financial difficulties. Its silk industry was a camel, as Dolly exclaimed. Interference and inexperience were two of its many humps.

A camel is a horse designed by a committee, the saying goes, and the NAEI showed how to do it. "The management of the affairs and undertakings of the Association shall be conducted by two distinct companies: 1st, a Stock Company; 2d, an Industrial Community," its first constitution declared. A by-law granted the members of each body the right to inspect the records of the other, and the directors of each to attend and speak at the meetings of the other (without a vote). Despite the companies' names, the Stock Company controlled the industries: the Stock Directors "shall determine in what manner their funds shall be invested, and shall make such appropriations for carrying on the different branches of business as they shall judge best." On the other hand, the Industrial Community "shall fix the rate of compensation for the various employments, awarding the highest compensation to the most necessary and disagreeable, and manage the purchase of materials and goods, and the sale of articles produced or manufactured." The Industrial Community did not control its funds: on appointing Oliver

Paine director of the silk-growing department, it resolved that he "be requested to prepare and present to the next meeting of the Stock Directors an estimate of the quantity and price of eggs, the expense of fixtures of every kind, and the amount of help required in that department, and obtainable within the community."[100] This form of industrial organization promised, at best, cumbersome decision making. After the Stock Directors and the Industrial Community were merged in 1843, everyone had a say in everything.

There seems to be a fatality attending our silk, wrote Dolly, and how could it be otherwise?[101] Almira mentioned "new hands put on to feed," James Atkins learned on the job, and no one seems to have known what to do in the finishing room.[102] Perhaps in response to the NAEI's decision to replace Vallentine, the professional dyer, with a beginner, Joseph Conant and his sons-in-law withdrew from the NAEI in October 1842 to start their own silk-manufacturing business, J. Conant & Co., in Northampton. With their departure, the NAEI lost its president (Conant) and silk department director (Swift) in one blow. William Adam explained later, "They are men of good private character as the world goes, but their object in joining us appears to have been from the first, pecuniary advantage, not moral improvement, or social usefulness, and we all feel that their departure has strengthened instead of weakened us."[103] This may have been post hoc wishful thinking. Swift's successor, E. H. Preston, had no experience in silk manufacture and resigned under pressure eight months later.

Over time, inexperience and mismanagement would have given way to expertise. And, over the next few decades, some of the technical problems the NAEI had faced were resolved in unexpected ways. The discovery of aniline dyes, the widespread acceptance of the germ theory of disease, and improvements in silk-manufacturing machinery changed the landscape of silk forever.[104] But time was running out.

THE STETSON letters chronicle the silk department's decline. But a silk thread phoenix rose from its ashes. By 1852, six years after the NAEI dissolved, Samuel Hill was manufacturing (not raising) silk in Northampton again.

I. M. Singer was an imaginative merchant, but his sewing machines sat idle in the absence of a strong, smooth thread. Hill accepted the challenge. "The silk was handed to Mr. Singer with the request that he would try it. He put a spool upon his machine, threaded up, and commenced sewing. After sewing sufficiently to enable him to judge of its merit, he stopped, and after examining the work it had done, exclaimed, 'Can you make any more like this?' (addressing the agent who stood watching the result with great interest:) 'I shall want all you can make.'"[105]

This first success, in Singer's shop, forced Hill to confront the problems of standardization and scale that had plagued the NAEI. "Although, in this first experiment of machine-twist, the invention was complete, the manufacturers still found great trouble in its production," explained the judges of the Centennial Exhibition, pronouncing Hill's company's exhibition of thread and machinery "splendid." For "the machine required a thread which, to be moved automatically, must be absolutely perfect, like the machine itself. It was by gradual improvements in machinery, and manipulations generally too minute to warrant description, that they succeeded in the result they have now so completely attained,—that of placing upon spools a definite weight of silk thread, of continuous length, entirely free from slugs, knots, and uneven places, and perfectly adapted to the machine which is to apply it." The NAEI could not have made such a thread: the crucial mechanism had not yet been invented.[106]

The box of ancient eggs, silkworms, cocoons, and skeins, and the Stetson letters, tell a story of a many-humped camel and a many-lumped thread. But the camel's offspring—machine twist—passed through the eye of the sewing machine needle. Hill's Nonotuck Silk Company quickly grew to be one of the nation's leading silk-thread manufacturers, famed for its Italianate "Corticelli" thread.[107] The Stetsons stayed in touch with Northampton throughout their lives and witnessed this remarkable epilogue. They knew their work had not been in vain.

Notes

I would like to thank Marian Goldsmith, Barbara Janssen, and Stan Sherer for their invaluable assistance, and Kerry Buckley, Chris Clark, and Paul Gaffney for their thoughtful suggestions.

1. The term *raw silk* is sometimes used for the unwound (but smothered) cocoons, but it usually means silk that has been unwound but not yet cleaned or dyed. In this essay I adopt the second meaning. One skein of silk is labeled "reeled at Florence, Mass., 1889," but the box and its other contents may be older.

2. Dolly W. Stetson to James A. Stetson [hereafter DWS and JAS], July 26, [1844]

(letter no. 13). Stetson Family Correspondence, Manuscript Collection, Historic Northampton, Northampton, Mass. References are to letters in this collection unless otherwise indicated, and include the letter number assigned in this volume.

3. This apt expression is the title of chapter 5 in Christopher Clark, *The Communitarian Moment: The Radical Challenge of the Northampton Association* (Ithaca, N.Y., 1995; Amherst, Mass., 2003).

4. Ibid., 20.

5. *First Annual Report of the New-England Silk Convention, at its session held at Northampton Massachusetts, September 28, 1842* (Northampton, 1843).

6. Shang dynasty oracle bones date silk in China to at least 3000 B.C.E. See Joseph Needham, *Science and Civilization in China*, vol. 5, part 9, "Textile Technology, Spinning and Reeling," by Dieter Kuhn (Cambridge, Eng., 1988), 278–284.

7. Sericulture ultimately failed in the southern colonies for many reasons, some economic, some technical. Sericulture is highly labor-intensive and the colonists had many other things to do; tobacco and other crops were easier to raise and more lucrative; reeling silk from cocoons requires years of experience and expert skill. For more details, see Gertrude Brown Working, "The History of Silk Culture in the North American Colonies" (Ph.D. diss., Radcliffe College, 1932).

8. King James I, *A Counter-blaste to Tobacco* [1604], ed. Edmund Goldsmid (Edinburgh, 1884).

9. Tobacco destroyed silk figuratively, in the market, and also literally: nicotine is toxic to silkworms. Contrary to the assertions of Edward Digges, governor of the Virginia Colony (1655–1658) and silk enthusiast, the two crops are incompatible.

10. Alfred Lilly, *The Silk Industry of the United States from 1766 to 1874* (New York, 1882), 2–4.

11. As yields vary with the climate, soil, and type of tree, calculations of them are at best approximate. Mine are based on those in Jonathan Cobb, *A Manual containing information respecting the growth of the Mulberry Tree with suitable directions for the Culture of Silk, in three parts* (Boston, 1833). The quotation is from Lilly, *The Silk Industry*, 4.

12. L. P. Brockett, *The Silk Industry in America* (New York, 1876), 52.

13. In the 1870s techniques for summer hibernation were developed, but in the 1840s, each crop of eggs had to be kept over the winter to hatch the following spring.

14. Cobb, *Manual*, x.

15. Brockett, *The Silk Industry*, 53.

16. B. S. Lathrop, "History of Dr. Daniel Stebbins [and] of his connection with the silk industry of Northampton," (c. 1929) Manuscript Collection, Forbes Library, Northampton, Mass.

17. Charles A. Sheffeld, ed., *A History of Florence, Massachusetts, Including a Complete Account of the Northampton Association of Education and Industry* (Florence, Mass., 1895), 56. Florence is the name later adopted, in honor of its Italian counterpart, by the citizens of the Northampton suburb in which the factory was located. A proposal to rename the Mill River the Arno was rejected.

18. Agnes Hannay, *A Chronicle of Industry on the Mill River*, Smith College Studies in History, 21 (Northampton, Mass., 1935–36), 60.

19. Both steam engines were built by John Gore of Brattleboro, Vt., who built six of the seven other engines in western Massachusetts at that time. See U.S. Treasury Dept., *Letter from the Secretary of the Treasury, Transmitting in obedience to a resolution of the House of the 29th of June last, information in relation to Steam-Engines, &c*, 25th Cong., 3rd. Sess., House Doc. no. 21 (1838).

20. Mary Stetson to JAS, June 26, 1845 (letter no. 63).

21. Sheffeld, ed., *History of Florence*, 82.

22. Northampton Association of Education and Industry, Records, 1836–1853, American Antiquarian Society, Worcester, Mass. (hereafter cited as follows, using the volume numbers under which items are cataloged: Record of Proceedings, 1842–1848: NAEI, Records, vol. 2; Northampton Silk Company Account Book: NAEI, Records, vol. 3; Letterbook, 1843–1847: NAEI, Records, vol. 4; Silk Manufacturing Department Account Book: NAEI, Records, vol. 8), vol. 3.

23. Samuel Whitmarsh, *Eight Years Experience and Observation in the Culture of the Mulberry Tree, and in the Care of the Silk Worm, with remarks adapted to the American system of producing raw silk for exportation* (Northampton, 1839), 10–11.

24. Brockett, *The Silk Industry*, 111–112. The witness was John Ryle, who later helped found the silk industry of Paterson, N.J.

25. Like their American counterparts, Italian farmers debated the merits of varieties of mulberry, including the *Morus multicaulis*. See Giovanni Federico, *An Economic History of the Silk Industry, 1830–1930* (Cambridge, Eng., 1997), 86. For a detailed discussion of the *multicaulis* mania, see David Rossell, "The Culture of Silk: Markets, Households, and the Meaning of an Antebellum Agricultural Movement" (Ph. D. diss. SUNY–Buffalo, 2001).

26. Kate deNormandie Wilson, *Dolly Witter Stetson: A Sketch of Her Life* (Brooklyn, Conn., 1907), 1–2.

27. W. Adam, in *The Silk Question Settled. Report of the National Convention of Silk Growers and Silk Manufacturers, held in New York October 13th and 14th, 1843* (New York, 1844), 69.

28. See Barbara Suit Janssen, *Technology in Miniature: American Textile Patent Models 1819–1840* (Washington, 1988).

29. Cobb, *Manual*, 44.

30. Ralph Waldo Emerson, "The American Scholar," an oration delivered to the Phi Beta Kappa Society, Cambridge, Massachusetts, August 31, 1837. The exact quotation is, "A strange process too, this, by which experience is converted into thought, as a mulberry leaf is converted into satin. The manufacture goes forward at all hours."

31. David Mack to A. T. Taylor, April 23, 1843, NAEI, Records, vol. 4, p. 29.

32. *The Phalanx* 1, no. 18 (September 7, 1844): 275.

33. Almira Stetson [hereafter ABS] to JAS, [June 3, 1844] (letter no. 8).

34. [Anna Benson Percy?], "When I Was a Girl," in Sheffeld, ed., *History of Florence*, 124–125.

35. "Oliver Paine's History from the time he was born to February the 10, 1844," 1844, Manuscript Collection, Historic Northampton, Northampton, Mass.

36. DWS to JAS, August 4, 1844 (letter no. 17).

37. George Stetson, "When I Was a Boy," in Sheffeld, ed., *History of Florence*, 122.

38. William Kenrick, *The American Silk Grower's Guide; or the art of raising the mulberry and silk on the system of successive crops in each season* (Boston, 1835), 43–44.

39. DWS to JAS, August 4, 1844 (letter no. 17).

40. ABS to JAS, [July 27, 1844] (letter no. 14).

41. Thomas Moffett, *The Silkwormes and their Flies*, (1599; facsimile edition, Binghamton, N.Y., 1989).

42. U.S. Treasury Dept., *Growth and manufacture of silk. Letter from the secretary of the treasury, transmitting the information required by a resolution of the House of Representatives, of May 11, 1826, in relation to the growth and manufacture of silk, adapted to the different parts of the Union, February 7, 1828*, 20th Cong., 1st Sess. House Doc. no. 158 (1828).

43. Lathrop, "History of Dr. Daniel Stebbins." Mrs. Lathrop, Stebbins's granddaughter, cites diseases and deaths of silkworms among the problems he encountered. Others included the difficulty of retarding the egg hatching until the foliage was ready to feed the worms. "My grandfather did not seem as anxious to keep records of the failure of the silk culture as of the first successes."

44. Whitmarsh, *Eight Years Experience*, 102–104. In response to my query, Vyacheslav Klymenko, a contemporary geneticist, wrote "often not 'thunderstorm' was important but high humidity after the heavy rain. It's well known that high humidity . . . is very dangerous as favoring many diseases especially at high density of larvae." Email message to Marian Goldsmith (who passed on my question), September 7, 2001. I wish to thank Professor Goldsmith for her assistance with this question and for her critical reading of an early draft of this essay.

45. Whitmarsh, *Eight Years Experience*, 92–93.

46. DWS to JAS, August 4, 1844 (letter no. 17).

47. For lists of prize winners, see *Hampshire Gazette*, October 18, 1842; October 24, 1843; October 15, 1844; October 21, 1845.

48. Whitmarsh, *Eight Years Experience*, 67. See also Patrizia Sione, "From Home to Factory: Women in the Nineteenth Century Italian Silk Industry," in D. Hafter, ed., *European Women and Pre-Industrial Craft* (Bloomington, Ind., 1995).

49. In 1843, wrote Paine, "we had Mary Munson, Sarah Wite, Almira Stetson, and Lyda Pearce" to do the reeling. "Oliver Paine's History."

50. ABS to JAS, [June 3, 1844] (letter no. 8).

51. Kenrick, *The American Silk Grower's Guide*, 71.

52. DWS to JAS, June 3, [1844] (letter no. 7); DWS to JAS, August 4, 1844 (letter no. 17).

53. DWS to JAS, August 25, [1844] (letter no. 20).

54. Mary Stetson to JAS, October 13, 1844 (letter no. 29).

55. Holland was granted Patent no. 977 on October 10, 1838, and in 1841 another patent for improvements to this machine. See Janssen, *Technology in Miniature*, 46–47.

56. "At a meeting of the Stock Directors held May 28th 1842 . . . It was resolved . . . That Mr. Conant be requested to ascertain the terms at which the Holland's machine jointly belonging to himself and Mr. Russell may be purchased by the Association." NAEI, Records, vol. 2, p. 13. Evidently the NAEI did not buy the machine at that time, as several months later, when Conant withdrew from the Association, he sold it to the NAEI. "September 4, 1842 . . . It was further resolved that the directors accept the offer of Holland's Silk Spinner belonging to Messrs. Conant and Russell at $155 including the right to use it." NAEI, Records, vol. 2, p. 29.

57. Sarah Stetson to JAS, February 17, 1845 (letter no. 37).

58. DWS to JAS, March 18, 1845 (letter no. 45).

59. Kenrick, *The American Silk Grower's Guide*, 72.

60. DWS to JAS, July 26, [1844] (letter no. 13).

61. Brockett, *The Silk Industry*, 134.

62. "Ward Cheney . . . himself spent some months in Northampton, acquiring 'all the secrets of the art' from Mr. Vallentine for the sum of three hundred dollars. In Mr. Cheney's case, Mr. Vallentine afterwards occasionally boasted that he kept some of his knowledge in reserve; but at all events, the Cheney Brothers never appeared conscious of the deficiency." Ibid.

63. David Mack to W. C. Locke, September 16, 1843, NAEI, Records, vol. 4, p. 55.

64. Degumming is not an optional step unless your goal is a rather stiff silk of natural color, which is exactly what some uses of silk require. See, e.g., Cara McCarty and Matilda McQuaid, *Structure and Surface: Contemporary Japanese Textiles* (New York, 1998).

65. DWS to JAS, August 25, [1844] (letter no. 20).

66. Elijah Bemiss, *The Dyers Companion* (1815; rpt. ed., New York, 1973), 97.

67. "Blue vitriol" is hydrated copper sulfate.

68. Bemiss, *The Dyers Companion*, 59.

69. ABS to JAS (letter no. 40).

70. See NAEI, Records, vol. 2, p. 65 and vol. 4, p. 40.

71. DWS to JAS, June 3, [1844] (letter no. 7).

72. Luca Molà, *The Silk Industry of Renaissance Venice* (Baltimore, 2000), 137.

73. Brockett, *The Silk Industry*, 135–136. But now, he assured his readers, "American manufacturers justly pride themselves on having discountenanced this species of fraud: pure dye silks are with them the rule; weighted goods, the rare exception."

74. An advertisement in the *Hampshire Gazette* in January 1845 stated that "a German dyer would color dresses, shawls, and stockings, wool, cotton, or linen." Cited by Sheffeld, ed., *History of Florence*, 98.

75. ABS to JAS, December 1, 1844 (letter no. 33). "Black has but one shade," says Bemiss, *The Dyers Companion*, 254, "that of black or darkness, yet it is denominated as having four, blue black, because the blue is not absorbed; grey black, for pores or bodies

are not filled; brown black, for want of a neutral to correct the vitriolic acid and the slightly parts of the logwood; and the coal black, that is, perfectly fine and velvety."

76. On September 1, 1842, the Stock Directors resolved "that Mr. [illegible]'s offer to introduce the manufacture of tram and organzine at a fixed rate of wages be declined and that it be proposed to him to remain for that purpose without at present becoming a member but in every respect under the same conditions to which members are subject and with the same advantages . . ." NAEI, Records, vol. 2, p. 28. The agreement with White was reached on February 4, 1843, NAEI, Records, vol. 2, p. 46.

77. DWS to JAS (letter no. 25).

78. Hall Judd to G. & D. Taylor, May 15, 1846, NAEI, Records, vol. 4.

79. ABS to JAS (letter no. 40).

80. *Liberator*, May 1, 1844.

81. Quoted in *Hampshire Gazette*, September 6, 1842.

82. Brockett, *The Silk Industry*, 122.

83. Sheffeld, ed., *History of Florence*, 124.

84. DWS to JAS, June 16, [1844] (letter no. 10).

85. DWS to JAS, June 16, [1844] (letter no. 10). In Nathaniel Hawthorne, *The Blithedale Romance* (Boston, 1852), a novel set in the contemporaneous utopian community Brook Farm, one of the members knits silk purses for her father to sell on the streets of Boston. These purses were distinctive for their small size and lack of an evident opening.

86. Mary Stetson to JAS, October 13, 1844 (letter no. 29).

87. Clark, *The Communitarian Moment*, 157.

88. ABS to JAS, March 4, 1845 (letter no. 42).

89. ABS to JAS, April 25, 1845 (letter no. 50). Attar of Rose is an intensely concentrated distillation of rose petals.

90. DWS to JAS, March 18, 1845 (letter no. 45).

91. Brockett, *The Silk Industry*, 67.

92. For more about the silk producers' problems, see Rossell, "The Culture of Silk," passim.

93. For information on Shaker silk, see B. Gordon, *Shaker Textile Arts* (Hanover, N.H., 1980). The Harmonists' silk industry is discussed by Kristen Shutts in "The Harmonists and Their Silk Experiences," http://www.smith.edu/hsc/silk/Papers/shutts.html (posted May 26, 2000). The Shakers raised silk until the Civil War, the Harmonists until 1852. Both communities stopped production for financial reasons.

94. NAEI, Records, vol. 2, p. 14.

95. DWS to JAS, June 3, [1844] (letter no. 7).

96. Samuel Hill to Thos. J. Whittemore, January 28, 1845, NAEI, Records, vol. 2, p. 83.

97. Brockett, *The Silk Industry*, 88–89. Harrison Holland's family believed that he had invented the reeler eventually used in China: see Harriette M. Plunkett, *Josiah Gilbert Holland* (New York, 1894), 4–5.

98. For example, F. S. Hovey sold "Hovacci" and "Vitorelli" silks, the Cheney Brothers "Chincacci."

99. "Resolved, That this convention learns with deep regret that, as in other kinds of American manufacture, it has hitherto been deemed necessary to attach the foreign labels, English, French, and Italian, to the excellent sewings and fabrics of our own silk manufactures, in order to command a ready sale in our city market, superior as these sewings and fabrics are known to be, in strength, texture, and durability, to the foreign articles; And that we earnestly recommend to our silk manufacturers, now in the infancy of our enterprise, to set a good example to their brethren in other manufactures, by attaching their own name to their own goods." *The Silk Question Settled*, 17.

100. Minutes of the meeting of the Industrial Community, May 22, 1842, NAEI, Records, vol. 2, pp. 11–12.

101. DWS to JAS, June 3, [1844] (letter no. 7).

102. ABS to JAS, [July 27, 1844] (letter no. 14).

103. William Adam to John Bailey, March 16, 1843, NAEI, Records, vol. 4, pp. 16–17.

104. As did the successful invention of an "artificial silk," an unsuccessful passion of the good Dr. Stebbins. Stebbins claimed to have made silk from the inner bark of mulberry shoots, and in 1843 he persuaded the American Institute to offer a prize for a machine that would separate the inner from the outer bark (*The Silk Question Settled*, 77). The first English patent for artificial silk—made from the mulberry—was granted in 1855 to George Audemars of Lausanne, Switzerland, but the first "artificial silk" produced on a commercial scale was rayon, three decades later.

105. Alfred Lilly, quoted in the Report of the Judges of the 1876 International Exhibition, 180–181; National Museum of American History, Washington, D.C.

106. See Marjorie Senechal, "The Invention of Machine Twist," in *Silk Roads, Other Roads: Proceedings of the Eighth Biennial Symposium of the Textile Society of America, Northampton, Massachusetts, September 26–28, 2002*. (Earleville, Md.: Textile Society of America, 2003).

107. After merging with the Belding-Hemingway Company in the 1920s, the company was renamed the Corticelli Silk Company, but the brand name "Corticelli" was used much earlier. The company, once Northampton's largest employer, closed all operations in the area in the early 1930s.

Coloring Utopia

The African American Presence in the Northampton Association of Education and Industry

Paul Gaffney

In early 1892, as the fiftieth anniversary of the founding of the Northampton Association of Education and Industry approached, eighteen-year-old Charles A. Sheffeld, grandson of one of the founders, planned a small book on Florence, Massachusetts, the factory village that grew out of the Association's aftermath. It would feature illustrations—engravings from pen-and-ink sketches and photographs—of the "picturesque attractions" of local interest. The images were to be accompanied by six articles to be solicited from various residents, past and present. What began as a contribution in the "picturesque" genre so popular in 1890s New England soon expanded into a larger project. Sheffeld had found himself left with the task of writing "an adequate historical sketch."[1] Doing justice to what might be "adequate" propelled him into an extended history of the village, including a "complete account" of the communitarian experiment whose unacknowledged anniversary had no doubt spurred him on in the first place.

While filiopietistic interests drove the young man's efforts, it was an extraordinarily rich history he found himself researching. As his conception expanded, Sheffeld decided to solicit articles by former Association members such as Frances Judd and George R. Stetson and by significant visitors such as John W. Hutchinson and Frederick Douglass. While a spate of local history books dotted the 1890s landscape, Sheffeld's had become an amateur history and memory project that would address, however indirectly, the larger questions that the Northampton Association had so openly brought to center stage a half century before. Looking back from the waning days of his long, illustrious life, Frederick Douglass would remember what he had found on his visits in 1844 and 1845: the "high thought" of the men and women that "led them to dare and do startling things in contradiction to the common sense of the period." Among these startling things was a willingness to confront not just slavery but the everyday reality of race in American life.[2]

For his extended historical work, Charles Sheffeld had the records of the Northampton Association kept by his family or perhaps by Frances Judd, a former member who penned an article for the "Old Community Times" section in which Douglass's remembrance was also placed. Those records were subsequently lost until the 1980s. Using the rediscovered volumes, Christopher Clark began his definitive work on the community. Now the appearance of the letters of Dolly Stetson and her family coupled with Clark's research and probing analysis provide us with a wider window into the Northampton Association of Education and Industry. Here in the every-day world of this intentional community, the "radical challenge" of this band of reformers took shape.[3] A significant part of the cultural work these nineteenth-century men and women took on was the deliberate permeation of the color line. However limited in scope, however stumbling these efforts were, their aspirations and achievements deserve further investigation.

The Northampton Association from which Dolly Stetson looked out espoused a social philosophy of equality "without distinction of sex, color, or condition, sect, or religion."[4] While the negation of the distinction of color (and condition, for which we should read fugitive slave) was but one of the aims of their vision, we should underscore just how radical this was even in the context of antebellum communitarian efforts.[5] It is indeed striking that of all the challenges that communitarians took up, including confronting the organization of labor and the institution of marriage, the color line was so sacrosanct. Even in this age of great dreams, utopia itself was a coat of one color.[6] Within the rubric of "universal reform" the Northampton Association addressed, however inchoately, the crucial nexus of gender, class, and race. This essay looks at the lives of African Americans in the communitarian world of Dolly Stetson and in the emerging factory village that succeeded "utopia." What was the place of color in the model community of the Northampton Association that abolitionists and their kin and associates built? How did race work in this setting? How constrained and imperfect were their efforts? What place did African Americans carve out for themselves in this small industrial venture? Was there a sanctuary of brotherhood in coloring utopia?

The Northampton Association bought some 470 acres of land, a silk factory, and several dwelling houses in the outskirts of Northampton in early 1842. This area was crossed by the road that was the turnpike to Albany and by the Mill River that ran down through the burgeoning commercial center of Northampton. A tavern stood on the turnpike as a stage stop. A gristmill had long been located here, but settlement was thin and largely unorganized. Even the establishment of the Northampton Silk Company in 1835 had little impact on the development of the place but had instead drawn its workers from families scattered in the surrounding rural areas.

We know too little about African American life in the small towns and rural areas of New England. What people of color there were in Northampton seem to have been located nearer the center and to have been employed as laborers or servants. Adjacent to the Association property and the falls that provided the waterpower for their silk operation was the residence of Henry Anthony, an African American who farmed his own land, worked as a stonemason, and found occasional work as a fiddler at local dances in the decades to come. Anthony had married a recent Irish immigrant and was living on Spring Street in 1840. Whatever locals thought about this interracial couple, Anthony soon suffered the deaths to disease of their two children in March 1843 and, in June, of his wife, Maria. We do not know what Henry Anthony thought of the new associational experiment that had begun a year before his losses. While he did not seek to join in the effort, he did frequent the community store on a regular basis and bought land from the Northampton Association on the first anniversary of his wife's death. Complicating the usual picture of black-Irish relations, Anthony was living with another Irish woman in 1860 and boarding with a black family in an Irish-immigrant neighborhood in 1880.[7] Henry Anthony would witness the development of utopia and the arrival of several other black individuals and families throughout the 1840s. It is unclear whether these new African American residents were pulled to the area by the abolitionist sympathies of evangelical bent or by knowledge of the radical Garrisonian intentions of the Association. Perhaps they were merely seeking a relatively safe haven from southern life in out-of-the-way rural Massachusetts.

By 1850, Northampton was 3 per cent black, a percentage slightly above that of much of the rest of New England.[8] The increase of the black presence locally was certainly not insignificant: in 1840 Northampton's blacks numbered 58, in 1850 there were 152.[9] In the neighborhood of the Association two new black families would arrive during the 1840s and stay until well into the twentieth century: that of Basil Dorsey, a long-escaped slave from Maryland, and Nelson Askin, a free black from the Pittsfield area further west in Massachusetts. Although these blacks never joined or sought to enroll in the community, they were living and working close by and would become part of the neighborhood community that evolved after the Association itself ceased to function in 1846.[10]

Among these three families, the Anthonys, the Dorseys, and the Askins, only Basil Dorsey is known to have had any abolitionist connections. He and his brothers had voted with their feet in 1837, fleeing bondage in Liberty, Maryland, and finding refuge at Robert Purvis's farm in Pennsylvania. Purvis was a wealthy businessman and ardent abolitionist well known to William Lloyd Garrison and in the radical antislavery network. When the Dorsey brothers were found out, Basil was caught—the others slipped away—but the abolitionist lawyer David Paul Brown, whom Purvis had hired, got him freed temporarily on a technicality. Dorsey was whisked away and may have had contact with David Ruggles and the New York Vigilance Committee. As we shall see, Ruggles was a central, indeed intense and controversial, figure in the black abolitionist network in New York City and would later play an important role in the Northampton Association and in the Stetson letters. Dorsey's journey to freedom went through Northampton and eventually to Charlemont, Massachusetts. There he lived with the brother of Joshua Leavitt, an editor of the *Emancipator*, a New York–based newspaper that had employed Ruggles as an agent in the 1830s. Dorsey moved to the neighborhood of the Association in 1844 after the death of his first wife. Whether that was directly due to the presence of Garrisonians at the Association is unclear.[11]

THE APPARENTLY regular contact Association members had with their black neighbors was one thing. Integrating community life within the Association was a far more significant step toward a biracial republic, however small it was writ. The Northampton Association also had a small number of black members. The Stetson letters, which take us into the thick of community life, provide new and rare glimpses of its interracial character.

A few general observations about the African American presence in the Association might be made. Unlike other communitarian groups, the North-ampton community espoused a sort of affirmative action in reaching out to prospective black residents. Answering a letter from a white New Bedford abolitionist, John Bailey, who sought admission for a young black man into the community school, William Adam, Secretary, assured him that "of course, his colour is not a disqualification but rather a recommendation to us." Nonetheless, following a community policy of only accepting those who were known to members or to close friends, kin, or allies, they turned away the application until Bailey had personally met and interviewed the seventeen-year-old applicant.[12] And, despite such declared openness to new-comers of color, the Association drew only four permanent African American residents. Perhaps the very carefulness of considering membership, which only grew more painstaking as difficulties and tensions increased in the uto-pian project, meant that the community, given its insistence on close exami-nation of any prospective member's character, might only, no matter how resolute its ideals, replicate the color line of the outside world. This tension between principles and the larger reality of the color line would continue to place a great strain on what "sanctuary" the Association and its legacy could provide.

Of the four blacks who came to stay, our knowledge of only two reaches any depth. Of those, David Ruggles was well known in abolitionist networks as well as to New York City officials for his extensive legal interventions and run-ins associated with his underground railroad and anti-kidnapping work. The other, Sojourner Truth, who until 1827 had been enslaved in New York State, came to the Association late in 1843, having recently rechristened herself but basically unknown outside of evangelical and millenarian circles. Her later fame would ensure that some memory of the Northampton Asso-ciation's life would be preserved outside the context of local history.

Ruggles was the first African American to take up residence, arriving in November 1842, some six months after the community's founding. A year later, Truth arrived. In the meantime, the activities that would later become legendary throughout the North as the Underground Railroad were bring-ing in temporary sojourners. At this early stage, before postbellum legend had worn the ragged edges off the Underground Railroad and had given such titles as "conductors" and "stations" to these crucial efforts of antislav-ery resistance, the informality of the activities is apparent. A letter from

Sophia Foord at the community to a friend noted that a fugitive slave had just left after a stay and that another fugitive was soon to find respite there. Foord called it the "rail road under ground," a precious reference to an elusive reality.[13] This expected newcomer was undoubtedly Stephen C. Rush, who was "unanimously invited to consider the Community his home for the present" on May 13, 1843.[14] While it is unclear if Stephen Rush was ever formally accepted as a member beyond this invitation, he would stay on and figure in Dolly Stetson's daily life in the community boarding house, and he was clearly seen as a member by others. That this was true points to the paradox that even as the Association became more selective in its admissions policy, it was decidedly more cavalier about keeping up its membership records as time wore on. Rush is noted in the membership book as having entered in November 1843. Perhaps he was on a six-month probation, as more and more prospective members were, whites as well as blacks. A curious note in that log suggests the deeper meaning he and others in the Association might have ascribed to his freedom and community status: he is listed as born "Nov. 4, 1843."

If, as seems possible given the rather everyday tone of Foord's letter, the arrival and departure of fugitives was not uncommon, the Association might have found a source of black members. But the importance of trust and knowledge of character so vital to nineteenth-century Americans was underscored by the uncertainties and fears of their utopian experiment. As with all intentional communities, decisions to admit new members were fraught with anxiety and demanded vigilance. This held true for prospective white members as well, as the Association's records document.

We know little about the fourth permanent African American resident, George Washington Sullivan. He gave his birthday as July 4, 1825, in Baltimore and listed that city as his previous place of residence. Perhaps he too had come "under ground." He was admitted on November 3, 1843, and would achieve a brief splash of local fame for surviving a forty-five-foot fall from the factory belfry in 1844, an event duly noted in the Stetson letters. In the membership records, he has no color. It was the local newspaper write-up that made clear he was black.[15] Shortly after Sullivan's entrance, Sojourner Truth began what would be a fourteen-year residence in the area.

It is notable that the four black residents of the Association were single. In this intentional community dominated by settled families and a fair number of new marriages, this might tell us something about how the color line might be crossed. The centrality of family life is underscored by Dolly herself when she writes to her husband that she'd thought that "Association was to keep families together instead of seperating them."[16] Certainly Truth and Ruggles, the two most prominent African Americans, were decidedly not married: she a widow from a marriage which seems to have been an unhappy one, and he a lifelong bachelor in an era when that was uncommon indeed. Both of them may have had quite conflicted feelings about sexuality. Truth's relationships with men had included a forced separation from a young black lover who was then beaten. She was subsequently to marry, perhaps through coercion, another black, who belonged to her master. Ruggles later revealed in a water-cure writing a decidedly negative coupling of masturbation and disease. While such connections were relatively common in health reform literature, it may be significant that Ruggles was both single and so explicit.[17]

Three of the black members, then, were men; the one example we have of a black woman and of something akin to black family life is Truth and the presence of her daughters. It is not at all clear that the daughters were more than intermittent visitors. While they had sporadic accounts at the community store, Sojourner's own comings-and-goings, as seen in the Stetson letters, do not correlate directly with her daughters'. And, as the historian Nell Irvin Painter explains, at least some of the girls were still indentured to their previous owners. Moreover, in the biography of Truth that would be written by a community visitor and neighbor, Olive Gilbert, they are, in Painter's apt analysis, a "shrouded" presence.[18] If the Association saw itself as a family of families, it was a white reflection they found.

In fact, Truth's daughters seem a welcomed but possibly dangerous presence, "waltzing" into a circle that was in deep and voluble conflict over issues of dancing and bodily expression. If we take into account the long history of the conflation of race and sexuality in American life, we can find some resonance in the Association's choices in admitting (and possibly soliciting) black members.[19] The Northampton Association wanted to make it clear to the world at large that they were a community that saw monogamous marriage as an integral part of their vision. Its constitution affirmed that "the family relation, the relation between husband and wife, and between parents and children, has its foundation and support in the laws of nature and the will of God." No relations would be allowed that were "inconsistent with this which is sacred and permanent, the root and fountain of all human excellence and happiness." While there were single white members resident during the life of the community, they were in a minority; the fact that none of the black members were married emphasizes that the Association was not a place where African Americans participated in the family life that its founders idealized.[20] Would the ongoing sexual activities of black couples have been too challenging? Certainly the social proximity of the two races in Garrisonian abolitionist activities aroused considerable negative response throughout the North and only fueled the accusatory cries of the South. While an opposing argument could be made that the presence of black couples might have soothed anxieties about interracial bonds between single men and women, perhaps that possibility was implicitly seen as beyond the bounds, and erasure of the color line was, thus, best done one at a time.[21]

HOWEVER LIMITED the experiment of the Northampton Association in its interracial living arrangements, the very rarity of that occurrence invites us to take a closer look at the social and interpersonal lives of those involved.[22] On the face of it, the attitude of whites toward blacks within the Association, at least through the eyes of Dolly Stetson and her children, is remarkable. Poised somewhere between a neutral and a positive framing of black individuals, the Stetson family discusses the activities and presence of several people of color. We certainly have to be on the lookout for what George Fredrickson has aptly called "romantic racialism"—and indeed there was, no doubt, some of that behind the commentary we are privileged to overhear in the language of the letters. But overall the presence of color seems a rather natural part of the human landscape.[23]

Our first glimpse of the place of people of color in that landscape comes from a delightfully playful letter written by daughter Almira. She suggested that if she "should pursue the course of Mr Ruggles . . . I should be so smart that I should jump over the meeting house by spring."[24] With other references to fishes and swimming, this may refer to an early interest by Ruggles in water-cure, though it would predate what we know of his involvement in hydropathy. It does seem to show David Ruggles well ensconced in community life just weeks after his arrival and offering some sort of "course" to the children, perhaps water-cure oriented or simply athletic endeavors. We do know that cold-water swimming was recalled in memoirs about everyday life in the Association.

A group of letters mailed by Dolly to her husband in April 1844 refers to the kind of African American presence we would expect in a Garrisonian abolitionist community: appearances by touring speakers for the antislavery cause. Charles Remond, an important freeborn black orator from Massachusetts, was traveling with Sydney Howard Gay, a white journalist who became the editor of the *National Anti-Slavery Standard,* the official organ of the American Anti-Slavery Society. The well-educated Remond toured all over the North and the British Isles.[25] In fact, Remond, as the Anti-Slavery Society's premier African American spokesman, was in the process of being supplanted by the rising star Douglass. That a leading black orator would visit is not surprising given the community's close ties with the abolitionist circuit. As in so many of her letters, Dolly does not refer to Remond's color. We might interpret this as an instance of color-blindness, but it is more likely that James Stetson was familiar with Remond and others, and the designation would be unneeded.

Remond and Gay were out on the hustings as part of the Massachusetts Anti-Slavery Society's Hundred Conventions tour. The plan was to have five touring "conventions" traveling at the same time, a blanket strategy based on a successful canvassing of the West completed the year before. What seems to have happened is that the Association received Frederick Douglass, on a related but separate crisscrossing of the state, instead. The letter mentioned that the Hutchinson family, then a famous singing act converted to the antislavery cause, would be arriving on Sunday along with Gay and Remond. From the journals of the Hutchinsons, we learn that they came that Saturday and found the community in "simple, rough, pleasant condition," but with "care and study . . . written on every brow." At three o'clock that afternoon, a knock on the door revealed Douglass, preeminently filling the spot as his presence would increasingly do in the antislavery world from 1845 on.

Dolly's letters did not follow up on what happened because her husband had probably arrived in the meantime, but we learn from the Hutchinsons that John and Asa Hutchinson slept together in one dwelling and that Judson Hutchinson and Douglass bedded together in the next house. On Sunday morning, the Hutchinsons sang and Douglass "preached to them," telling the story of John L. Brown, a white South Carolinian who was threatened with the death penalty at first, later reduced to thirty-nine lashes, for helping a young black female escape bondage. Douglass brought many in the community to "shed tears of real grief, tears for suffering humanity. The room was full." That evening, members of the community went en masse to the

Town Hall in Northampton where the Hutchinsons sang "The Negro's Complaint" and "Over the Mountain." Douglass gave a "pithy and eloquent speech" opining that while the greatest enemy of the antislavery movement had once been the anti-abolition mobs, it was now the churches who stood in the way. This must have fitted well with the antisectarian leanings of community members. Douglass provided a mocking version of a Methodist preacher and of the "conversion" of his master. The noted tensions with the local "aristocracy" at the Town Hall would have matched the local image of the community as radical outsiders. A Boston paper reported that the Hutchinsons were considering joining the "social community" which was noted to "comprise all colors, from jet black to pure white." And Abby, the Hutchinson sister touring with her brothers, had "passed two or three days and nights at the 'community,' and on a Sabbath afternoon, was gallanted to her hotel by one of its members, and he a huge *black man*!" The colors of this utopia had set off alarms.[26]

Stephen Rush's presence in the letters showed him to be very much a part of everyday activities. An escaped slave who had an extended stay at the community, Rush was working in the boarding house, helping with the chores, and serving an important role in that work. It is notable that the Stetson letters accentuate the separate gender roles in the community—advocacy of women's rights largely did not involve close questioning of those Victorian "spheres"—and that we find Rush and Ruggles so closely tied to life in the boarding house. Women are doing the expanded version of women's work: keeping the boarding house, the table, and the onerous task of laundry for all those within. For Ruggles it was no doubt a matter of his infirmity; in Rush's case we might read an inclination to assign a black man to "women's work."

It may also be significant that Rush is one of the rare individuals outside the family whom the Stetsons referred to on a first-name basis. Others, with the important exception of Sojourner Truth, whose name(s) presented all kinds of variations, are Mr. or Mrs., or the full name is used. In the formality of nineteenth-century interpersonal relations, name usage had substantial meaning. Indeed, letters between spouses and family members were routinely signed with full names—and Mr. and Mrs. were not yet routinely universal. Stephen may have been born free on November 4, 1843, but he was not yet of the status of a Mr. Ruggles. While the use of the first name might imply kinship—George W. Benson, brother-in-law, is "George"—it seems doubtful that Rush had attained that sort of standing in the Stetson family world. More likely, Stephen was regarded as the children were. First-name use carried affection but also a reduction in status. The complex vision of slaves as victims, so necessary to both black and white abolitionists in their struggle against the "peculiar institution," portrayed, no doubt with some veracity, those in bondage as lacking the resources of fully developed "char-acter." The literary critics Charles T. Davis and Henry Louis Gates, Jr., have found the "relationship between the absence of selfhood and enslavement" in an anecdote in the autobiography of Calvin Fairbank, a fiery abolitionist who made forays into the South and who later became a resident of Florence. Fairbank had spied a young black on the south bank of the Ohio River, ax on his shoulder, singing, "De cold, frosty morning make a niggah feel good." Calling out, he asked if he was going chopping for himself. The young man answered, "Han't go no self." "Slave, are you? Dat's what I is."[27] The road from "no self" to "mister" was in some ways longer than the physical flight to freedom. We might see Stephen Rush as having completed the latter but only midway on the former despite his own assiduous efforts and the rare nurturance of community life.

As we have seen, Rush was certainly not the only fugitive slave to come to the community. Writing her husband in February 1845, Dolly includes a letter from a James Willson to his "mistress" which she avers will not bring harm to Willson if it is mailed in Boston. This almost certainly identifies him as an escaped slave daring to write back to his owner but wishing to conceal his whereabouts.[28] Whether the Stetsons had consulted the community leadership is not known.

George W. Sullivan's startling survival of his fall from atop the fourth story of the silk factory piqued the Stetsons' interest. Whether he had es-caped slavery or was a free black, Sullivan, all of nineteen years old, was also noted to be off to Boston to see James Stetson and may have been hoping to get employment there. Dolly passed along without comment that "David Ruggles wishes me to warn you agains trusting George W. Sullivan." As Ruggles seemed to stand well in the Stetsons' eyes, perhaps his word seemed sufficient.[29] However the Stetsons viewed Rush, Willson, and Sullivan, we see no obvious symptoms of romantic racialism in the letters. However we read Rush's place in the community, Sullivan is dealt with in a rather matter-of-fact manner. Willson was taken in but later left the community following criticism that he was not a "good workman."[30] Although in Willson's case, the pressing needs of the community's finances may have precluded any retention of unproductive labor, no romantic elevation of these blacks is evident.

One intriguing thread evident in the Association's social world is the relation of blacks to blacks. Truth's contemporary biographer would suggest a few years later that Sojourner harbored no romantic vision of fugitives, noting that she "declares of the slaves in their ignorance, that 'their thoughts are no longer than her finger.'"[31] Ruggles's view of Sullivan, noted above, contrasts with his advocacy for Stephen Rush. In August and September 1844 when Ruggles formed the Colored Citizens of Northampton, Rush was chosen to play a prominent role. In 1844 the Albany, N.Y., *Northern Star and Freeman's Advocate* offered Ruggles the editorship of the paper. Ruggles declined, no doubt for health reasons and possibly because of a reluctance to relocate; instead, he recommended his young protégé Rush.[32] Indeed, what evidence we have shows Ruggles far more engaged with other blacks than Truth is.

As we might expect, Sojourner Truth and David Ruggles emerge more fully fleshed out in the Stetson letters than the other black residents. Our own attention to these powerful figures and their legacy may highlight their presence, but their place was clearly near the center of Dolly Stetson's community. Truth's value as a worker is emphasized, and her evangelical, indeed moralistic, self seems much more prominent here than it would be in the *Narrative of Sojourner Truth* published a few years later. This biography, building on the popularity of slave narratives—certainly Douglass's had circulated through the neighborhood—was written by Olive Gilbert, a white woman living with her close friends the Bensons (in-laws of the Stetsons).[33] Close to the emotional heat of the moral conflicts within the community, Gilbert kept such issues from the public eye. What the Stetson letters open up for us is Truth's intense moral stance against physical affection between the young people, dancing, and card playing. This allied her with Samuel L. Hill, a community leader, and James Boyle, a radical perfectionist. Dolly Stetson took a more tolerant attitude and was somewhat taken aback by the ferocity of Truth, Boyle, and others, but suggested that allowing the dancing and card playing would forestall the dangers, in "a mixed company of boys and girls," of what she quoted Sojourner as calling "lolling on each other squeezing each others hands or sitting in each others laps."[34]

Sojourner Truth, c. 1867. Pencil drawing by Charles Burleigh. 6¾ × 4½ in.
(Courtesy, Historic Northampton)

We also learn more about the moral gulf between Truth and her daughters. Dolly noted that Sophia is "clearly 'encienta,'" using the (misspelled) Spanish word as a euphemism for pregnant.[35] This deepens our understanding of Olive Gilbert's disapproving account in the *Narrative* of Truth's daughters and how they weighed so heavily on a mother's heart. At the time of Dolly's "encienta" letter, Sojourner was away, a situation that seems to have occurred fairly often, leaving Dolly to take up the slack in the laundry work. If Truth's contribution was valued, Sophia was found wanting. As Sophia's pregnancy forced her to quit the hard work and thus put more on Dolly's shoulders, Stetson cannot resist noting that this is work that "she has done poorly enough."[36] Without being explicit, Stetson here drew a connection between sexual morality and work ethic—a key link in the free labor ideology that abolitionists trumpeted. We might note a presaging of abolitionists' doubts about African American character that would later come to play a role in their retreat from Reconstruction. Of course, this deficiency of character was seen as present in members of both races. Indeed, Dolly reports Samuel Hill holding forth at a gathering on "rational enjoyments and occupations that became rational beings."[37] Thus the weaknesses of those who strayed from the prevailing ethic need not be ones defined solely by color.

If Sojourner Truth is on the more upright side of the moral divide in the community, it is well to remember her background in evangelical concerns and causes before she joined the Northampton Association. As a preacher of the word, however uniquely defined, she had held forth at various religious gatherings from street corners to camp meetings. She had also been a staunch member of the ill-fated, indeed notorious, "Kingdom of Matthias" in New York City eight years before setting out on the life-changing journey that eventually led her to the Association.[38] One of the values of reading the Stetson letters is their corroboration of Sojourner Truth's deeply felt religious life which was so crucial to her identity and to her astonishing strength in advocating abolitionism and women's rights. Painter, her best biographer, has argued persuasively for the centrality of religion in her life, and traced the twentieth-century developments in the legend that have diminished her profound evangelical sensibilities. Clark has aptly listed her in the recent *Reader's Guide to American History* as "evangelist and abolitionist."[39] It was at the Association that Truth grafted the language of Garrisonian abolitionism and its women's rights connections onto her own special version of Bible-based wisdom and vernacular humor, creating a heady combination that would enthrall crowds for the next four decades.

What we find in the Stetson letters is a Sojourner in transition, with her "Matthias" side, absolutely forthright and unforgiving, still plainly evident. Later she would keep this inner strength but present the public with a healthy dollop of the more secular issues of the day undergirded with her old self-assurance. Soon after the publication of *Uncle Tom's Cabin* in 1852, Truth visited its author, Harriet Beecher Stowe. It has often been claimed that she was humbly seeking Stowe's approval, an imprimatur that others rightly sought for use in the American marketplace of reform publication. Yet as the literary critic Robert S. Levine has shown, the Stowe account of the meeting actually shows that Truth was "hardly nonplussed by Stowe's eminence [and] remain[ed] in control of the situation." Levine persuasively interprets Truth as not deferential but in fact aggressive. It is she who "looks down" on the author who had just published what would become the best-selling and arguably most influential book of the nineteenth century.[40] We see the same assured strength in dealings with whites in the woman Dolly portrayed.

The complicating factor in Truth's great popularity that we must assume as the deep background of her reception in the community is her status as what Painter deftly calls an "American Exotic."[41] While some scholars have criticized Stowe for commodifying Truth and focusing on her "Africanness and otherness," Levine argues that it was Truth herself who realized that her identity was what she had to sell. Thus, according to Levine, it was Truth's knowledge of whites' keen interest "when she theatricalized herself as an 'African' illiterate" that she used to build her career.[42] From the perspective of the Stetson letters that career is several years ahead. Clearly though, Truth was already well established as a fiery and "peculiar" character while negotiating her place in the utopian world of the Northampton Association.

The Stetson letters do not solve for us the enigma of Truth's agency or victimhood in the later portrayals. And looking back from the Sheffeld history, the whites of Florence who fondly remembered Sojourner Truth no doubt had tinged their admiration with the undertow of the 1890s popular discourse of "darky stories." Mindful of the dangers of such images of blacks in white minds, Douglass recalled her then as "a genuine specimen of the uncultured negro. She cared little for elegance of speech or refinement of manners." Douglass of course approached her fame, her place in the American collective memory, from a very different direction. It was, after all,

elegance of speech and refinement that he, as an African American man, so
adroitly sought and achieved. This was his prescription for equality. Garrisonians had complained in the 1840s, roughly around the time of his stay at
the Northampton Association, that Douglass did not sound enough like a
slave when he spoke on the lecture circuit. The requirements for a woman
of color in the nineteenth century in the public arena were different from
that of the manly eloquence that Douglass had so richly mastered.

Sojourner Truth. Woodcut illustration from the 1853 edition of the *Narrative of
Sojourner Truth*. (Courtesy, Historic Northampton)

Indeed, the two nineteenth-century black women most deeply etched in today's memory are Sojourner Truth and Harriet Tubman. Their images ring true precisely because of their uneducated and rough-hewn qualities. We want nineteenth-century "strong black women" to do the work of class in our revision of American history and culture. Yet, as Painter has shown, Truth's dress was decidedly middle-class and "respectable," thus complicating our understanding of her appeal in her time.[43] Douglass himself had wanted to emphasize his representative qualities as a polar opposite of the minstrelsy images so prevalent in American culture.[44] And to the Stetsons it is Sojourner's wit and wisdom, fueled by religion and an American folk humor, that is already assuming a shape that would give her a prominent place as a legend in her own time and since. In Painter's astute formulation, it is more the symbol that captures our collective memory than the flesh-and-blood woman.

If we see Dolly Stetson and family as beginning to receive a racial education through community life, their at times awe-struck appreciation of Truth foreshadows Sojourner's own later wide acceptance by the white public. The Stetsons saw a woman to whom the "Lord reveals everything." This sense of her profound connection to God was enlivened with an equal appreciation of her wit when, for example, Truth explained Sullivan's survival with her sharp one-liner that "if it was the Devil that made him fall it was the Lord that prepared a place for him to land." Clearly the Stetsons were enthralled with Truth's religiosity and vernacular humor, both key elements in the later exotic Sojourner persona. Yet the letters also give us a more measured appreciation of her eloquence when her speech on the simple beauties of the newly refurbished community room was prominently featured in Dolly's letter to James before she noted the remarks of community leaders George W. Benson and Samuel L. Hill.

By the time Douglass wrote his memoir for Sheffeld's history he was far and away the most prominent African American. He recalled of Sojourner Truth that it was "her duty to trip me up in my speeches and to ridicule my efforts to speak and act like a person of cultivation." Yet while he might portray her as a "genuine specimen," he also suggests a self-fashioning in her manner: "she seemed to please herself and others best when she put her ideas in the oddest forms."[45] The place of color brought forth strikingly different strategies. Those methods were auditioned in the struggling interracial theater of the Northampton Association. Yet for Douglass, and certainly for the many black women espousing uplift in the "woman's era," the dangers of an unsophisticated image were stunningly clear in the Jim Crow world of the 1890s. As Painter's analysis of Truth's visual presentation of her self makes plain, Sojourner herself was rather more complex in her self-portraiture than our collective memory suggests.

IF THE STETSONS observed Sojourner Truth in transition, they also caught glimpses of Frederick Douglass at a point of change. The young Douglass was sitting for a portrait by Elisha Hammond. This painting may well have been the basis for the engraving that graces the frontispiece of the *Narrative of the Life of Frederick Douglass* published the month after his 1845 visit. Hammond had already done a portrait of Garrison in January 1844.[46] Now Douglass, with his portrait, his growing fame on the lecture circuit, and the publication of his *Narrative*, would rival his white benefactor. And indeed, Douglass's presence in the community's life, however fleeting, would have significant impact. Despite his status as visitor, it is his presence that would come to occupy so much of Florence's memory of its interracial heritage. His portrait and his 1890s contribution to Sheffeld's book would come to bookend the coloring of the village's sense of brotherhood.

That portrait was but part of a momentous year in Douglass's life and career. By June, Dolly was writing to her husband that David Ruggles was "very much disappointed that he did not receive 1½ doz more of the F Duglass Narritive by the box."[47] Soon after publishing the *Narrative*, Douglass would be off to Great Britain, where his self-confidence would rise with his spreading fame. On his return he would purchase his freedom with help from British friends and begin to break away from William Lloyd Garrison to publish his own newspaper. Increasingly viewed by Garrisonians as beyond their control, he would cross over to political abolitionism and to advocacy of a more assertive role for African Americans in the freedom struggle. In an important sense, the talk by Douglass to the community that Dolly recorded as "upon prejudice against color" portends his later role within the abolitionist movement. It certainly served as a key text in the racial education of the Stetsons, for Dolly noted that it was "an old subject but one upon which I never heard a colored person speak in public—he did very well."[48] As she made clear, it was not the novelty of the subject that drove home the young man's argument but rather that it was coming from a black man himself. Douglass would press white abolitionists, no matter how radical their antislavery and reform agendas, to educate themselves on their own racial ways.

By 1855, independent and even more widely known, Douglass published his second autobiography. This one, far longer and more writerly in tone than the first, brought his story up to date, emphasizing his freedom years as well as his bondage. In it he is far more critical of the North, even jabbing those who espouse racial equality, recounting how he found the prejudice against color "very strong" even among the abolitionists of New England.[49] His treatment at the hands of Garrisonians while he was in Great Britain and upon his return certainly underscored his perceptions. Whatever the specific thesis of his presentation that day in April 1845 at the community, that night he delivered a more standard stump speech. His talk to the Association may well have been the seed of what he later made explicit. In 1855 his warning was straightforward: "If the anti-slavery movement shall fail now, it will not be from outward opposition, but from inward decay."[50] Unlike many fugitives, Douglass may have never known the extreme wants of "han't got no self," but he had traveled a long psychological road from his first days of freedom in David Ruggles's apartment in lower Manhattan. He always remembered his "old friend," he of such "sterling sense and worth" and included him in all three of his autobiographies.[51]

DAVID RUGGLES is today unknown outside scholarly circles, and even within he occupies a small place. Usually noted as the Underground Railroad conductor who shepherded Frederick Douglass from New York to New England on his way to freedom, Ruggles himself returned to his native New England when he came to the Northampton Association in the fall of its first year. Whereas Truth was unknown outside evangelical circles when she took the long walk toward a new home at the Association, abolitionists, principally Lydia Maria Child, then editor of the *National Anti-Slavery Standard*, guided Ruggles there. Ruggles was suffering from broken health and a wounded reputation.[52]

Widely admired within abolitionist circles for his personal courage and intense dedication to the cause, Ruggles was also a figure of considerable controversy. Seen by many as too extreme in his strategies and actions, he had also become a target of criticism, caught up in the crossfires of the split of the abolitionist movement in the late 1830s. He found in Child a writer and activist of considerable renown, a deeply moral and levelheaded advocate who had lived in Northampton from 1838 until moving to take up the editorship.[53] She also had extensive contacts in the abolitionist movement, including the Garrisonians in the Northampton Association, who had set up their utopian experiment next door to where her husband, David Lee Child, was engaged in his own experiment, growing sugar beets as an alternative to slave-grown sugar. Although Ruggles was nearly blind and suffering from poor health, he had characteristically had confrontations with officials for their attempted Jim Crow treatment of him the summer before on a Nantucket steamboat and a New Bedford railroad.[54] Thus Ruggles was a wounded warrior finding sanctuary in the Association.

David Ruggles had been born in 1810, in Norwich, a seaport in New London County, Connecticut, to a free black family that had received patronage from some prominent whites in the town. Yet apparently all did not sit well with this bright young man. In 1833 a convicted murderer, in a published confession, recounting his life of crime, claimed that as youths he and Ruggles committed thefts together.[55] The condemned man acknowledged his regrets but bitterly wondered if a more moral life would have made any real difference in his prospects, given that he was black. Whatever the source of Ruggles's misbehavior, the picture of him as an angry young man, well aware of his blackness and the limits it placed on him accords well with the shape of his life as we know it. By 1827, at the age of seventeen, Ruggles was off to New York City as a mariner. In this venture his life echoes the experiences of Peter, Sojourner Truth's troubled son.[56] The life of a mariner, with its threat of rough justice, was commonly seen as a turn-around experience for wayward young men. And it was also one of the few occupations relatively open to blacks.[57]

This was an auspicious moment for a young African American to enter the city: that year emancipation became official in New York State; the first African American newspaper, *Freedom's Journal*, was published; and a great optimism seized the black leadership, who challenged the Colonization movement and sought to galvanize the black community.[58] Within two years Ruggles had opted for a different career path, opened a grocery store, and then publicly announced that he would no longer sell alcohol. Samuel Cornish, editor of *Freedom's Journal*, lauded this in the paper and called on all readers to frequent Ruggles's establishment.[59] The long road in a life of reform had begun. As with so many others, including the Stetsons, temperance was the signal step. Moreover, Ruggles formed a connection with the prominent black leadership of the city. Anger found activism. Indeed, Ruggles's advertisement ran alongside that of David Walker's clothing store in Boston even as Walker published his incendiary *Appeal* to the "coloured citizens of the world."[60]

As Cornish and others took the young man under their wing, he became an agent for the *Emancipator*, official organ of the American Anti-Slavery Society, and a fledgling representative at the National Negro Conventions held annually.[61] By the mid-1830s he had published articles in the *Emancipator* and his own pamphlet attacking the American Colonization Society and, especially, one of its spokesmen, Dr. David Reese, who became something of a recurring nemesis for the young black activist. Ruggles's voice was a fiercely logical one, contrasting with the homemade wit and religious dictums of Sojourner Truth and the soaring eloquence of Frederick Douglass.[62] By 1835 he was selling books instead of groceries and building a career as an author and editor. As his reputation as radical challenger to the status quo grew, his bookstore was set afire and accusatory placards were put up around the city reading: "black amalgamator who lately married a white wife! Let him be lynched!" Ruggles not only denied the interracial marriage but also made it plain that he had never been married to any woman.[63]

At the same time, the New York Committee of Vigilance was formed to fight kidnappers of blacks and to protect runaway slaves. Ruggles served as secretary and point man for all activities, confronting authorities, visiting slaveowners, and would-be kidnappers alike. He was the victim of arson and several assaults and repeatedly ran afoul of the law; his confrontational brand of abolitionism resulted in court appearances and stints in jail. The black leadership increasingly saw him as too radical, too dangerous for the stability of African American reform strategies. Tensions erupted when the funds raised for the Vigilance Committee were found to be depleted. Functioning, at least in his own eyes, as the committee's sole active employee, Ruggles worked closely with white abolitionists such as the Quaker radical Isaac T. Hopper. He was accused at a large special meeting of misusing, or at least not accounting for, the committee's funds. Ruggles claimed not to have used any funds for personal gain but admitted to sloppy bookkeeping. He was also in the crossfire of the widening and increasingly bitter split between political abolitionists and Garrisonians. And while some of his troubles came from white attitudes, especially from the Tappanite political abolitionists who tended to be more prejudiced against blacks, Ruggles had finally exhausted the patience of the African American leadership in the city.[64]

The Vigilance Committee case was coupled with a controversy over Ruggles's giving haven to a slave who had stolen a large sum of money from his master while visiting the city. The resulting notoriety signaled the end of his abolitionist career in New York. Continually referring to him as the "young man," Samuel Cornish professed great sympathy and patience for Ruggles over the years but noted that "we never had confidence in his judgment nor prudence." Cornish concluded that as the "fingers of scorn and the clamors of denunciation" were now almost everywhere, it was necessary to give up the "vain hope that he would out-live youthful blunders."[65] Struggling to maintain and, in fact, enhance his standing, Ruggles started a periodical, *Mirror of Liberty*, and published *A Plea for "A Man and A Brother"* in pamphlet form.[66] However, his health was steadily deteriorating. Destitute and in considerable debt, alienated from black and white New York abolitionists, he repaired to the utopian possibilities of the Northampton Association. There he was welcomed with open arms and deep respect. He had, after all, helped some 600 slaves to freedom and was probably seen as a wounded veteran of the abolitionist wars. He was also the first African American resident in a community that saw itself as racially enlightened.

Ruggles emerges in the Stetson letters as close both to the inner circle of leadership of the community and, as a result of his infirmity, to the women workers in the boarding house. His move to yet another career change as water-cure physician is shown in its early stages. Frederick Douglass would later nicely sum up this evolution: "In search of health, he became a physician."[67] Ruggles penned a request to James Stetson to purchase an "India-rubber syringe" in Boston, explaining that it was "indispensible to my progress in the 'Water Cure.'"[68] Helping with chores, he delighted in Dolly's reading aloud James's letters—one describing a "temperance Jubilee" he found especially "rich."[69] Ruggles also continued, at least minimally, his book-selling business.[70] That he was close to the Association's leadership is made plain when Dolly discussed the proposals being entertained by the Executive Committee to rent or sell the factory to an outsider for the manufacture of cotton: "I obtained these facts by pumping David Ruggles."[71]

The most astonishing revelation is that Ruggles is reported rather matter-of-factly to have taken Harriet Hayden and Sydney Southworth aside to discuss their strained relations with the rest of the Association after their "marriage" without a justice of the peace.[72] This was a tense controversy for the communitarians. It violated their sense of propriety and would seem to have given credence to the most dangerous of accusations hurled at them by outsiders—that they were immoral free-love advocates. Their constitution, after all, had specifically underscored the sacredness of matrimony. When the two sought to present their union as sacred in a transcendental fashion and forged under God's eyes, community members were shocked. They saw themselves as open-minded but also deeply believed in moral constraints, as we have seen in the dancing and card-playing episodes. That a black man would have a talk with a young white couple, advising them that "they never could be admitd here as members and they had better go while the weather was warm" certainly violated the social code on color and sexuality.[73] Yet Dolly Stetson reported it to her husband rather plainly. It fitted her sense of Ruggles as close to the leadership and as a member of the community with a decided moral authority.

Ruggles seems never to have taken a role in the morality wars between the camps that Clark terms "puritans" vs. "liberals." While Sojourner Truth was at the forefront of this debate, Ruggles's image may have been clearly above any considerations of sexuality. While not a man of notable religious concerns, he had in 1835 published a powerful indictment of slavery under the provocative title *The Abrogation of the Seventh Commandment*, which argued that the sexual exploitation of slave women violated the sanctity of marriage. Akin to William Lloyd Garrison's call for separation from the slaveholding South, this was a "No Union with Adulterers" diatribe. Characteristically, he signed it "A Puritan."[74] A single man but without any apparent interest in marriage, he might well have fit the honorary "uncle" role that whites liked to assign to older black men—much as Sojourner Truth would become "auntie" to Abraham Lincoln and countless others in later years.[75] And indeed, though but thirty-four years of age, Ruggles seemed to have undergone a remarkable transformation in the community setting from the impetuous young man of his New York days to a wise old man. His infirmities, including blindness, certainly would have played into this. Yet he may well have encouraged this change himself—after all, youth had brought him to grief and shame in the city and Samuel Cornish, among others in the African American elite, had repeatedly emphasized his youth and impetuosity.

David Ruggles's place in the Northampton Association ultimately came to rest on two seemingly different roles: abolitionist extraordinaire and water-cure physician. The two are not, or at least may not have been to Ruggles and his fellow utopians, unrelated. Clark convincingly posits the shift to water-cure as one of three retreats from the radical challenge that the Northampton Association posed.[76] Yet, while that analysis is valid, we should note the logical development in Ruggles's thought. His call in the 1830s was "to vindicate outraged human nature." The Garrisonian diagnosis of the national sin of slavery in the body politic had chased down the suspect. To the Northampton Association, that sin, that outrage against human nature, was increasingly found not just in the public sphere but also in their bodies themselves. This echoed the language of the temperance movement that saw alcohol addiction as internal slavery.

While limited by his health and his need to build a new career, Ruggles did not give up his abolitionist activities. In 1844 he and Erasmus Darwin Hudson, a former member of the Northampton Association, were brought to court in nearby Springfield for convincing a slave to declare her freedom from her visiting master. And, as mentioned above, Ruggles used the community organizing techniques from his New York days to rally the "Colored Citizens of Northampton," including giving support to two white radical abolitionists who had been jailed in the South trying to liberate slaves.[77] Stephen Rush was appointed secretary of this short-lived group and Sojourner Truth spoke at the second of their rallies. The rest of the "Colored Citizens" were local blacks, including neighbors of the Association such as Henry Anthony.

As he wielded his new identity Ruggles may have seen no discontinuity in his struggles "to vindicate outraged human nature." Wielding a sort of Swedenborgian logic of "correspondences," he perhaps saw the disease of the American world as equally social, political, spiritual, and physical.[78] It was, then, ubiquitous: from plantations to streetcars to the very physical being of whites and blacks alike. To be sure, the necessities of making a living, especially as the Association began to seem likely to fall apart, must have suggested a course of action for him to survive. In the years after the demise of the community, he borrowed heavily from local whites to purchase land and build up his water-cure facility. And the inventory taken after his death showed a series of well-appointed rooms with extensive furnishings including a piano.[79] His journey from mariner to proprietor marked a precarious but determined effort to negotiate the ladders of class and race.

When the Association disbanded in late fall 1846, the slow shift toward a "neighborhood community" had been under way for some time. Samuel L. Hill and Elisha L. Hammond had built private houses (as Dolly Stetson noted), and Ruggles himself seems to have been living in separate quarters. Ruggles's water-cure seemingly prospered, although his debts would out-weigh his assets—and there were competitors setting up nearby. Finally, the "physician" could not heal himself. He died in December 1849 without see-ing the Compromise of 1850 or the dispiriting challenges to black Americans the next decade would bring. His mother and sister came to take his body back to Norwich. When his estate was probated, his erstwhile antagonists in the abolitionist culture wars from New York City put in a claim.

AFTER THE COMMUNITY closed, Sojourner Truth moved in with George W. Benson and his wife, James Stetson's sister, Catharine Stetson Benson. Truth occupied an ambiguous role, both domestic servant and housemate, suggesting the complexities of her place in the white North. The runaway success of *Narrative of the Life of Frederick Douglass, An American Slave, Writ-ten by Himself*, and the market for slave narratives in general, no doubt rein-forced the impulse, born of her financial needs, to publish her own "free story." As Painter has shown, the *Narrative of Sojourner Truth* was a far cry from others in the genre. The intricate ambivalence toward her former mas-ter and his family had been clear in her daughters' changing identities in the Association's store accounts.[80] Throughout the *Narrative* we can hear the voices of Gilbert and Truth tangling and not always resolving. Contrary to abolitionist sentiment—and strategy—she closes with a deeply felt forgive-ness of her former owner John Dumont.[81] This would perhaps have been more congruent with the intensely religious, if nonsectarian, thought of a Samuel L. Hill than with the radical convictions of a more conventional Garrisonian. Here again, Truth's religious worldview reminds us not to re-member her solely by her abolitionist and reformist identity.

For whatever reasons, Stephen C. Rush and George W. Sullivan did not stay on to help build the neighborhood community. In fact, little is known of either man's later life. In 1844, Sullivan had removed to Springfield. Be-fore Rush disappeared from the record, he had left the Association under a cloud and had come back seeking redemption. We know nothing of what his transgression was, and Rush's poignant 1846 letter of apology seeking read-mission to the community is an intriguing puzzle. Preserved as a loose doc-ument in the Association records, the one-page appeal explains that his "mind was much excited" and that he had been writing "a book of my life." This may well have been his own attempt at crafting a narrative, perhaps inspired by Douglass. Unlike Sojourner Truth, he apparently did not suc-ceed. Having sought his chances in the outside world of the antebellum North, he reported back, "I don't find no place like the association yet for I believe that they live out a principle that the world no nothing about . . . I want to help you to do more good yet in weak ways no more at present but I am still a friend of humanity."[82] Rush had been praised by Garrison in the *Liberator* and championed by Ruggles. While Garrison seems to have thought that he had learned to read and write only recently, perhaps befitting the importance of freedom, it seems very unlikely that Ruggles would have suggested him as an editor if this was true. We are the poorer for not know-ing more of this young man and for not having his "book." His obscurity and more ordinary status would offer a somewhat different view of the lives of African Americans than the powerful personalities of Truth, Ruggles, and Douglass, even though, as his attempt to tell his own free story suggests, he may have wanted to see himself as in their league.

Upon the formal dissolution of the community in late 1846, Samuel L. Hill had assumed all the debts and all the assets of the Association, and he and others began the process of subdividing land. Among the many former members of the Association who stayed on to develop the village, soon to be named Florence, the only black member remaining after David Ruggles died in December 1849 was Sojourner Truth. When the Benson family fled cred-itors in 1850, Sojourner Truth turned to Hill for a mortgage for a house and lot on nearby Park Street. In doing so she became a homeowner, a full-fledged member of the "neighborhood community." We would do well to underscore the importance of this achievement and the sense of security it represented for an African American woman. Now she could provide a home for her daughters and grandchildren.[83] Nearby were the African American households of Sarah Askin, Basil Dorsey, and Henry Anthony. There is no evidence of any connections between Truth and these blacks. In fact, in a later memoir, Hill's son claimed that Sojourner would not allow her grand-son to play with the Askin children; Arthur G. Hill remembered Jimmy

Caldwell taunting his grandmother with a playful charge of color prejudice.[84] While we should approach this anecdote with caution, it may have had more to do with class bias, or, if we recall the similar conflict in the Stetson letters, with Truth's proscription of sexual contact, however innocent the grandson's intentions.

Sojourner Truth launched a new career as orator and author with her electric appearance at the Woman's Rights Convention in Worcester, Massachusetts, in October 1850.[85] Now mixing her unique evangelism with the abolitionist and women's rights language of the Garrisonians in the Association, she would sell her book (and, later, photographs and song lyrics) and pay off Samuel Hill within four years. Truth would become a national figure even as she kept her Florence home. But, perhaps missing the close ties of community and surmising that her future as an orator on tour was in the Midwest, she sold the Florence house in 1857 and moved to Battle Creek, Michigan, where white women friends and a Spiritualist community had gathered.

After the demise of the community, Dolly Stetson and most of her family moved back to Connecticut, but the Stetsons kept up contact with their friends as the village struggled to gain its feet. By the late 1850s Florence was a growing industrial center for Northampton and the surrounding area. The remaining community members drew kin and associates to the area. The former Associationists would largely become the middle class of Florence, occupying important niches in the economic and social life of the village. The expanding industries would come to employ large numbers of immigrants, chiefly Irish and Germans, who flocked to the area. Hill and his associates built a "neighborhood community" that emphasized family dwelling houses instead of the boarding house system used in Lowell and other factory towns. To be sure, boarding houses existed in Florence, but they were few in number, and the overwhelming preference of Hill and others was for underscoring the importance of family.

Echoing the pattern of life within the utopian experiment, a few blacks would develop close relations with the former communitarians in the factory village. Prominent among them were those who had begun their Florence years as nearby neighbors of those so intently devoted to exploring a community of equality. Henry Anthony stayed on for decades, largely marginalized with his stonemason and musician's work, associating more with the working class than the burgeoning middle class dominated by the former communitarians. Basil Dorsey was working as a teamster for the cotton mill and lived in his home just across the dam from the factory canal. He became an esteemed resident of the town from the 1850s on as antislavery became an increasingly popular cause. As a fugitive slave he seemed to enjoy a special if limited authenticity for whites.[86] His son went on to become a successful contractor in Florence and bought a fine home, moving the Dorseys up from "under the hill," where the community and its silk operations had once set up, an area increasingly given over to the working class. The Askins endured, suffering the desertion of Sarah Askin's husband and the untimely death of her two oldest children. The surviving children moved into work in the mills and helped pay off the various mortgages on their home across from the silk company.

Aside from Basil Dorsey's niche as heroic escaped slave, there remained no powerful personages such as Truth, Ruggles, or Douglass among the African Americans of Florence. There certainly is no record of those black families most closely associated with the former Associationists testing the newly established order after utopia—an order presumed, at least in the memory of Arthur Hill or Charles Sheffield and his co-authors, to be a sanctuary for people of color. Yet, however limited in their participation in the social and economic life of the village, these blacks were surviving and, indeed, to a modest extent, succeeding in an increasingly white world.

The 1860s saw the building of more social and cultural institutions in the village. Where once the members of the community had shared their gains and losses, now there was a definite class structure. While an idealism of giving still held sway, it was more clearly a paternalistic endeavor. After utopia, in Clark's fine summary phrase, "Equality had yielded to philanthropy."[87] Most important in representing the developing vision of the former communitarians was the Free Congregational Society, a unique nonsectarian organization that embodied the free religious ideology that had begun to take shape in the Association. Implicit within this new creedless society were the limited lessons of the racial education of community days. Formed in 1863, the year of the Emancipation Proclamation, it espoused the friendship of humanity Stephen Rush had so poignantly missed. Still, freedom was now another word, a word addressing matters of religious conscience and moral uplift—and deeply imbricated with the fierce individualism of free labor ideology. The Free Congregational Society would make Florence well known, notorious even, but it now sheltered white infidels rather than fugitives from bondage. The desire to continue to honor the cause of African American rights was strong enough to make Frederick Douglass one of the four speakers for the dedication of the Society's new home, Cosmian Hall, in 1874. And the Dorsey and Askin families were respected members in the Free Congregational Society. Yet the locus of change was now more a podium for big-name speakers from Ralph Waldo Emerson, to Elizabeth Cady Stanton, to Douglass than a crucible where issues of class and race were directly embraced.

Those issues were the stuff of the lives of the Askin family. A working-class African American, Mrs. Askin did washing and "working out by the day" to earn a living.[88] Yet the Askins aspired to middle-class status. If the children grew up to work in the mills, they participated in much of the social life of respectable Florence, including the Free Congregational Society. Luther Askin, the oldest son, was in three local orchestras, a founding member of the otherwise all-white Nonotuck Fire Company No. 1, and a proud member of the Florence Eagles, the local amateur baseball team that enjoyed considerable success in the Northeast. The baseball historian Brian Turner has discovered that the 1865–1867 Eagles are the earliest known integrated team in American history. If the eyes had strayed after utopia from the prize of racial equality, there was still glimmer enough for Luther to participate in a team made up of Irish-American millworkers and the sons of Association families (and now Free Congregationalists). As the Eagles' fame spread after their first two seasons, at the end of the Civil War, however, an unexplained illness "forced" Luther Askin to withdraw from the team.[89] While the record obscures what role the increasingly segregated American world may have played in Askin's demotion, larger regional and national realities may have been too insistent, too intrusive to be ignored. Luther Askin's illness did in fact coincide with the team's trip to New York to meet the national champion Brooklyn Atlantics. There they would enter the larger, strictly segregated world of baseball.

Memory increasingly shouldered the responsibilities of Florence's self-image. What was not accomplished wore memory's clothes: the failures were recalled as valiant trials. The young Charles Sheffeld may have been pleasantly surprised by the breadth and depth of his forebears' community experiment, but in the 1890s he was more engaged in recounting the past than in making history. Labor wars were tearing at the nation's fabric and threatening to come to Florence itself. Lynchings were legion in the South, and backsliding in racial matters was established as a new "normalcy" in the white North. Asked to contribute to the book, Douglass fondly recalled the "old Community times" and how the "place and people struck me as the most democratic I had ever met. It was a place to extinguish all aristocratic pretensions. There was no high, no low, no masters, no servants, no white, no black."[90] If Florence could still be seen as a different place, as an island of toleration and hope, it was because of the now fading shape of those community dreams. Arthur G. Hill, son of Samuel and uncle of Charles Sheffield and shortstop for the Florence Eagles, would leave a manuscript draft of an article in his papers called "Florence, Sanctuary of the Colored Race."[91]

The Askins were among the "old colored families" living in the sanctuary, Hill said. Few new black families had moved in, opting instead for urban havens such as Springfield where there was at least the promise of solidarity of color. Luther's son and namesake declined a life of factory labor and chose to become a traveling musician. Leaving Florence in 1906 or 1907, he became a successful cornetist with a number of barnstorming brass bands. Light-skinned, he lived away from the post-utopia sanctuary as a white man. He married a white woman and settled in upstate New York, eventually taking a position as a music teacher in a local school. While his wife knew of his "colored" past, none of his family or neighbors saw him as anything but white. Later descendants had always wondered why they never saw the "Florence side of the family."[92] Memory had no place for color. The long and powerful history of the construction of race in the larger world overwhelmed the dreams of utopia, as limited as they were. The sanctuary could not hold.

Notes

I thank Kerry Buckley and Christopher Clark for their warm and expert editorial work. Marjorie Senechal has unfailingly lent her keen insights and understanding. Chris Clark has been a supportive and intellectually stimulating "co-conspirator" on the Northampton Association for many years, and his scholarship is the edifice on which this book builds. To work with Kerry, Chris, and Marjorie has been a collaborative experience of "education and industry." I also want to give special thanks to Brian Turner and Frances V. Krumpholz, both members of the Florence History Project, for all their invaluable and thoughtful help. This essay is dedicated to Fran Krumpholz for her thoughtful support in a community of two.

1. Charles A. Sheffeld, ed., *The History of Florence, Massachusetts, including a Complete Account of the Northampton Association of Education and Industry* (Florence, Mass., 1895), 3–4. A close associate, publisher Charles F. Warner, had published such volumes on two counties: *Picturesque Hampshire: A Supplement to the Quarter-Centennial of the Hampshire County Journal* (Northampton, Mass., 1890) and *Picturesque Hampden* (Northampton, Mass., 1891).

2. Frederick Douglass "What I Found at the Northampton Association," in Sheffeld, ed., *History of Florence*, 129–132. The quotation is on 129.

3. For the scope and thrust of this community, see Christopher Clark, *The Communitarian Moment: The Radical Challenge of the Northampton Association* (Ithaca, N.Y., 1995; Amherst, Mass., 2003). Clark's cogent study probes the historical context of the NAEI as well as the historiographical literature of intentional communities. An earlier study of the NAEI, done as a Master's thesis, is Alice Eaton McBee, 2nd, *From Utopia to Florence: The Story of a Transcendentalist Community in Northampton, Mass., 1830–1852*, Smith College Studies in History, 32 (Northampton, Mass., 1947.) An illuminating study of the intellectual life of Garrisonian abolitionists is Lewis Perry, *Radical Abolitionism: Anarchy and the Government of God in Antislavery Thought* (Knoxville, 1995); this reprint of the 1973 edition has a thoughtful, self-critical "Preface to the New Edition" which notes the need to pay more attention to the role of black abolitionists.

4. NAEI Constitution and By-Laws, reprinted in Sheffeld, ed., *History of Florence*, 76.

5. The late American Studies scholar Sidney Kaplan saw the Northampton Association as not only antislavery but also antiracist.

6. On the very different community experiments for African Americans, see William H. Pease and Jane Pease, *Black Utopia: Negro Communal Experiments in America* (Madison, Wis., 1963).

7. The Anthony family information is from Frances V. Krumpholz, typescript of Park Street cemetery burials compiled (and updated) from index cards of genealogists Walter and Lottie Corbin, Florence History Archives, Florence Association, Florence, Mass., and U.S. Sixth, Eighth, and Tenth Censuses, Population Schedules, Massachusetts, 1840, 1860, 1880. Also see *Hampshire Gazette*, September 7, 1880, where Anthony was given a rather extensive death notice describing him as "the aged mulatto . . . the oldest inhabitant of the village." The article goes on to mention his "remarkably social nature" and that he "enjoyed the companionship of his kind." This latter reference is clearly racial marking. Yet Anthony's living among working-class whites and marrying across the color line might suggest that paternalism's two faces, race and class, were not always neatly separated.

8. The percentage was decidedly higher in Boston, in parts of Rhode Island, and in New London County, Connecticut. Although we still know too little about the life of blacks in the North, especially in rural areas, some fine works include the still valuable Leon Litwack, *North of Slavery: The Negro in the Free States, 1790–1860* (Chicago, 1961); Leonard P. Curry, *The Free Black in Urban America, 1800–1850: The Shadow of*

the Dream (Chicago, 1981); Graham Russell Hodges, *Slavery and Freedom in the Rural North: African Americans in Monmouth County, New Jersey, 1665–1865* (Madison, Wis., 1997), and idem; *Root and Branch: African Americans in New York and East Jersey, 1613–1863* (Chapel Hill, N.C., 1999); James Oliver Horton, *Free People of Color: Inside the African American Community* (Washington, D.C., 1993); James Oliver Horton and Lois E. Horton, *Black Bostonians: Family Life and Community Struggle in the Antebellum North* (New York, 1979), and idem, *In Hope of Liberty: Culture, Community, and Protest among Northern Free Blacks, 1700–1860* (New York, 1997). Pioneering in its time and still useful is Lorenzo J. Greene, *The Negro in Colonial New England* (1942; rpt. ed., New York, 1968). Slave narratives of African Americans who became New Englanders are collected in Arna Bontemps, ed., *Five Black Lives: The Autobiographies of Venture Smith, James Mars, William Grimes, the Rev. G. W. Offley, and James L. Smith* (Middletown, Conn., 1971), which offers works of Connecticut residents, and Robert J. Cottrol, ed., *From African to Yankee: Narratives of Slavery and Freedom in Antebellum New England* (New York, 1997). Arna Bontemps's *Great Slave Narratives* (Boston, 1969) includes *The Fugitive Blacksmith; or Events in the History of James W. C. Pennington, Pastor of a Presbyterian Church, New York, Formerly a Slave in the State of Maryland*. Pennington was called by David Ruggles to marry the young Frederick Douglass and Anna Murray in his apartment in New York. Robert J. Cottrol has also contributed *The Afro-Yankees: Providence's Black Community in the Antebellum Era* (Westport, Conn., 1982). A provocative and deeply researched recent study, Joanne Pope Melish's *Disowning Slavery: Gradual Emancipation and "Race" in New England, 1780–1860* (Ithaca, N.Y., 1998) continues the recent investigations into "whiteness." Melish is perhaps a little too inductive in her approach but reveals much of the workings of race and the African American experience in New England.

9. U.S. Sixth Census, 1840, Population Schedules, Massachusetts, and U.S. Seventh Census, 1850, Population Schedules, Massachusetts.

10. Nell Painter, *Sojourner Truth: A Life, A Symbol* (New York, 1996), 95, has Dorsey as a resident of the community, but this seems to be based on his appearance in the store accounts of the Association. The store accounts, however, include many local people, and there is no record of his being anything but a neighbor. On the Askins, see Brian Turner, "Baseball's Earliest Integrated Team?" *The National Pastime* 22 (2002): 81–90. I am indebted to Turner for his assiduous research and collegial sharing of his work.

11. Basil Dorsey was profiled in a number of the *Hampshire Gazette* given over largely to Florence that was published April 2, 1867, silently commemorating the twenty-fifth anniversary of the Northampton Association of Education and Industry. This portrait was repeated in edited form in the *Gazette* after his death, February 20, 1872, and again June 15, 1900, and February 15, 1902. For a brief account of Dorsey's escape (with his brothers) from slavery in the 1830s that may have established some renown for him in the North, see Nick Salvatore, *We All Got History: The Memory Books of Amos Webber* (New York, 1996), 13, 331, and Janice L. Painter, "The Blacks in Bucks County," *Bucks County Panorama* 18, no. 11 (November 1976): 64.

12. William Adam to John Bailey, February 13, 1843, in Northampton Association of Education and Industry Records, 1836–1853, American Antiquarian Society, Worcester, Mass. (hereafter cited as NAEI, Records), vol. 4, p. 7. Bailey was one of the most radical white abolitionists in New Bedford. See Kathryn Grover, *The Fugitive's Gibraltar: Escaping Slaves and Abolitionism in New Bedford, Massachusetts* (Amherst, Mass., 2001).

13. Sophia Foord to Robert Adams, Northampton, May 8, 1843, in the collection of Lisa Baskin, Leeds, Mass., whose generosity toward historical research is matched by her present-day activism.

14. NAEI, Records, vol. 2, Record of Proceedings, 1842–1848, entry for May 13, 1843.

15. On Sullivan's fall, see *Hampshire Gazette*, June 4, 1844.

16. Dolly W. Stetson to James A. Stetson [hereafter DWS and JAS], (letter no. 5), Stetson Family Correspondence, Manuscript Collection, Historic Northampton, Northampton, Mass. References are to letters in this collection unless otherwise indicated, and include the letter number assigned in this volume.

17. On Truth's relationship with Robert, her cruelly treated lover, see Painter, *Sojourner Truth*, 18–19. On her husband, Thomas, see Painter, 18–21, 23, 24, 60, 75, 296, 328; see also Carlton Mabee, with Susan Mabee Newhouse, *Sojourner Truth: Slave, Prophet, Legend* (New York, 1993), 5–7. Painter posits a possible romantic interest of Ruggles toward Truth's daughter Elizabeth (100). But while the considerable expense of the shawl in the store accounts is, as Painter notes, "intriguing," there is no other evidence on this and certainly, as Painter makes clear, nothing came of the "romantic" gesture by this very serious man.

18. Painter, *Sojourner Truth*, 100–101. As Painter notes, there were three young women connected to Truth's store accounts, Elizabeth, Sophia, and Jane. While Elizabeth and Sophia are known to be Truth's children, Painter's research found no other mention of a "Jane" as a daughter. Painter offers a fine, intriguing look at the naming of the "daughters" in the records, taking the changing last names associated with them to be a record of the ambiguities of postslavery identity.

19. There is a vast literature on race and sexuality. Much of the anxiety came to a head in the supposed link between lynching and rape. See, for example, Jacqueline Jones Royster, ed., *Southern Horrors and Other Writings: The Anti-Lynching Campaign of Ida B. Wells, 1892–1900* (Boston, 1997); Paula Giddings, *Where and When I Enter: The Impact of Black Women on Race and Sex in America* (New York, 1984); Bettina Aptheker, *Woman's Legacy: Essays on Race, Sex, and Class in American History* (Amherst, Mass., 1981).

20. Christopher Clark has calculated that 55 of the 240 members of the Association were single. Clark, *The Communitarian Moment*, 78.

21. While certainly not directly related to our concerns here, Thomas C. Holt, *The Problem of Race in the Twenty-First Century* (Cambridge, Mass., 2000), addresses the issue of how race works in American culture. Holt argues that while race and racism were once closely tied to slavery and labor, they play a different role now in our heavily

commodified, consumer culture. Within the NAEI, we might see, correspondingly, that admittance of blacks to the community occurred on a one-by-one basis because the free labor system structured race that way. Celebrity, certainly the province of Douglass and Truth, allowed for other crossings in later nineteenth-century America. While nothing like the celebrity culture we are a-swim in now, the orator's circle was a major forum and a central part of popular culture.

22. The most extensive analysis of the black presence in the NAEI is in Clark, *The Communitarian Moment*, esp. 71–75.

23. George Fredrickson, *The Black Image in the White Mind: The Debate on Afro-American Character and Destiny, 1817–1914* (Middletown, Conn., 1971).

24. Almira B. Stetson to JAS, January 13, 1843 (letter no. 1).

25. On Remond, see C. Peter Ripley et al., eds., *The Black Abolitionist Papers*, vol. 3: *The United States, 1830–1846* (Chapel Hill, N.C., 1991), 318–319; Walter M. Merrill and Louis Ruchames, eds., *The Letters of William Lloyd Garrison*, 6 vols. (Cambridge, Mass., 1971–1981), 3:26; Rayford W. Logan and Michael R. Winston, eds., *Dictionary of American Negro Biography* (New York, 1982), 520–522.

26. On the Hundred Conventions Tour of Massachusetts, see Gregory P. Lampe, *Frederick Douglass: Freedom's Voice, 1818–1845* (East Lansing, Mich., 1998), 207–226. On the Hutchinsons: Dale Cockrell, ed., *Excelsior: Journals of the Hutchinson Family Singers, 1842–1846* (Stuyvesant, N.Y., 1989), 264–270, provides transcriptions of the journals and the newspaper reports of the *Hampshire Gazette*, April 30, 1844 (the Town Hall abolition meeting), and the subsequent article besmirching the family and the Association from the Boston *Atlas* (undated).

27. Charles T. Davis and Henry Louis Gates, Jr., "Introduction: The Language of Slavery" in *The Slave's Narrative* (New York, 1985), xxx.

28. DWS to JAS, February 20, [1845] (letter no. 38).

29. DWS to JAS, July 26, [1844] (letter no. 13). Sullivan is discussed in Clark, *Communitarian Moment*, 73 and 239–240.

30. DWS to JAS, May 4, 1845 (letter no. 52).

31. [Olive Gilbert and Frances Titus], *Narrative of Sojourner Truth; A Bondswoman of Olden Time, Emancipated by the New York Legislature in the Early Part of the Present Century; with a History of Her Labors and Correspondence Drawn from Her "Book of Life"; Also, a Memorial Chapter*, ed. Nell Irvin Painter (New York, 1998).

32. On the *Northern Star and Freeman's Advocate*, see Ripley et al., eds., *The Black Abolitionist Papers*, 3: 379. On the recommendation of Rush, see the *Liberator*, May 24, 1844.

33. There are three editions of Truth's *Narrative* generally available in reprint editions: [Olive Gilbert] *Narrative of Sojourner Truth* (New York, 1993), ed. Margaret Washington, a reprint of the 1850 edition; [Olive Gilbert and Frances Titus], *Narrative of Sojourner Truth; A Bondswoman of Olden Time, Emancipated by the New York Legislature in the Early Part of the Present Century; with a History of Her Labors and Correspondence Drawn from her "Book of Life."*, Introduction by Jeffrey C. Stewart (New York, 1991), a reprint of the 1878 edition; and Painter's Penguin reprint of the 1884 edition, for which

see note 31. All editions include the original narrative written when Truth was living with the Bensons. The 1878 and 1884 editions include the "Book of Life," a scrapbook of articles collected by Titus on Truth, newspaper notices, letters (including some from Florence and Northampton friends and associates such as Samuel Hill), and autographs of nineteenth-century notables. A "Memorial Chapter" in the 1884 edition includes accounts of her death and funeral.

34. DWS to JAS, September 1, 1844 (letter no. 22); DWS to JAS, October 6, 1844 (letter no. 27); DWS to JAS, November 19, 1844 (letter no. 32).

35. DWS to JAS, October 12, 1844 (letter no. 28).

36. Ibid.

37. DWS to JAS, March 18, 1845 (letter no. 45).

38. The Matthias involvement is discussed by Gilbert in the *Narrative*. For a delightful exploration of all that can be found with a close look at this phenomenon of the Second Great Awakening, see Paul E. Johnson and Sean Wilentz, *The Kingdom of Matthias* (New York, 1994). The best modern biography of Truth, which gives substantial coverage to her religious life, is Painter, *Sojourner Truth*, which does valuable and convincing work at separating the two Sojourner Truths implied in the subtitle. See also Mabee, *Sojourner Truth*.

39. Painter, *Sojourner Truth*. Clark's entry on Truth is in Peter J. Parish, ed., *Reader's Guide to American History* (Chicago, 1997), 700–701.

40. Robert S. Levine, *Martin Delaney, Frederick Douglass, and the Politics of Representative Identity* (Chapel Hill, N.C., 1997), 153–155.

41. Nell Irvin Painter, "Sojourner Truth in Life and Memory: Writing the Biography of an American Exotic," *Gender & History* 2, no. 1 (1990): 3–17.

42. Levine, *Martin Delaney, Frederick Douglass, and the Politics of Representative Identity*, 153–155 and 277. His argument is with the interpretations of Carla L. Peterson, *"Doers of the Word": African American Women Speakers and Writers in the North (1830–1880)* (New York, 1995), and Painter, "Representing Truth: Sojourner Truth's Knowing and Becoming Known," *Journal of American History* 81 (1994). Solomon Northup's strange tale of his kidnapping from his life as a free black in the North and subsequent sale into slavery clearly was meant to echo Stowe's *Uncle Tom's Cabin* soon after its publication; [David Wilson], *Twelve Years a Slave, A Narrative of Solomon Northup, a Citizen of New York, Kidnapped in Washington City in 1841, and Rescued in 1853, from a Cotton Plantation Near the Red River in Louisiana* (Baton Rouge, 1968), shows the power of Stowe's name. It was dedicated to her and became a best seller. It also demonstrates some of the ironies of interdependence in that Stowe was publishing a key to her famous novel to show the authenticity of her fiction while Northup and others were seeking her fictive power to enhance their "true stories." Stowe's *Atlantic Monthly* article on Truth, published in 1863, a decade or so after her interview with Sojourner, shows Truth as African Sybil with a heavy southern dialect. By including the Stowe work in her "Book of Life," Truth was knowingly fictionalizing her own image to better sell her own "truth." For other valuable works on Truth by literary critics with an emphasis on historical context see Frances Smith Foster, *Written by Herself: Literary*

Production by African American Women, 1746–1892 (Bloomington, Ind., 1993), and Jean Fagan Yellin, *Women and Sisters: The Antislavery Feminists in American Culture* (New Haven, Conn., 1989). Yellin looks at images of Truth in an iconographical analysis in chap. 4: "Sojourner Truth and Harriet Jacobs," 77–96. A fine interdisciplinary collection is Jean Fagan Yellin and John C. Van Horne, eds., *The Abolitionist Sisterhood: Women's Political Culture in Antebellum America* (Ithaca, N.Y., 1994). Painter's essay "Difference, Slavery, and Memory: Sojourner Truth in Feminist Abolitionism," in that volume probes Truth's building of her public self and her use of that image to differentiate her from her white audiences.

43. For a succinct portrait of Tubman, see Darlene Clark Hine's biographical sketch in Darlene Clark Hine, Elsa Barkley Brown, and Rosalyn Terborg-Penn, eds., *Black Women in America: An Historical Encyclopedia* (Bloomington, Ind., 1993), 2:1176–1180. On Truth's image see especially Painter, *Sojourner Truth*, 185–199.

44. For works on minstrelsy and its uses in nineteenth-century America, see Alexander Saxton, "Blackface Minstrelsy and Jacksonian Ideology," *American Quarterly* 27 (1975): 3–28; Eric Lott, *Love and Theft: Blackface Minstrelsy and the American Working Class* (New York, 1993); and Robert C. Toll, *Blacking Up: The Minstrel Show in Nineteenth-Century America* (New York: Oxford University Press, 1974).

45. Douglass, "What I Found at the Northampton Association," in Sheffeld, ed., *History of Florence*, 132.

46. See Garrison's letters to his wife Helen Benson Garrison, to George W. Benson, and to the *Liberator* in Merrill and Ruchames, eds., *The Letters of William Lloyd Garrison*, 3:246–254.

47. DWS to JAS, June 19, [1845] (letter no. 61).

48. DWS to JAS, April 13, 1845 (letter no. 47).

49. See *My Bondage and My Freedom* in Frederick Douglass, *Autobiographies* (New York: Library of America, 1996), especially chap. 25, "Various Incidents," 389–398, and in the Appendix, "The Anti-Slavery Movement: Extracts from a Lecture before Various Anti-Slavery Bodies, in the Winter of 1855," 445–452.

50. Douglass, *Autobiographies*, 449.

51. Douglass, "What I Found at the Northampton Association," in Sheffeld, ed., *History of Florence*, 131.

52. On Ruggles see Dorothy B. Porter, "David M. Ruggles, An Apostle of Human Rights," *Journal of Negro History* 28 (January 1943): 23–50. Many of Ruggles's writings are in two edited works by Porter: *Negro Protest Pamphlets: A Compendium* (New York, 1969), and *Early Negro Writing, 1760–1837* (1971; rpt. ed. Baltimore, 1995). Fortunately, we have Graham Russell Hodges's biography of Ruggles to look forward to.

53. Child was an articulate writer of many genres and a thoughtful moral force in nineteenth-century reform, recognized as such in her own time. Her reputation, however, like those of many women writers, faded quickly in the twentieth century. She has finally been brought back to something like her justly deserved status. See Carolyn L. Karcher, *The First Woman in the Republic: A Cultural Biography* (Durham, N.C.,

1994), a scholarly and exhaustive work. Deborah Pickman Clifford, *Crusader for Freedom: A Life of Lydia Maria Child* (Boston, 1992), is more of a traditional life-and-times approach and readily accessible to the general reader. Child was notable, among other things, for addressing the issue of race (including Indians) and not just slavery in her writings. See especially *An Appeal in Favor of That Class of Americans Called Africans*, ed. Carolyn L. Karcher (Amherst, 1996), a reprint of the 1833 edition. Karcher's edited volume, *A Lydia Maria Child Reader* (Durham, N.C., 1997), gives a comprehensive sampling of Child's many concerns and venues of publication.

54. The incidents are recounted in Henry Mayer, *All on Fire: William Lloyd Garrison and the Abolition of Slavery* (New York, 1998), 304–305.

55. *Confessions of Two Malefactors, Teller & Reynolds, Who were Executed at Hartford, Connecticut, on the Sixth of September, 1833, for the Murder of Ezra Hoskins at the Connecticut State Prison, Containing an Account of their Numerous Robberies, Burglaries, &c* (Hartford, 1833), 52–54.

56. Peter's troubles in the city, his going to sea, and three letters from him to his mother are in [Gilbert and Titus], *Narrative of Sojourner Truth*, ed. Painter, 49–54. Painter discusses this in *Sojourner Truth*, 66–68.

57. W. Jeffrey Bolster, *Black Jacks: African American Seamen in the Age of Sail* (Cambridge, Mass., 1998), explores the rough but relatively wide-open world of opportunity for young black men who went to sea.

58. On African Americans in New York in this period see Rhoda Golden Freeman, *The Free Negro in New York in the Era before the Civil War* (New York, 1994), and George E. Walker, *The Afro-American in New York City, 1827–1860* (New York, 1993).

59. On *Freedom's Journal*, see Bella Gross, "*Freedom's Journal* and *The Rights of All*" *Journal of Negro History* 17 (July 1932): 241–286.

60. Ruggles and Walker advertised in *Freedom's Journal* and its renamed successor, *Rights of All* throughout 1828 and 1829. In September 1829, David Walker published his pamphlet. See Herbert Aptheker, *"One Continual Cry": David Walker's Appeal to the Colored Citizens of the World, 1829–1830, Its Setting and Its Meaning, Together with the Full Text of the Third, and Last, Edition* (New York, 1965).

61. For the perspectives and experiences of free black leadership see Frederick Cooper, "Elevating the Race: The Social Thought of Black Leaders, 1827–1850," *American Quarterly* 24 (December 1972): 604–625; Howard Holman Bell, *A Survey of the Negro Convention Movement, 1830–1861* (New York, 1969); Ira Berlin, "The Structure of the Free Negro Caste in the Antebellum United States," *Journal of Social History* 9 (1976): 297–318; and Robert L. Harris, "The Free Black Response to American Racism, 1790–1863" (Ph.D. diss., Northwestern University, 1974). The classic account, Benjamin Quarles, *Black Abolitionists* (New York, 1969), is still valuable.

62. See for example his "Appeals to the colored citizens of New York and elsewhere in behalf of the press. By David Ruggles, a man of color," originally in the *Emancipator and Journal of Public Morals*, February 17, 1835, and reprinted in Porter, ed., *Early Negro Writing*, 637–655. For example, "A, B, or C calls upon E, and puts the question, "Will

you assist in sustaining the cause of suffering humanity by subscribing to this paper?" He then goes on to refute the possible replies of E and of F, etc., 640–641.

63. *Emancipator*, November 1835.

64. Lewis Tappan's summary of the Vigilance Committee incident does not mention the fierce infighting between abolitionists as a cause but instead opines, "Like most every other colored man I have ever known, he was untrustworthy about money matters. I do not accuse him or others as deficient in integrity, but no regular account appears to be kept of moneys received or paid." Quoted in Bertram Wyatt-Brown, *Lewis Tappan and the Evangelical War against Slavery* (Cleveland, 1969), 180. The Tappans, wealthy abolitionists, never had black clerks.

65. *Colored American*, February 23, 1839.

66. The *Mirror of Liberty* (1838–1841) was published, edited, and largely if not wholly written by Ruggles. *A Plea* plays on the widely used abolitionist appeal to public pity for the enslaved which featured an abject victim and the heading "Am I Not A Man and A Brother"—a fascinating use of the phrase by a free black to counter his accusers.

67. This is in Douglass's second autobiography, *My Bondage and My Freedom* (1855), available in Douglass, *Autobiographies*, 353.

68. David Ruggles to JAS, June 20, 1844 (letter no. 12).

69. DWS to JAS (letter no. 9).

70. DWS to JAS, June 19, [1845] (letter no. 61).

71. DWS to JAS, April 15, [1845] (letter no. 48).

72. An 1860s article giving a somewhat fictionalized treatment to the episode was written under a pseudonym by an unidentified former community member and published in a local newspaper: "Harriet Hayden, A Story of Florence in the Days of the 'Old Community,' by Richard," *Northampton Free Press*, May 16, 1862.

73. DWS to JAS, July 26, [1844] (letter no. 13).

74. David Ruggles, *The Abrogation of the Seventh Commandment, by the American Churches* (New York, 1835), reprinted in Porter, ed., *Early Negro Writing*, 478–493. I am indebted to David Blight for the delightfully succinct summary (playing on Garrison's famous phrase "No Union with Slaveholders") of Ruggles's thesis in this pamphlet.

75. Truth's meeting with Lincoln is described and analyzed by Painter, *Sojourner Truth*, 203–207. Examples of references to her by others as "Aunt" or "Aunty" can be found in Painter's edited volume of the 1884 edition of the *Narrative of Sojourner Truth*, 182, 190, 196.

76. The others are to political abolitionism and acceptance of the dictates of labor-capital relations in industrial capitalism. See especially Clark, *The Communitarian Moment*, 183–219.

77. Reported in the *Liberator*, August 30, 1844.

78. See Robert C. Fuller, "Alternative Medicine," in Mary Kupiec Cayton, Elliott J. Gorn, and Peter W. Williams, eds., *Encyclopedia of American Social History* (New York, 1993), 3:2382–2384. Fuller discusses Swedenborgian influences on practitioners of ho-

meopathy and of mesmerism. While Fuller does not specifically mention Sweden-borg's influence in the section on hydropathy, Ruggles was almost certainly exposed to the theories of homeopathic medicine—and, indeed, he utilized a sort of derivative of mesmerism in his theory of hydropathy (or water-cure) in that he claimed to be able to diagnose patients by feeling the electrical charge in their bodies upon examination. Clark discusses hydropathy and Ruggles's practice of it in *The Communitarian Moment*, 196–203.

79. Ruggles died intestate. His estate was probated in 1850; see Box 242, No. 51, Registry of Probate, Northampton, Mass.

80. See note 18.

81. On Truth's daughters, see Painter, *Sojourner Truth*, 100–102. On the *Narrative*, ibid., 103–112 and her Introduction to the Penguin edition, vii–xx.

82. Stephen Rush letter, 1846, loose, included with NAEI, Records. The handwriting is difficult to decipher, especially the date. It may be "7th 7 1846," or "7th 1846."

83. The 1850 U.S. Census lists Isabella Van Wagener (note the ambiguity of names again) as living with Diana, 28 years old and Sophia, 21; all are listed as born in New York. Unlike Diana and her mother, Sophia is said to be able to read and write. There is some doubt as to the accuracy of that. The 1855 Massachusetts state census lists Isabella as "Sojourner Truth" with Elizabeth Williams, 30 years of age, and her grandson, Samuel B. Williams, 4, along with Diana Dumont (still using her slaveowner's name), aged 44, and her grandson, James E. Caldwell, 10. All were born in New York with the exception of grandson Samuel, born in Massachusetts.

84. Arthur G. Hill, "Anti-Slavery Days in Florence," typescript, Florence History Museum, Florence, Mass., n.d., n.p.

85. On the conference see John F. McClymer, *This High and Holy Moment: The First National Woman's Rights Convention, Worcester, 1850* (Fort Worth, 1999).

86. On Dorsey, see note 11.

87. Clark, *The Communitarian Moment*, 211.

88. Quoted from a handwritten, 1930s memoir of the Free Congregational Society: Anna Pauline Friedrich, "Recollections of Florence People who attended Cosmian Hall." Records of The Free Congregational Society of Florence, Unitarian Society of Northampton and Florence, Northampton, Mass. Here Mrs. Askin was remembered as "a jolly good natured colored woman . . . friendly kind and sociable . . . fleshy . . . a splendid house keeper and was noted for her cooking."

89. Turner, "Baseball's Earliest Integrated Team?"

90. Douglass, "What I Found at the Northampton Association," in Sheffeld, ed., *History of Florence*, 130.

91. Arthur G. Hill, manuscript in possession of a descendant who wishes to be unidentified. Photocopy in my possession. Hill had originally titled the draft, probably written around 1912 and intended for publication in a newspaper, "Florence, the Mecca of the Colored Race," but had crossed out Mecca and inserted "Sanctuary."

92. Brian Turner and I reconstructed the Askin story in the spring of 2001. On

May 29 we set out to interview the descendants of this African American family and found remarkably personable Askins eager to share family photos and memorabilia. They were also clearly "white folks." They had been told that Luther Askin, Jr., had eloped when he married, little realizing that his marriage had been planned to take place in Northampton and to coincide with his parents' wedding anniversary at the family home in Florence which was rather prominently written up in the local papers. In Florence, the Askins were of color, as confirmed by Brian Turner, Interview with James Ryan, 1999. Ryan was then nearing 100 years old and knew the Askin family as a young man.

NOTES ON CONTRIBUTORS

CHRISTOPHER CLARK is professor of North American history at the University of Warwick, England. He is author of *The Roots of Rural Capitalism: Western Massachusetts, 1780–1860* (1990), which won the Frederick Jackson Turner Award of the Organization of American Historians; *The Communitarian Moment: The Radical Challenge of the Northampton Association* (1995); and (with Nancy Hewitt) the second edition of *Who Built America?: Working People and the Nation's Economy, Politics, Culture, and Society*, vol. 1, *From Conquest and Colonization through 1877* (2000).

KERRY W. BUCKLEY is executive director of Historic Northampton Museum and Education Center. He is the author of *Mechanical Man: John Broadus Watson and the Beginnings of Behaviorism* (1989) and editor of *A Place Called Paradise: Culture and Community in Northampton, Massachusetts, 1654–2004* (forthcoming, University of Massachusetts Press).

MARJORIE SENECHAL is Louise Wolff Kahn Professor in Mathematics and History of Science and Technology at Smith College, where she leads the Program in the History of Science and Technology and directs the Edmund J. and Louise W. Kahn Liberal Arts Institute. She is a cofounder and director of the community-wide Northampton Silk Project. In addition to six books in mathematics, she is the author of *Long Life to Your Children! A Portrait of High Albania* (1997) and *Silk Threads, A History of the Science and Technology of Silk* (in preparation).

PAUL GAFFNEY teaches history, American studies, and African American studies in the Humanities Department at Landmark College, Putney, Vermont.

INDEX